C000297962

Broadway Remembers

by

Debbie Williamson

Published by
Debbie Williamson
The Manor House
West End
Broadway
Worcestershire
WR12 7JP

Copyright © Debbie Williamson, 2014

ISBN 978-0-9929891-0-1

The moral right of Debbie Williamson to be identified as the author of this work has been asserted by her in accordance with the Copyright, Designs and Patents Act of 1988.
All rights reserved. No part of this publication may be reproduced, stored in a retrieval system or transmitted in any form or by any means (electronic, mechanical, photocopying, recording or otherwise), without the prior permission of the copyright owner and the publisher of the book.
All photos are used by permission of the photographer or print holder. Unacknowledged photos are by the author, copyright expired or those where the copyright holder has proved impossible to trace.

Designed by Debbie Williamson

Printed and bound in Great Britain by
Vale Press Ltd, Willersey, Worcestershire

Dedication

This book is dedicated to those men of Broadway who gave their lives in the First World War and their comrades who fought with them.

They shall grow not old, as we that are left grow old:
Age shall not weary them, nor the years condemn.
At the going down of the sun and in the morning
We will remember them.

Robert Laurence Binyon, *For the Fallen* (1914)

Acknowledgements

It has been educational and extremely rewarding to research the stories behind the 48 men from Broadway who died in the First World War and whose names are inscribed on the Broadway War Memorial. I have spent many hours researching their families, their comrades and other Broadway men who gave their lives in the First World War who are not commemorated on the war memorial.

Some of the information that has been used to compile the biographies about each of the men was readily available, such as in the UK, Soldiers Died in the Great War, 1914-1919 database and on the website of the Commonwealth War Graves Commission. Other information took longer to find either by researching family histories using a number of online sources, by visiting The National Archives at Kew, or by reading various accounts of the First World War published online, in books, or in local newspapers. Hours have been spent reading the microfilmed copies of the Evesham Journal at Evesham Public Library. Special mention must be made of The Long Long Trail website, the most useful website about the First World War I have come across.

So many people have been very generous with their time, memorabilia and knowledge. I would like to thank the Committee of Broadway Remembers and particularly Mary Smith who has supported me from the start and helped me obtain much of the information about many of the men and their families. I have been amazed by the generosity of people who have provided me with information, some of whom have visited cemeteries across Europe and beyond to take photos for me. I am very grateful to: Susan Appleby, Cyril Banks, Jane M. Barker, Eman Bonnici, Elizabeth Bubb, Robin Cartwright, Jacky Cook, David Cotterell, Margaret Dufay, Colin Ellis, Robert Emms, Harry Fecitt, Sybilla Flower, Jeff Fox, Julie Green, Peggy Hancock, Charlie Hulme, Sarah Huxford, Graham Knight, Perran Newman, Norman, Keith Pearey and The British School of Paris, Mark Porter, Aurel Sercu, the Wale family, Jacqueline Walker, Marguerite Wiewel, Peter Woodger, Susan Woodhouse, Kim Workman, Len Wright, the Commonwealth War Graves Commission, the Berrows Worcester Journal and the Evesham Journal for providing me with photographs and information. Thanks must also go to all those who have answered questions and provided information via the online forum, the Great War Forum. I would also like to thank Broadway Parish Council for their generous donation towards the printing of this book. Without the help of all these people and many others this book would not have been possible.

As the centenary of the outbreak of the First World War approaches on 4th August 2014, this is my tribute to the men of Broadway who made the ultimate sacrifice.

Debbie Williamson
Broadway
July 2014

Contents

Introduction

In the spring of 1911 the population of the Worcestershire village of Broadway, measured by the census taken on the night of Sunday 1st April 1911, was just 1,793. Just over three years later, on 4th August 1914, Great Britain declared war on Germany and by the end of the following month the Evesham Journal[1] had published the names of 14 Broadway men who had enlisted in the first few weeks of the war. By the end of 1914 the number of men who had enlisted had risen to 116 (see page 133) and by April 1915 over 170 men from the village had joined up to fight for their country.

Following the introduction of conscription at the beginning of 1916, a total of over 300 men from the village served and were involved in conflicts not only on the Western Front[2] which for many symbolises the war, but across Europe, Africa and the Middle East. The war memorial, erected in 1920 on the village green, commemorates 48 of the men from the village who lost their lives in the First World War and this book is a series of biographies about each of them.

Not all of the men commemorated on the memorial were born in Broadway and some had moved away from the village in the early 1900s in search of work in other parts of the country. During my research I came across a number of men who had either been born or lived in Broadway and had died whilst serving during the war but had not been considered by the Broadway War Memorial Committee for inclusion on the memorial. I have included these men in Appendix III at the end of the book.

When the memorial was being planned, a number of meetings took place in the village to discuss how best to remember not only the men from the village who had died but also the sacrifice of those that had served and returned home, several of whom were badly wounded. It was agreed that the memorial would be dedicated to the war dead and their comrades, and I have included information in the appendices about many of the men from Broadway who went to war and returned home.

All of the 48 men on the war memorial are included in the Roll of Honour in St Michael and All Angels' Church[3], Broadway. The Roll of Honour 1914-1918 lists 49 men as it also includes Albert Daffurn (see page 122) who was born in Broadway but had moved to Willersey before emigrating to Canada where he was working when he was mobilized.

Although this book is about the Broadway men of the First World War, the war memorial also commemorates 21 men killed in the Second World War and Kenneth Hensley who died in Malaya in 1955. All 70 of the men commemorated on the memorial laid down their lives for their country.

Roll of Honour in St Michael and All Angels' Church, Broadway.

Lest we forget.

---

1   The Evesham Journal and Four Shires Advertiser is hereinafter referred to as the Evesham Journal.
2   The Western Front was an entrenched line that stretched from the Belgian coast to Switzerland.
3   St Michael and All Angels' Church, Broadway, is hereinafter referred to as St Michael's Church.

The Broadway War Memorial

At the end of the First World War, Broadway, like many other communities, sought to honour the men of the village who had died fighting for their country. On Wednesday 30th April 1919, Broadway Parish Council held a public meeting in the Lifford Memorial Hall[4] to obtain the views of the villagers about how best to remember the village's war dead and all those who had fought with them in the war. The meeting was chaired by George Beale Game, JP of Barn House, whose sons had all served during the war and whose youngest son, Lieutenant Hubert John Game (see page 53), had died whilst serving with the Royal Flying Corps in June 1917. The meeting opened with the proposal by Sir Richard Amphlett Lamb of Tudor House, that "a war memorial, protected by railings and independent of any ecclesiastical building or project, be built in an open public place in the village and that the names of the men of Broadway who had fallen in the war be inscribed on the memorial." Discussion then followed about where the memorial should be located either outside the Lifford Hall or on the village green where the old boundary cross had stood. A number of other schemes were also suggested including a recreation ground and the building of public swimming baths. The meeting ended with Herbert Edward Collier (Farnham House) proposing that a cross be erected in a suitable spot in the village and the motion was carried.

The Village Green, Broadway, c1910 before the building of the War Memorial.
(J. Jacques Jnr., Broadway)

After the public meeting a committee was appointed to oversee the Broadway War Memorial Project chaired by Parish Councillor Alfred Parsons[5] (Luggershill). The members of the Broadway War Memorial Committee were: Secretary and Treasurer Horace Gill (Bell Farm), Albert William Billey[6] (Tower View), Henry Gordon Clegg (Bibsworth House), James William Folkes[7] (Church Street), George Game (Barn House), Arthur Harold Keyte, Sir Richard Lamb, Theodore Howard Lloyd (Pear Tree House),

---

4   The Lifford Memorial Hall (Lifford Hall) is Broadway's village hall that was built in 1915 as a private theatre in memory of James Wilfred 5th Viscount Lifford (1837-1913).
5   Alfred William Parsons, RA (1847-1920) was an English artist, landscape painter, illustrator and garden designer, see page 115.
6   Father of William Robert Billey, see page 12.
7   Father of Francis Alfred Folkes, see page 50.

John Morris (The Green), Richard Slingsby Peirse-Duncombe (Copgrove), Captain Theodore Emmanuel Rodocanachi, DSO, MC (The Hill), Captain Henry Seymour Ayshford Sanford (The Court), Dr Charles Turner Standring (Laurels), Albert Day William Stokes[8] (High Street) and Austin Read Williams (West End). The committee met again a fortnight after the public meeting and decided that the most suitable site for the memorial would be on the village green between Holcroft's Road and Cotswold House. The committee asked for designs for a memorial to be submitted to them and by the end of May 1919, a number of designs had been passed to Alfred Parsons who had agreed to prepare a sketch of a memorial embodying the views received. Based on the suggestions, Alfred Parsons designed a memorial consisting of a bronze figure of an upright soldier to be sculpted by William Silver Frith[9] on top of a stone monolith.

The committee received a number of objections from villagers to a memorial to the fallen and these were discussed at a committee meeting held at the beginning of June. Many alternatives were considered as there was strong feeling that the purpose of a memorial was not only to remember the dead but also to remember and give thanks to those who had fought and returned. It was finally agreed that a memorial should be built and that the inscription of the proposed memorial should read: *In Memory of those men of Broadway who gave their lives in the Great War 1914-1919 and of their comrades who fought with them.*

The following month Captain Henry Sanford submitted a sketch of a cross to be erected on the Lower Green opposite Fairview the home of Miss Ada Faraday[10]. Although this idea was turned down by the committee, Captain Sanford requested that the proposal be put before a public meeting. After considerable discussion about the design of the memorial, John Morris suggested that the committee should visit surrounding villages to see what they had done but this idea was rejected and it was decided instead to hold a second public meeting to obtain the villagers' views.

The second public meeting was held in the Lifford Hall on 26ᵗʰ September 1919 at which Alfred Parsons's design of a bronze Frith figure of a soldier on top of a stone monolith to be built on the green by W. & H. Gardiner[11] of Evesham at a total cost of £300 was approved. The design was subsequently exhibited in the window of John Morris's shop on the village green. It had been agreed that the memorial would be funded by public subscription and in October 1919, a circular was sent to every household in the parish asking for the promise of a subscription however small. By December 1919, 480 circulars had been distributed but only 78 subscriptions had been received or promised so the committee agreed to display the list of subscribers in the post office to encourage more villagers to subscribe, and in January 1920 another public meeting was called to report on the status of the subscriptions.

The January public meeting did not take place. Chairman Alfred Parsons died on 16ᵗʰ January 1920 following a period of declining health after an operation in November 1919. Following his death, a committee meeting was not held until March 1920. The meeting was chaired by Antonio Fernando de Navarro (Court Farm) and a new committee was elected. The members were: Henry Clegg, Charles Stuart Drury (Farnham House), George Game, William Lissaman (Islay House), John Morris, Archibald Renfrew, MRCVS (Croft Villa) and Austin Read Williams. The committee agreed that another design for the memorial was needed and that members should visit other villages to view their memorials.

The committee hired a car to take them to Ashton-under-Hill, Elmley Castle, Saintbury, Stanton, Toddington and Wyre Piddle and following their visits agreed that a memorial cross similar to the one in Saintbury, and the obelisk on a stepped base at Wyre Piddle, be built in Broadway. William Lissaman agreed to draw up some designs and George Game subsequently also submitted a design. However,

---

8   Brother of Susan Alice Box (née Stokes), see page 16.

9   William Silver Frith (1850-1924) was an English sculptor and wood carver and fellow of the Royal Society of Sculptors.

10   Ada Faraday (1854-1936) was the great niece of the scientist Michael Faraday (1791-1867). Her sister, Alice Faraday (1847-1924), married the Victorian illustrator and painter Frederick (Fred) Barnard (1846-1896). In the late 1880s/early 1890s, Alice and Fred Barnard lived in Broadway. Their daughters Dorothy Barnard (1877-1949) and Marion Alice (Polly) Barnard (1874-1946) were the models for John Singer Sargent's iconic painting *Carnation, Lily, Lily, Rose* which he painted in Broadway during the summers of 1885 and 1886.

11   W. & H. Gardiner built Sedgeberrow War Memorial, see page 78.

Antonio de Navarro suggested that the architect and artist Frederick Landseer Maur Griggs[12], who had designed the Chipping Campden War Memorial[13] and the Willersey War Memorial, should also be asked to prepare a design for Broadway.

Frederick Griggs submitted a design and just over a year after the first meeting, a third and final public meeting was held on 3rd May 1920 and it was agreed to accept his design, a framed Latin stone cross on top of a tapered single monolith 14 feet in length set on a three stepped octagonal base. Following the meeting, a number of local builders were asked to tender for the work and relatives of the war dead were requested to send in the names of the fallen for inscription on the memorial. The committee also discussed whether or not the inscriptions on the memorial should include rank, service numbers and regiment details.

By July 1920, £285 1s 7d had been promised in subscriptions and the committee agreed to accept the tender from Jewson and Berkeley of South Cerney of £345 to erect the memorial in Box Ground Stone, a hard wearing premium limestone. A month later the cost of the memorial increased to £383 due to an increase in the price of the stone and an extra labour charge of 2d per hour for the stone masons. Once the costs were agreed, the work started on building the memorial on the village green.

Total subscriptions promised had reached £407 7s 1d by October 1920 and a sub-committee of the War Memorial Committee was formed to agree the names to be inscribed on the memorial. Arthur Keyte, John Morris, Austin Read Williams and Horace Gill were tasked with putting a list of names together. It was suggested by John Morris that an unveiling and memorial service should be held and that Colonel Edward Hankey[14] be asked to unveil the memorial.

The sub-committee initially drew up a list of 59 names to be inscribed on the memorial and they were put before the War Memorial Committee on four separate lists: 'Undoubted', 'Doubtful as to Date and Cause of Death', 'Non-Residents' and 'Alive' (indeed two men considered for inclusion on the memorial, Ernest Clarke and William J. Clarke, were found to be alive and well). It was finally agreed that the names of 42 men should be included and that a further request for names be circulated around the village. Finally the committee settled on 48 names which would be inscribed on the memorial in alphabetical order, six names on each of the eight sunken panels around the memorial. The date of the unveiling and dedication service was set as 16th December 1920 and the inscription was shortened to: *In memory of the Men of Broadway who Died in the War of MCMXIV-XIX and in Honour of their Comrades.*

At 8.15am on Thursday 16th December 1920, a Requiem Mass for the men of the parish who had lost their lives during the war was held at St Saviour's Church conducted by the Very Reverend F. George whose brother had died at Gallipoli. Broadway's school children were given the afternoon off and at 2pm a Memorial Service was held at St Michael's Church conducted by the Reverend Leonard Staniforth, MA. At 2.45pm, hundreds of villagers, school children and the congregations of all the Broadway churches gathered on the village green, and the soldiers who had safely returned home to Broadway at the end of the war formed a guard of honour around the memorial. Colonel Hankey, in the presence of the Bishop of Worcester, Ernest H. Pearce, unveiled the memorial, the foot of which had been covered by a Union Jack provided by Antonio de Navarro. Colonel Hankey then gave a short speech during which he said that he hoped that future generations would never forget what the men had given their lives for and that one day their sacrifice would be realised. The Bishop then followed with a prayer and a dedication of the cross. Antonio de Navarro read out the names of the 48 men and said "Forty-eight gallant men, forty-eight glorious bodies scattered in British and foreign graveyards, but whose individualities assemble here to spiritualise this inanimate stone." He promised that as long as he lived in Broadway he would "remove his hat every time he passed the memorial as a silent homage to the dead and to keep alive through them the

---

12   Frederick Landseer Maud Griggs, RA, RE (1876-1938) had settled in Chipping Campden in 1903.

13   The Chipping Campden War Memorial, designed by Frederick Griggs was unveiled on 9th January 1921.

14   Colonel later Brigadier General Edward Barnard Hankey, CB, DSO (1875-1959) commanded the 2nd Battalion Worcestershire Regiment from September 1914 to December 1914 and the 3rd Battalion from August 1915 to November 1915. He won the DSO at Ypres in 1917 and was presented with the freedom of the City of Worcester in the form of a silver tank in 1917. He was created CB in 1927, awarded the Croix de Guerre and was three times mentioned in despatches.

remembrance of the noble deeds and great sacrifice." The ceremony concluded with prayers including the *Lord's Prayer*, the hymn *O God, our help in ages past* and the laying of wreaths at the foot of the memorial.

The total cost of the memorial and the dedication service was £414 19s 3d which was covered by the subscriptions received, and surplus funds of £1 12s 7d were donated by the War Memorial Committee to the Trustees of the Lifford Hall.

The names of 21 men were added to the memorial at the end of the Second World War and a bronze plaque inscribed with the details of Second Lieutenant Kenneth Andrew Hensley[15], Royal Warwickshire Regiment attached Northern Rhodesia Regiment, was added in the late 1950s following his death on 12th May 1955 whilst serving in Malaya during the Malayan Emergency 1948-1960. The memorial was listed as a Grade II structure in 1987 and work was carried out to partially restore it in May 2014.

Unveiling and Dedication of the Broadway War Memorial, Thursday 16th December 1920.
(Antona)

---

15   Kenneth Andrew Hensley was the great nephew of George Hensley, see page 68. He is buried in Cheras Road Christian Cemetery, Kuala Lumpur.

George Barnett
Private 9562, 1ˢᵗ Battalion Royal Warwickshire Regiment

Pte George Barnett.
(Evesham Journal)

George Barnett was born in Broadway in 1886, the youngest of seven children of William Barnett from Childswickham, and Mary Ann Smith Barnett (née Chadd) from Aston on Carrant near Tewkesbury. George's parents had married in Droitwich on 22ⁿᵈ February 1874 and at the time of their marriage William was working as a grocer. By 1881 William and Mary had moved to Phillipps Cottages[16], Willersey Road (later known as Leamington Road), Broadway, where they raised their family before moving to 29 Council Cottages further along Leamington Road after the new houses were completed in 1913 (see page 14).

George attended Broadway Council School and after leaving school worked as a plough boy in the village before working as a milkman for Henry J. Patten at The Kite's Nest Dairy. On 4ᵗʰ December 1914, George enlisted with the Royal Warwickshire Regiment in Stratford-upon-Avon with fellow Broadway men; Joseph Badger[17], Frederick Goddard (older brother of Arthur Goddard, see page 59), Reginald Hill (see page 71), Algernon John Keyte, Walter Meadows, Frank Phillips (see page 136), Thomas Stanley (younger brother of Charles Stanley see page 102) and Felix Wilfred Lambley[18], a baker from Childswickham, and Charles Herbert Keyte[19] from Snowshill who worked with George at the dairy.

George, along with Frederick Goddard, Reginald Hill, Frank Phillips and Walter Meadows, trained on the Isle of Wight and was posted to the Western Front on 2ⁿᵈ May 1915 with the 1ˢᵗ Battalion. The battalion formed part of the 10ᵗʰ Brigade of the 4ᵗʰ Division of the British Army and in June 1915 was in the trenches at Lancashire Farm outside Ypres.

During the first week of July 1915 part of the battalion was lent to the 11ᵗʰ Brigade and was called on to support troops fighting to capture the International Trench between Pilkem and Boesinghe, along the Yser Canal in Flanders. Casualties were high during the ensuing days and on 9ᵗʰ July 1915 George was killed in action, aged 28. George was initially declared as missing and a possible prisoner of war. The Evesham Journal reported on 7ᵗʰ August 1915:

Nothing has been heard for a month of Pte. George Barnett, of the 1ˢᵗ Batt. Royal Warwick Regt., and at the end of last week his parents, Mr. and Mrs. William Barnett, of the Council Cottages, Broadway, received an official intimation that he was missing. Pte. Barnett had been at the Western front for a couple of months. Several men writing home have stated that they had heard he had been killed, but no direct knowledge or evidence of the fact is forthcoming, so that there is a possibility of his having been taken prisoner. Previous to enlistment Pte. George Barnett was at work for Mr. H. Patten of The Kite's Nest Dairy and was employed as delivering milk in the village. He was generally liked and esteemed, and obliging and trustworthy. General sympathy is felt for the parents in their anxiety and troubles.

Following a request for news, George's parents received the following letter, dated 31ˢᵗ December 1915, from George's commanding officer, C.S. Hewitt, Lieutenant Commanding 'B' Company, 1ˢᵗ

---

16   Phillipps Cottages were named after Sir Thomas Phillipps (1792-1872), 1ˢᵗ Baronet of Middle Hill, Broadway, a collector of books and manuscripts. The Barnett family were neighbours of William and Mary Vincent, parents of Ernest Edward Vincent, see page 113.

17   Pte 30833 Joseph Lawrence Badger, MM (1896-1983), see page 137.

18   Pte 9579 Felix Wilfred Lambley (1896-1949) served with the 1ˢᵗ Battalion Royal Warwickshire Regiment (see letter from Frederick Goddard on page 60). He received a gunshot wound to the head at Arras in November 1915 and was discharged on 18ᵗʰ July 1916 under Section 392(xvi) of the King's Regulations 1912 as he was deemed no longer fit for military service.

19   Pte 9575 Charles Herbert Keyte lived at Earl's Cottage, Broadway. He was employed at The Kite's Nest Dairy as a groom and was discharged on medical grounds from the 3ʳᵈ Battalion Royal Warwickshire Regiment on 13ᵗʰ February 1915 under Section 392(iii)(c) of the King's Regulations 1912 (unfit for service and not likely to become an efficient soldier).

Warwickshire Regiment:

I regret to inform you that your son was killed near Ypres on the 9th-7th-1915. You should have had this information long ago from the War Office. Hoping this will not be too severe a blow for you. With deepest sympathy from his comrades.

BARCLAY A.
BAREFOOT C. H.
BARLEY F.
BARNETT E. W.
BARNETT G.
BARRATT F.
BASTABLE W. H.
BATSFORD W.

Pte George Barnett's inscription on the
Ypres (Menin Gate) Memorial. (Sarah Huxford)

George's body, along with many others who lost their lives during the battle near Boesinghe, has never been recovered and he is commemorated on the Ypres (Menin Gate) Memorial, Belgium (Panel 8). George is also commemorated on the Broadway Council School Memorial Board (see page 128).

George completed an 'informal' will in his army pay book shortly after he enlisted leaving his effects to his mother.

A year after his death the following in memoriam announcements were published in the Evesham Journal on 8th July 1916:

In loving memory of our dear son George, killed in action July 9, 1915.
Sadly missed and mourned by his loving mother and father, brothers and sisters.
A link of a united family broken.

To the memory of our brother George, who fell in action July 9, 1915
In the bloom of his life God claimed him,
In the pride of his manhood days,
None knew him but to love him,
Nor spoke to him but to praise.
Never forgotten by Maud and Charlie.

Ypres (Menin Gate) Memorial.
(Commonwealth War Graves Commission)

Between the 6th and 11th July 1915, over 360 British soldiers lost their lives at Boesinghe. Five other men from the George's battalion died on the same day as George, three are commemorated with him on the Menin Gate and two others, including Harvey Bertram Carter[20] from Childswickham, are buried at Lijssenthoek Military Cemetery.

---

20 Private 9759 Harvey Bertram Carter (1896-1915), 1st Battalion Royal Warwickshire Regiment, who also enlisted in December 1914, died at No. 10 Casualty Clearing Station near Abele in Belgium on 9th July 1915 of a gunshot wound received in action the previous day while carrying grenades to the firing line. Harvey is buried in Lijssenthoek Military Cemetery, Poperinge, and is commemorated on Childswickham's Memorial Board in Childswickham Memorial Hall.

Josiah James Bayliss
Private 25249, Worcestershire Regiment transferred to 278004, Labour Corps

Josiah James Bayliss, known as James, was born in 1882 at Pathlow near Wilmcote and was baptised in the Parish Church of St Andrew, Wilmcote, on 28th August 1882. James was the third and youngest son of Josiah Bayliss, a highways' surveyor from Little Rissington, and Eliza Bayliss (née Harvey) from Oxfordshire. James's parents had married in 1873 and after he was born the family moved to Cromwell House[21], Mickleton. Whilst in Mickleton, James's father worked as a surveyor to the Campden Highways Board, kept the village post office and ran a stationery business. James's mother died in 1886 and his father remarried Susannah Jackson in 1888 and had six further children.

By 1901 James was working as a telegraph messenger living with his eldest brother John Thomas[22] and his wife Martha at Mickleton Post Office where his brother was the postmaster. His father, step-mother and half-brothers and sisters had moved to Gretton near Winchcombe where his father continued to work as a highways' surveyor.

In 1912, in Stow-on-the-Wold, James married Minnie Elizabeth Ann Mustoe, the daughter of James Mustoe, an agricultural labourer, and Elizabeth Ann Mustoe. Prior to their marriage Minnie was living with her brother George in one of the estate cottages in the grounds of Eyford Park, Upper Slaughter. After they married James and Minnie moved to Broadway.

Following the outbreak of war, James enlisted with the Worcestershire Regiment and was later transferred to the Labour Corps. The Labour Corps was formed in January 1917 and was manned by officers and other ranks, often wounded or older men, who had been medically rated below the A1 condition needed for front line service.

In 1919, whilst stationed at the Southern Command Labour Centre, Fovant, on Salisbury Plain, James caught influenza[23] which he suffered with for 42 days before he developed pneumonia. James died, aged 36, on 2nd March 1919 in Fovant Military Hospital. The hospital, staffed by Royal Army Medical Corps personnel and nursing staff, was housed in a row of huts in a field which is still called 'Hospital Field' between Fovant and Compton Chamberlayne. His death certificate states his name as 'James Bayliss' and his occupation as 'Private 27800[24] Southern Command Labour Centre'.

At the time of his death, James's widow Minnie was living along Davies Alley off the High Street. James's coffin was transported to Broadway where a funeral service was held at St Eadburgha's Church on 8th March 1919 prior to his burial in the churchyard (grave N2. 4. 8). His headstone is inscribed with his Worcestershire Regiment service number 25249, and the name 'J. T. Bayliss' which is how James is recorded by the Commonwealth War Graves Commission. James is recorded as 'John Bayliss' in the Roll of Honour 1914-1918 in St Michael's Church.

Following his death, probate was eventually granted to his widow Minnie on 5th February 1925, total effects £81 3s 1d.

The grave of Pte Josiah J. Bayliss
(headstone engraved J.T. Bayliss),
St Eadburgha's Churchyard, Broadway.

---

21 Cromwell House was located next to Cotswold House, Mickleton, opposite the gardens of Mickleton Manor.

22 John Thomas Bayliss was postmaster of Mickleton until 1916 when he moved to Nineveh Farm.

23 The 'Spanish' flu pandemic of 1918-1919 killed an estimated 50 million people worldwide and is estimated to have infected up to one billion people, half the world's population at the time.

24 The Commonwealth War Graves Commission records his service number as 278004.

St Eadburgha's Church, Broadway, where Privates J.J. Bayliss (see page 10), E.E. Emms (see page 40), A. Folkes (see page 48), T. Gould (see page 126), W.J. Tebby (see page 109) and Capt W.R. Ponsonby, DSO (see page 126) are buried.

Worcestershire Regiment
First World War silk embroidered postcard.
(Mary Smith)

Worcestershire Regiment Cap Badge 1902-1923.
(Mary Smith)

William Robert Billey

Private 34604, 2nd Battalion Worcestershire Regiment

Pte William R. Billey.
(Evesham Journal)

William Robert Billey was born in Broadway and baptised at St Michael's Church on 28th March 1897. His parents, Albert William Billey, a builder from Willersey, and Lilian Billey (née Moseley), the daughter of Broadway tailor Charles Moseley, had married in Broadway on 26th December 1895 and moved to the High Street where they had a grocery shop between Fox Yard and Ram's Alley. As well as running the grocers, William's father worked as a builder and decorator. William had one sibling, a younger sister, Annie Louisa, who was born in 1899.

William was a pupil at Broadway Council School before he was sent to The Douglas School, Douglas House, Vittoria Walk, Cheltenham, a small private boarding school for boys under the ownership and headmastership of Joseph Leonard Butler, BA. On leaving The Douglas School in 1912, William joined the office staff of the Great Western Railway (GWR) in Broadway. In July 1914 he moved to the GWR's offices at Chepstow. He later took up posts at Llantrisant and was later appointed head clerk in the railway's Passenger Department at Ebbw Vale in Wales. It was whilst in Ebbw Vale, William turned 18 and in September 1915 he enlisted with the Worcestershire Regiment.

William joined the 2nd Battalion of the Worcestershire Regiment and trained at Devonport before being posted to the Western Front where on 20th December 1915 his battalion joined the 100th Brigade of the 33rd Division at St Hilaire in north east France. During 1916 his battalion took part in the Battle of the Somme and in early 1917 the 1st and 2nd Battles of the Scarpe (the Arras Offensive).

From mid-April 1917, the battalion was stationed in the Croisilles Valley, south east of Arras in the Pas de Calais. On 20th May 1917, his battalion attacked the Hindenburg Line north east of Croisilles. From 3.30am, through thick mist, the battalion attacked the enemy line, made it through the wire and into the German trenches without being detected. They then advanced towards the enemy's support line but the smoke from the shells had thickened the mist into a dense fog and many of the men lost contact and direction in the poor visibility. At several points the German's support line was seized but heavy bombardment caused the men to retreat and by the end of the day the whole of the valley was under fire. All that night and the next day bombing attacks went on up and down the Hindenburg Line. The captured position was held and by night fall on the 21st May the battalion was relieved by the 2nd Royal Welsh Fusiliers and returned to the support trenches west of Croisilles. The casualties had been very heavy. The battalion had gone into battle with 530 officers and men but nearly half their fighting strength had been killed or was missing. One of the casualties of the Actions of Croisilles, the last great fight in the Battle of Arras, was William who died, aged 20, on 21st May 1917.

On 9th June 1917, the Evesham Journal printed an extract from a letter from Private James Stanley, of Broadway, to William's father:

I expect by now you have been informed of your son's death in action. A shell came over and burst amongst a party of our boys, and I am very sorry to say that your son was one of them that was killed.

At the time of William's death his parents were living at Tower View, Broadway. William is buried at Croisilles British Cemetery (grave I. B. 19), just outside the village of Croisilles, to the south east of Arras. His epitaph reads: THY WILL BE DONE. Croisilles British Cemetery, designed by Edwin Lutyens, contains 1171 Commonwealth burials and commemorations of the First World War of which 647 are unidentified. In 1919 William's father joined the Broadway War Memorial Committee (see page 4) and he contributed towards the building of the war memorial in memory of his son. William is also commemorated on the Broadway Council School Memorial Board as 'Robert Billy' (see page 128).

Croisilles British Cemetery, Croisilles, Pas de Calais, France.
(Commonwealth War Graves Commission)

The grave of Pte William Billey,
Croisilles British Cemetery.
(Sarah Huxford)

The entrance to Croisilles British Cemetery,
Croisilles.
(Commonwealth War Graves Commission)

William Bishop
Private 203259, 10th (Service) Battalion Worcestershire Regiment

William Bishop was born in 1888 in Temple Guiting, Gloucestershire, the son of Thomas Bishop, a blacksmith from Broadway, and Sarah Ann Bishop (née Handy). His parents had married in 1881 and William had five siblings, a younger brother and four older sisters. In the 1901 census the family are recorded as living in Temple Guiting where William, aged 12, was working with horses on a farm and his father as the village blacksmith. By 1911 William's father had retired and the family had moved back to Broadway and were living at Hillside Cottages next to Bertram Clarke (see page 21). William found work in the village as a builder's labourer with his cousin, Albert Handy[25].

On 13th April 1914, William married Fanny Malin at St Michael's Church. Fanny had been born in Broadway in 1896, the daughter of Charles Henry Malin, a shepherd, and Elizabeth Malin of Hicks Yard, Broadway. Prior to their marriage, Fanny had worked as a servant for John Dudfield, a farmer at nearby Bourton-on-the-Hill. After their marriage William and Fanny moved to 45 Council Cottages[26]. Their daughter, Kathleen, was born in 1914.

Council Cottages, Leamington Road, Broadway. 60 cottages were built by the Broadway Rural Housing Scheme and completed in 1913.

William enlisted with the Worcestershire Regiment in Evesham and was posted to the 10th (Service) Battalion on the Western Front. When William enlisted he was given the regimental number 20205. He was later reissued with a new number 203259 following the renumbering of the territorial battalions in December 1916.

On 7th March 1918, the battalion moved forward from the reserves near Bapaume to billets in Barastre in readiness for the expected German Spring Offensive which started with the Battle of St Quentin on 21st March 1918. The opening bombardment of the German attack was unprecedented in its intensity with German shells nearly reaching the battalion's billets at Barastre. The British line was heavily bombarded with artillery and gas and an estimated 3,500,000 shells were fired in five hours, the biggest

---

25   Albert Handy served with 440th Agricultural Company, Labour Corps.
26   The Commonwealth War Graves Commission records William Bishop's address as 48 Council Cottages, Broadway, which is where Henry Harold Edwards lived, see page 38.

barrage of the entire war. Dense mist and poor visibility prevailed over the battle site throughout the day allowing German stormtroopers to penetrate deep into the British lines undetected and large parts of the British army had to retreat as forward positions were overwhelmed. At 1pm that afternoon the battalion, part of the 57th Brigade, moved forward to the ridge west of Velu Wood ready to attack Doignies. By 6pm the attack had been cancelled but the order was not received by the brigade in time and the attack on Doignies went ahead at 6.40pm. The battalion met heavy rifle and machine gun fire throughout the night, and thick fog hampered the fighting on both sides the following day. However, by the evening of 22nd March the battalion had managed to hold their line along a sunken road between Beaumetz and Doignies. Several British and German battalions were wiped out on the first day of the German Spring Offensive. During the second day of the offensive, 22nd March 1918, William was declared as missing in action.

Four months later William was still missing, and on 27th July 1918 the Evesham Journal appealed for information about William:

Mrs. W. Bishop, of 45, Council Cottages is most anxious to hear news of her husband, Pte. W. Bishop, of the Worcesters, who has been missing since March 22 last. If any of his comrades can give his wife any information concerning him she will be very grateful.

William was later declared as having been killed in action, aged 29, on 22nd March 1918 and he is buried at Beaumetz Cross Roads Cemetery, Beaumetz-les-Cambrai, France (grave D. 28). 250 casualties are commemorated in Beaumetz Cross Roads Cemetery.

Beaumetz Cross Roads Cemetery, Beaumetz-les-Cambrai, France.
(Commonwealth War Graves Commission)

William Arthur Box
Private M/340163, Mechanical Transport Spare Parts Depot, Army Service Corps

Born in Broadway in 1879, William Arthur Box, known as Arthur, was the son of Joseph Box, a groom from Blockley, Gloucestershire, and Fanny Box (née Kempson). William's parents had married in 1876 and moved to the High Street, Broadway. Arthur was baptised on 29th June 1879 at St Michael's Church. He had an older sister, Annie Elizabeth born in 1877, and a younger brother Tom, born in 1885.

Arthur was a pupil at Broadway Council School and after leaving school worked as a groom in the village. On 30th August 1899, aged 20, Arthur married Susan Alice Stokes at St Michael's Church. Susan[27], known as Alice, was from Evesham, the daughter of wheelwright Frederick Stokes and his wife Rebecca. After their marriage, Arthur and Alice lived in Broadway where their first daughter, Elsie Nellie, was born on 22nd November 1900. Shortly afterwards, the family moved to Toddington where Arthur continued to work as a groom until he learnt to drive and found work as a chauffeur. Their second daughter, Mabel Kathleen, was born in Dumbleton in 1903 and shortly afterwards the family moved to Laverton, where their third daughter Edith Annie was born in 1905 followed by their only son Willie George in 1907. Arthur and Alice's youngest daughter, Doris, was born in 1912.

Arthur enlisted in Broadway with the Army Service Corps[28] and he served at a Spare Parts Depot of a Mechanical Transport Company in East Africa. At the outbreak of the First World War, Tanganyika (now Tanzania) was the centre of German East Africa. From its invasion in April 1915 by Commonwealth forces, a long and difficult campaign was fought against a small but highly skilled German force, led by Colonel Paul Emil von Lettow-Vorbeck, commanding officer of the Colonial Army of German East Africa, which eventually surrendered on 25th November 1918 as required by the armistice signed in Europe.

Whilst in Tanganyika, Arthur died of nephritis (inflammation of the kidneys) on 14th January 1918, aged 39. He is buried in Dar Es Salaam War Cemetery, Tanzania (grave 4. E. 9). The cemetery contains 1,764 Commonwealth burials of the First World War, of which 60 of them are unidentified. Arthur is commemorated on the Broadway Council School Memorial Board (see page 128) and he is also commemorated on the stone memorial tablet inside St Michael's Church, Buckland, alongside the names of seven other casualties of the First World War including John William Grimmitt of Broadway (see page 129).

The grave of Pte William Box (right), Dar Es Salaam War Cemetery. (Harry Fecitt)

---

27   Susan's brother, Albert William Day Stokes, was on the Broadway War Memorial Committee, see page 4.
28   The Army Service Corps received the 'Royal' prefix in late 1918. The Royal Army Service Corps was responsible for delivering equipment, ammunition, food and other supplies from Britain to the various front lines by motor vehicles, railways or waterways.

Dar Es Salaam War Cemetery, Tanzania.
(Commonwealth War Graves Commission)

Stone Memorial Tablet inside St Michael's Church, Buckland, Gloucestershire, designed by the
architect Alexander Fisher, which was unveiled in 1920.

Albert Henry Clarke
Private 15372, 11th (Service) Battalion Worcestershire Regiment

Albert Henry Clarke was born in Broadway in 1893 and baptised at St Michael's Church on 12th April 1893. Albert was the third son of Albert Clarke, a butcher and slaughter man from Dumbleton, and Emma Mary Clarke (née Keyte) of Broadway. Albert's parents had married in Broadway in 1889 and lived along Back Way before moving to live with Mary Keyte, Emma's mother, in China Square at the foot of Springfield Lane (see page 77). Albert had seven siblings and was first cousin to Charles Hubert Keyte (see page 80). Albert grew up in Broadway and after leaving school worked as a groom for Thomas Bayliss, grocer, corn and offal dealer of Sheldon House.

Pte Albert H. Clarke.
(Evesham Journal)

In September 1914, aged 21, Albert enlisted in Broadway with Kitchener's Army[29] and joined the 9th (Service) Battalion Worcestershire Regiment. Albert trained at Tidworth, Basingstoke and Aldershot before moving to Blackdown on Salisbury Plain by May 1915. The battalion formed part of the 39th Brigade of the 13th (Western) Division which was made up of four battalions including the 9th (Service) Battalion Royal Warwickshire Regiment[30]. Fellow Broadway man Wilfred Tandy (see page 107) who was with the 9th Royal Warwicks would have been at Blackdown with Albert where the division amassed prior to being posted to Gallipoli[31] in June 1915.

The 13th Division was posted to Gallipoli to reinforce the allied forces made up of British, Australian, New Zealand, Indian and French troops, who were engaged in an attempt to seize the Dardanelles from the Ottoman Empire[32]. On 20th June 1915 the division left Blackdown on Salisbury Plain by train for Avonmouth. At Avonmouth the battalion boarded the transport ship SS Cawdor Castle and set sail for Mudros on the island of Lemnos, briefly stopping at Malta and Alexandria en-route. The battalion arrived at Cape Helles (see map on page 108) on the Gallipoli peninsular during the first week of July and the following month was involved in the Battles of Sari Bair, Russell's Top and Hill 60. Soon afterwards they were transferred northwards to Suvla and by the end of the year the battalion had moved back to Helles before being evacuated from Gallipoli to Egypt in early January 1916 when the allied forces withdrew from the peninsula. During his time in Gallipoli, Albert was injured by a kick from a horse and was transported back to England to recover from his injuries where he spent some time in a military hospital in Stockport.

After a period of recuperation, Albert rejoined his regiment and in August 1916 was posted to the 11th (Service) Battalion. The battalion was in Salonika, now Thessaloniki, in Macedonian Greece, with the 78th Brigade of the 22nd Division, part of the British Salonika Force engaged in battles against the Austro-Hungarian and Bulgarian forces on the Macedonian (Salonika) Front.

The harsh winter of 1916/17 in Salonika immobilized both sides and there were few casualties during that time. The 11th Worcesters alternated between the forward trenches near Horseshoe Hill and

---

29   Kitchener's Army, K1 the 'first hundred thousand', was collectively the six new Army Divisions created from new infantry battalions made up of volunteers who enlisted after *Your King and Country need you: a call to arms* was published on 11th August 1914. The new Divisions moved overseas in early 1915.

30   The 39th Brigade of the 13th (Western) Division comprised the 9th (Service) Battalion Royal Warwickshire Regiment, 7th (Service) Battalion Gloucestershire Regiment, 9th Battalion Worcestershire Regiment and the 7th Battalion North Staffordshire Regiment.

31   The Gallipoli Campaign, also known as the Dardanelles Campaign took place on the Gallipoli peninsula in the Ottoman Empire between 25th April 1915 and 9th January 1916. The campaign was fought by Commonwealth and French forces in an attempt to force Turkey out of the war, to relieve the deadlock on the Western Front and to open a supply route through the Dardanelles and the Black Sea.

32   Turkey formally entered the war on 28th October 1914, and on 5th November 1914 France and Britain declared war on the Ottoman (Turkish) Empire.

their reserve trenches. By March the weather had improved and the Allied forces prepared for active operations in the trenches at Senelle Ravine, near Lake Doiran. The battalion was relieved by the 9th (Service) Battalion Gloucestershire Regiment on 31st March and retired to the reserve at Pearse Hill where they received further training in preparation for a planned attack on the enemy's position. On 8th April, the battalion relieved the 9th Battalion Gloucestershire Regiment in the front line trenches where they remained until 13th April. On 13th April the battalion marched back to camp at Pivoines where they spent six days' training before moving to forward to shelters in the Senelle and Elbow Ravines, close behind the front trenches. On 23rd April word came that they were to attack the following night with a direct frontal attack across the Jumeaux Ravine. Throughout the night of 24th April the battalion came under heavy fire and repeated counter-attacks and gradually the length of the trench held by the battalion became shorter and shorter and eventually they were ordered to retire. Out of battle strength of around 500, the 11th Worcesters had lost over 350 officers and men. One of those men was Albert who was killed in action during the night of 24th/25th April 1917[33] in the battle that became known as the First Battle of Doiran. The Evesham Journal reported on 19th May 1917:

A letter written a day before his death was received by his parents on Monday. In it he stated that he had for the first time met his cousin, Pte. T. Handy[34], and that they had together been to the hospital and seen another cousin, Pte. W. Keyte[35], who was a patient therein. Since the writing of that letter it has been officially notified that Pte. T. Handy was killed in action on the same date, April 24.

Albert is commemorated on the Doiran Memorial in the north of Greece near the villages of Drossato and Doirani at the western end of the old Allied front line, an area held by the British Salonika Force between 1916 and 1918. The memorial stands on what used to be called Colonial Hill and marks the scene of the fierce fighting of 1917-1918, which caused the majority of the Commonwealth battle casualties.

Doiran Memorial, Greece, designed by Sir Robert Lorimer with sculpture by Walter Gilbert. The Memorial serves the dual purpose of Battle Memorial of the British Salonika Force and a place of commemoration for more than 2,000 Commonwealth servicemen who died in Macedonia and whose graves are not known.
(Commonwealth War Graves Commission)

33   The Commonwealth War Graves Commission records his date of death as 25th April 1917.
34   Pte George Thomas Handy was killed in action in Salonika on the same date, 24th April 1917, see page 129.
35   Pte Wilson William Keyte, see page 138.

Inscription on the Doiran Memorial.
(Commonwealth War Graves
Commission)

Men of the 11th (Service) Battalion Worcestershire Regiment, 1915.
(Berrows Worcester Journal)

Men of the 11th (Service) Battalion Worcestershire Regiment, 1915.
(Berrows Worcester Journal)

Bertram Clarke
Private 30483, 2nd Battalion Worcestershire Regiment

Bertram Clarke, known as Bert, was born Bertram Shirley in Birmingham 1896, the only son of John Shirley and Caroline Shirley (née Masters). Bert's mother was born in Great Bridge, Staffordshire, the daughter of a baker. Bert's parents had married in Birmingham in 1894 and at the time of their marriage his mother, Caroline, was living with her widowed mother, Mary Ann Masters, at 253 Heath Street, Rotton Park (now Winson Green), Birmingham, where they had a butcher's shop.

Pte Bertram Clarke.
(Evesham Journal)

Bert's father died, aged 36, in 1900 when Bert was three years of age. The following year, Bert, his mother Caroline and grandmother Mary, are recorded in the 1901 census as living at 39 Foundry Road, Winson Green. Lodging with them was Charles Clarke[36], aged 25, from Broadway who was working as a bedstead maker. Charles was the son of Job Clarke and Emma Clarke (née Adams) and the uncle of Jack Tustin (see page 111).

Bert's mother married Charles Clarke in King's Norton in 1912 and they had two daughters, Laura Maud born later that year and Winifred Mary born in 1910. Shortly after Winifred was born the family moved to Hillside Cottage, London Road, Broadway, next door to William Bishop (see page 14). Bertram was enrolled at Broadway Council School where he finished his education before finding work in the village as a farm labourer.

Bert enlisted with the 2nd Battalion Worcestershire Regiment in Evesham during the autumn of 1915 in the name Bert Clarke. Bert served on the Western Front with the 100th Brigade of the 33rd Division. His battalion took part in the battles of the Somme in 1916, the First and Second Battles of the Scarpe (the Arras Offensive) in early 1917 and the Third Battles of Ypres later that year.

In April 1918, the battalion was involved in the Battle of Lys (the Fourth Battle of Ypres) during the German Spring Offensive. The battle began on 7th April 1918 and part of the battalion became surrounded in the town of Neuve Église[37] near Ploegsteert in Belgium. Bert was subsequently reported as missing in action between 11th and 17th April 1918. Several months later, on 3rd August 1918 the Evesham Journal published a request for information about Bert along with a request for information about Private Alec Stanley (see page 101) also of the 2nd Battalion Worcestershire Regiment who had been reported as missing in action at the same time.

A year later on 19th April 1919, Bert's parents and sisters placed the following announcement in the Evesham Journal:

Clarke - Reported missing, 16th of April 1918. Pte. Bert Clarke, 2nd Worcesters, of Broadway. The hardest and bitterest blow of all, is not knowing where he is.

Bert's body was never found and he is commemorated on the Ploegsteert Memorial, Belgium (Panel 5). His date of death is given as 16th April 1918. The Ploegsteert Memorial to the Missing (also known as Hyde Park Corner and referred to colloquially at the time as 'Plug Street') stands in the middle of Berks Cemetery Extension, which was founded by Commonwealth troops in June 1916 and lists almost 11,500 missing Commonwealth soldiers from battles in the area. The memorial was designed by Harold Chalton Bradshaw, CBE with sculpture by Gilbert Ledward and the grounds were assigned to the United Kingdom in perpetuity by King Albert I of Belgium in recognition of the sacrifices made by the British in the defence and liberation of Belgium during the war. Bert is also commemorated on the Broadway Council School Memorial Board as 'Bertram Clark' (see page 128).

---

36   Charles Clarke's sister, Annie, married Algernon Tustin, father of Jack Tustin, see page 111.
37   After the Battle of Neuve Église in April 1918, Pte Charles Jarrett 2nd Battalion Worcestershire Regiment, of Bury End, Broadway, was awarded the Croix de Guerre (see page 139).

Ploegsteert Memorial, Berks Cemetery Extension, Belgium. The panels inside the memorial are inscribed with the names of the missing.
(Fédération du Tourisme de la Province de Hainaut)

Gilbert Ledward was the sculptor of the memorial which includes two large recumbent lions.
(Len Wright)

Pte Bertram Clarke's inscription on the Ploegsteert Memorial.
(Sarah Huxford)

Archibald William Collins

Private 16263, 10th (Service) Battalion Gloucestershire Regiment

Pte Archibald W. Collins.
(Evesham Journal)

Archibald William Collins, known as Archie, was born in Broadway in 1896 the second son of Charles William Collins, a farm labourer from Broadway, and Mary Jane Collins (née James) from Cutsdean. His parents had married in 1891 in Childswickham and lived at Mount Pleasant Cottages before moving to live on the High Street, Broadway.

Archie was a pupil at Broadway Council School and after leaving school was apprenticed as a baker in the village. By 1911 Archie's father was working as a builder's labourer in the village and his sister, Elsie, was employed as a parlour maid at The Lygon Arms Hotel.

Archie enlisted with the 10th (Service) Battalion Gloucestershire Regiment in January 1915 and joined the battalion in billets in Cheltenham. During their stay in Cheltenham the battalion trained at Cleeve Hill with the 9th (Service) Battalion Gloucestershire Regiment and Cheltenham College Officer Training Corps. On 6th May 1915, the Mayor of Cheltenham, Alderman William Nash Skillicorne, saw the battalion off from Cheltenham station and the battalion moved to Sutton Veny, Salisbury Plain, to complete their training. The battalion then spent a short time at Longbridge Deverill, Wiltshire, before being posted to France.

On 8th August the battalion crossed from Southampton to Le Havre arriving in France the following morning where the battalion joined the 1st Brigade of the 1st Division on the Western Front. In September the battalion moved to the trenches at Bois Carré, west of Hulluch, in the Pas de Calais. During the artillery bombardment of the German trenches in the days preceding the Battle of Loos[38], north west of Lens, on 22nd September 1915, Archie was wounded and died four days later, aged 19, on Sunday 26th September 1915. He is buried in Noeux-les-Mines Communal Cemetery, in the Pas de Calais, France (grave I. B. 26). His epitaph reads: *THERE IS A LINK DEATH CANNOT SEVER LOVE AND REMEMBRANCE LIVE FOREVER.*

On 23rd October 1915, the Evesham Journal reported:

General regret is expressed at the loss of Pte. Archibald Collins, of the 10th Gloucesters, who was wounded on September 22 and died on the 26th. He was the second son of Mr. and Mrs. Charles Collins, jun. of the Council Cottages[39], Broadway – a nice lad, and only nineteen years old. He was a baker by trade, and had worked for Messrs. Biles[40] (Broadway), Stanley (Stanton), and Davis (Broadway). Pte. Collins joined the army in January last, and trained at Cheltenham and Aldershot. In August he went out to the French front, where he had been engaged as a bomb thrower. Sincere sympathy is felt for his parents and family in their trial. Mr. and Mrs. Collins have two other sons serving in the army.

Archie is also commemorated on the Broadway Council School Memorial Board (see page 128).

The grave of Pte Archibald W. Collins,
Noeux-les-Mines Communal Cemetery.
(Margaret Dufay)

---

38   The Battle of Loos, 25th September to 18th October 1915, was the first battle where the British Army used gas. Over 12 British Divisions were involved, totalling approximately 150,000 men.

39   11 Council Cottages, Leamington Road, Broadway.

40   The three sons of William Henry and Gertrude Biles served: Pte Frank Arthur Biles with the Army Service Corps and the Royal Sussex Regiment, Pte William Henry Biles as a baker in the Army Service Corps and Gordon Highlanders, and Pte Percy George Biles as a signaller with the 9th (Service) Battalion Gloucestershire Regiment.

Noeux-les-Mines Communal Cemetery, Pas de Calais, France. The cemetery was designed by Sir Edward Lutyens.
(Margaret Dufay)

Archie's brothers, Pte Oscar Collins and Pte Horace Collins.
(Evesham Journal)

Gloucestershire Regiment
Cap Badge.
(Mary Smith)

Archie's eldest brother Oscar, who had entered service and worked as a house boy in the village, had moved to London where he was employed as a valet for Mr. S. Bruce, 23 Cromwell Road, London. Oscar enlisted in Chipping Campden with the 11th (Reserve) Battalion Gloucestershire Regiment on 27th August 1915. From March 1916 Oscar served as an infantryman with the 3/4th Battalion and was transferred to 1/4th Battalion on 8th April 1916. Whilst in Egypt, on 26th March 1917, Oscar received a gunshot wound to his left forearm and was treated in the 15th, 17th and 19th General Hospitals[41] in Alexandria. Oscar later served in Palestine, and in November 1917 was transferred to the Labour Corps (808th Area Employment Company) attached to the Royal Engineers until he was discharged from the army on 17th March 1919.

In 1916 the Evesham Journal reported that Archie's brother Horace, who had worked as a farm labourer in the village prior to his enlistment in February 1915, was serving with the 9th (Service) Battalion Gloucestershire Regiment. The Absent Voters' List 1918[42] for Broadway lists Horace as serving with 'C' Company 1/4th Battalion Welsh Regiment (see page 139).

---

41   5th General Hospital, Alexandria, was set up in April 1915 in the buildings of the Abbassieh Secondary School (an Egyptian Government School). The officer in charge was Colonel Herbert E.R. James, Royal Army Medical Corps. The hospital provided over 1,000 beds for the sick and wounded. 17th General Hospital, Alexandria, was set up in Victoria College and eventually had over 2,000 beds.

42   There was a General Election on 14th December 1918 and men (over the age of 21) serving in the war were recorded in Absent Voters Lists.

Two of Archie's uncles also enlisted: his uncle Albert Collins served as a driver with the Army Service Corps, and his uncle George Collins served on the Western Front with the 10th (Service) Battalion Royal Warwickshire Regiment. Archie's cousin, Hubert Collins (son of Archie's uncle William Collins), served with the Bedfordshire Regiment.

Archie's uncles: Pte Albert Collins and Pte George Collins.
(Evesham Journal)

Archie's cousin: Pte Hubert Collins. (Evesham Journal)

Archie Collins (centre front row) and Childswickham men who
enlisted with the 10th (Service) Battalion Gloucester Regiment.
Back row left to right: Privates Cecil Smith, Reginald William
Gilder, Charles Stephen Carter, Walter Jones.
Front row: Privates Frank Wilfrid Hodgkins, Archibald William
Collins, Alfred Lloyd Carter (brother of Pte Charles Carter).
(Evesham Journal)

The above photo was published in the Evesham Journal on 13th November 1915. Four of the Childswickham men pictured above with Archie were killed during the Battle of Loos. Three are commemorated together on the Loos Memorial (Panel 60 to 64): Private Cecil (Charles E.) Smith who was gassed and died on 13th October 1915, Privates Reginald William Gilder and Frank Wilford (Wilfrid) Hodgkins who were both killed in action on the first day of the battle on 25th September 1915. Pte Alfred Lloyd Carter also died on 25th September and is buried in Cabaret-Rouge British Cemetery (grave XXVI. D. 10), Souchez, Pas de Calais, France.

William George Crump
Yeoman of Signals, 220097 HMS Revenge, Royal Navy

William George Crump was the eldest son of George Crump of Bromsgrove, and Prudence Delsaux Emily Fricker Crump (née Keeling) of Dunkerton, Somerset. William's father, George, had originally worked as a nail maker and had been brought up on Willow Lane, Bromsgrove, the centre of the nail making industry. George married Prudence Keeling on 18th December 1883 in Dunkerton and they moved to Gallipot Farm, Laverton, Gloucestershire, where George took up farming. William was born in Laverton on 9th December 1886 and he had four brothers and five sisters. By 1901 the family had moved to Tuck Mill, Broadway, where his parents ran a beerhouse and farmed the surrounding land.

After leaving school, aged 15, William joined the Royal Navy. He served on destroyers and dreadnoughts and once qualified served as an instructor for 18 months at the Royal Navy School, Plymouth, prior to the outbreak of the war. William excelled at sports and won several rowing and boxing championships.

At the time of the 1911 census William was serving as Leading Signalman on the destroyer HMS Goldfinch which was in dock at Devonport. The following year William married Mary Edith Cotterell, the eldest daughter of Frank Cotterell and Edith Cotterell

Yeoman of Siganls William Crump.
(David Cotterell)

(née Upton) of Willersey Hill Farm, Willersey. William and Mary had three children. Their two daughters, Margaret born in 1912 and Dorothy in 1914, were both born in Somerset and in 1917 their son Raymond was born in Broadway whilst the family were living along Leamington Road.

In June 1914, William was commissioned to HMS Marlborough, an Iron Duke-class battleship, named in honour of John Churchill, 1st Duke of Marlborough. The Marlborough, flying the flag of Vice-Admiral Sir Cecil Burney, joined the 1st Battle Squadron of the Grand Fleet based at Scapa Flow and William served on the admiral's staff as a Yeoman of Signals. During the first two years of the war, the Marlborough did not engage in any direct combat but was involved in blockade activities out of range of German U-boats in the North Sea.

Mary Edith Crump, née Cotterell.
(David Cotterell)

On 31st May and 1st June 1916, the Marlborough was engaged in the Battle of Jutland between the British Grand Fleet and the German High Seas Fleet off the mainland of Denmark. The Marlborough was hit by a torpedo in the diesel engine room but was able to retaliate before being towed back into port. Two men were killed and two were injured. After the battle, William left the Marlborough with eight of the staff when the Admiral transferred his flag to HMS Revenge, the lead ship of the Revenge class of battleships. At the end of 1916, HMS Revenge became the flagship of Admiral Charles Edward Madden, second in command of the Grand Fleet.

William was taken ill in early 1919 with a gastric ulcer and died of peritonitis at the Royal Naval Hospital, Plymouth, on 16th March 1919. His funeral took place with full naval honours in the city and he is buried in Ford Park Cemetery, formerly known as Pennycomequick or Plymouth Old Cemetery, Devon (grave General L. 5. 26). His epitaph reads: I LIGHT THE TAPERS AT MY HEAD & FEET AND LAY THE CRUCIFIX ON THIS SILENT HEART.

William's widow Mary, who had moved to Elm Tree House, High Street, Chipping Campden, received the following letter, dated 22nd March 1919 from Captain George P. Ross[43]:

Dear Mrs. Crump, I was so shocked to hear the sad news about your poor husband, and I sympathise with you and your children. Having known him in the Marlborough and Revenge since 1915, I have always looked on him as one of the finest characters of petty officers I have ever met. Always cheerful, encouraging the youngest, a very fine oar and good all round sportsman and gentleman. We will sadly miss him. He is a great loss to the navy, and all in this ship, from the admiral to the latest joined boy, I am sure deeply feel your great loss.

William's brother, Francis Laurent Delsaux, who had been born in Broadway on 19th January 1897, enlisted in 1914. He served on the Western Front with the Worcestershire Regiment (Private 15857) from 22nd September 1915. Francis was later commissioned and as a Second Lieutenant was attached to the 21 Squadron Royal Flying Corps. He was killed during a practice flight on 16th October 1918 when his RE8[44] aeroplane (number E246) stalled in a sharp turn coming into the aerodrome at Floringhem. Francis is buried in Lapugnoy Military Cemetery in the Pas de Calais, France. His epitaph reads: MERCIFUL JESUS GIVE HIM ETERNAL REST. At time of his death Francis's address was 30 Craven Park Road, Harlesden, Middlesex. Both Francis and William are commemorated on the City of Gloucester Cenotaph in Gloucester Park.

The grave of Yeoman of Signals
William G. Crump,
Ford Park Cemetery.
(Ford Park Cemetery Trust)

The grave of Second Lieutenant
Francis D.L. Crump,
Lapugnoy Military Cemetery.
(Margaret Dufay)

City of Gloucester Cenotaph where Yeoman of Signals William G. Crump and his brother
Second Lieutenant Francis L.D. Crump are commemorated.

---

43   Rear-Admiral George Parish Ross, CB (1875-1942), commanded HMS Marlborough from 25th May 1914 until his transfer to HMS Revenge on 11th February 1917.

44   The Royal Aircraft Factory RE8 was a two-seater biplane reconnaissance and bomber aircraft designed by John Kenworthy.

John Sydney Cull

Private 47558, 15th Squadron Machine Gun Corps 6th (Poona) Cavalry Brigade
formerly 1/1st Worcestershire Yeomanry (Queen's Own Worcestershire Hussars)

John Sydney Cull, known as Jack, was born in Badsey on 2nd November 1890 and was baptised at St James Church, Badsey, on 25th January 1891. Jack was the third son of John Ernest Cull, born in Bengeworth, Evesham, and Ruth Cull (née Silvester) from West Bromwich. His parents had married in Dudley in 1881. His father was a baker and confectioner and his mother a teacher. After his parents married in Dudley in 1881 they moved to The Sumacs, 18 High Street, Badsey, where they opened a bakery and raised Jack and his nine brothers and sisters.

John S. Cull's parents
Ruth Sylvester and John Cull.
(Audrey New/Badsey History Society)

J. E. CULL,
BAKER AND CONFECTIONER,
Dealer in Flour and all kinds of Meals
BIRTHDAY, WEDDING AND FANCY CAKES of all Descriptions.
HOVIS BREAD A SPECIALITY.

HIGH STREET, BADSEY.

1900s advert for J.E. Cull, Badsey.

Jack started at Badsey Infants School on 5th April 1897, leaving, aged 12, on 22nd September 1903. In the 1911 census, Jack is recorded as assisting his father in the bakery which was run from the bakehouse at the back of the family home at The Sumacs. Jack tried to enlist at the outbreak of war but was rejected on medical grounds. He was finally accepted in October 1914 and enlisted with the Queen's Own Worcestershire Hussars. Jack subsequently trained as a gunner and was transferred to the 15th Squadron Machine Gun Corps which was formed on 29th February 1916.

Whilst on leave from King's Lynn where he was stationed, Jack married Maud Marion Richardson of Broadway at St. Michael's Church on Saturday 5th February 1916. Their son, Robin John, was born the following summer on 19th June 1917. The following report of Jack and Maud's wedding was published in the Evesham Journal on 12th February 1916:

Khaki Wedding – A quiet but pretty wedding was celebrated at St. Michael's Church on Saturday between Miss Maud Marion Richardson, only child of the late Sergt. F. Richardson, gymnastic instructor of Cheltenham College, and Mrs. Maud Richardson, of the White City, Broadway, and Mr. John Sydney Cull, of the Queen's Own Worcestershire Hussars, and the third son of Mr. J.E. Cull, of The Sumacs, Badsey. The ceremony was performed by the Vicar (the Reverend F. Trevelyan Snow, M.A.). The bride, who looked very charming, was attired in a dress of white velvet trimmed with old rose point lace and a wreath and veil; also a diamond and pearl pendant and brooch the gift of the bridegroom. The bride was given away by her mother, who wore a navy blue costume. The bride was attended as maid by her cousin, Miss Molly Dudfield, who wore a violet velvet coat and cap. The wedding party all wore Christmas roses and a number of children of friends strewed snowdrops in the path of the bride as she left the church.

Jack served with the Mesopotamia Expeditionary Force on the Tigris Front with the 6th (Poona) Cavalry Brigade (also known as the 6th Indian Cavalry Brigade), which was made up of units from the British Army and the British Indian Army stationed in India. The initial reason for British involvement in the Ottoman province of Mesopotamia (modern day Iraq) was to secure oil supplies from neighbouring Persia and to safeguard the Shatt Al-Arab waterway. However, British forces were drawn further into Mesopotamia as the fighting continued and the Ottoman forces remained undefeated.

Jack died, aged 27, from influenza on 25th October 1918 a month before the war in Mesopotamia ended and he was buried in Bijar Cemetery, Iran. Bijar is in the northwest of modern day Iran, about 100 miles from the border with Iraq and about 600 miles south of Baku (the capital of Azerbaijan and the centre of important oil fields). Bijar was perhaps one of the most remote places where British and Commonwealth troops were stationed. The cemetery where Jack was buried has since been obliterated and he is commemorated as Private John Sydney Cull on the Tehran Memorial (Panel 5, Column 1) within the grounds of the British Embassy at Gulhak.

At the time of Jack's death, his widow Maud's address was given as 4 White City Estate, Broadway. The news of Jack's death was reported in the Badsey Parish Magazine in December 1918:

On November 11, just as the bells were celebrating the armistice with a merry peal, Mr. Cull received a telegram to the effect that his son, Pte. J.S. Cull, had died of influenza at Basra, on the Tigris, on October 25. Pte. Cull offered his services for his country in August 1914, but was rejected on medical grounds. Two months later he was passed as "fit" and enlisted in the Worcestershire Yeomanry. After a machine-gun course he went out to Mesopotamia as a mounted machine-gunner, in which capacity he saw a considerable amount of fighting. He was formerly a chorister at Badsey Church. Mrs. Cull recently received a letter written by Pte. Cull on October 9 in which he stated that, although there had been fatal cases of influenza, he was in the best of health. A memorial service arranged for November 22 was postponed owing to the Vicar's illness.

A memorial service for Jack was held on 19th December 1918 and the following April the Parish Magazine reported:

Mrs J.S. Cull has received from one of the late Cpl. Cull's officers a letter of sympathy in the course of which he says: "I have found your husband the most willing and obliging man I have ever met. I can honestly say that he was the best man I had under my command. We have been together under fire, and he displayed a coolness and courage any man might envy. He was most popular amongst all ranks and his loss is keenly felt amongst both officers and men."

Jack's name is also inscribed on his parents' headstone in the churchyard at St James Church, Badsey, with the epitaph: FOR YOUR TOMORROW I GAVE MY TODAY. Jack is also commemorated on the stone plaque inside the church which commemorates the men of the parish who died in the war and on the war memorial in Badsey First School (formerly Badsey Council School).

Tehran Memorial, Gulhak, Iran.
(Commonwealth War Graves Commission)

Stone Memorial Plaque,
St James Church, Badsey.

Jack's younger brother, Edgar George, born on 25th February 1897, served with the 1/8th Battalion Worcestershire Regiment (Private 6638). Edgar was wounded in the head by a bullet at Festubert on 24th June 1915 and was admitted to a military hospital in Rouen before being transferred to the Red Cross Hospital, Winchcombe. The hospital which opened in 1915 was housed in two buildings a few hundred yards apart in The Unionist Workmen's Club and the old Infant Schoolroom. The Evesham Journal reported in July 1915:

Pte. Edgar Cull, of Badsey, of the 8ᵗʰ Worcesters (Evesham Co.) came to Hospital A at Winchcombe on Wednesday afternoon. Interviewed by our Winchcombe correspondent on Thursday, Pte. Cull was in bed with a bandage all round his head. He does not appear to be very ill and hopes to be about soon. He received a bullet wound in the head, but not a very serious one, on the night of the previous Thursday, Midsummer Night. The Germans had been shelling them all day giving them a hot time and the infantry followed with a night attack. The Worcesters were down in the valley and the Germans were up on the hill. After his injury Pte. Cull was at hospital in Rouen: he was then brought to Southampton and then per rail to Cheltenham and by motor car to Winchcombe. Some of the other Worcester men were injured at the same time as our Badsey friend, but he thinks they were sent on to Harrogate. All the other Evesham men, Cull said, seemed to be getting on very well. The patient said he was very comfortable indeed at Winchcombe. Cull's opinion of the war is that the Germans will take a lot of moving, but they will get shifted in time. The German artillery, he believes, is very fine.

Edgar later returned to France (Private 242194) and in 1918 news was received that he was being held as a prisoner of war in Germany. Edgar was released from prison in early 1919 and returned home to Badsey. After the death of his father in 1929 Edgar continued to run the bakery business with his brother Alfred. Edgar lived in Badsey until his death in 1969.

The Cull family grave, St James Churchyard, Badsey.

Tom Daffurn
Driver 17522, 'B' Battery 98th Brigade (XVI Corps HQ) Royal Field Artillery

Tom Daffurn[45] was born in Broadway in early 1888 and baptised a few weeks later on 12th February at St Michael's Church. Tom was the only son of Charles Edward Daffurn, a stonemason from Broadway, and Eliza Ann Daffurn (née Ingles) from Willersey. Tom's parents, Charles and Eliza were first cousins. When Tom was young his parents adopted his cousin Francis Henry Ingles (see page 75), son of his father's sister, Emily Ingles. Tom and Francis were brought up together in the village and attended Broadway Council School.

Driver Tom Daffurn.
(Elizabeth Bubb)

Tom grew up working with horses and after leaving school, Tom went to work at the kennels of the North Cotswold Hunt in Broadway before obtaining work as a groom for Percy John Pelly, JP[46] at Stanton Court, Stanton, and later for Captain Arthur Edward Wrigley, JP[47] at Kiftsgate Court near Chipping Campden.

In the 1911 census Tom, who was still working as a groom, is recorded as boarding with Ezra Webb and his family at the White Hart Inn, 4 Sheep Street, Bicester. Tom later moved to London and worked as a bus conductor prior to enlisting, in the name of Thomas Daffurn with the Royal Field Artillery in London in March 1915.

The North Cotswold Hunt on the Village Green before 1920. (J. Jacques, Jnr., Broadway)

---

45 Tom Daffurn was first cousin to Francis Henry Ingles (see page 75) and Charles Robert Stanley (see page 102).
46 Percy John Pelly, JP (1853-1952) held the office of JP of Gloucestershire and hunted with the North Cotswold Hunt.
47 Captain Arthur Edward Wrigley, JP (1865-1952) served with the Manchester Regiment and the Lancashire Fusiliers during the war.

Given Tom's experience with horses it is no surprise that Tom enlisted and trained as a driver with the RFA. Tom trained firstly at Woolwich and transferred to Maidstone in April 1915. As a driver, Tom would have been put in charge of a team of up to six horses used to pull field guns or gun limbers. He was posted to Flesselles near Amiens, France, on 4th September 1915 with 'B' Battery of the 98th Brigade RFA, part of the 22nd Divisional Artillery. His stay in Flesselles would have been short as on 25th October 1915, the brigade moved on to Marseilles by train where it embarked for Salonika on 27th October 1915, part of the British Salonika Force. The brigade disembarked at Salonika in November with the final artillery units arriving in December.

In 1916 the 98th Brigade took part in the Battle of Horsehill Hill from 10th to 16th August 1916 and the Battle of Machukovo on 13th and 14th September 1916. However, Tom was invalided with malaria during the year and was transferred by hospital ship to a military hospital in Malta[48] for treatment.

Tom was deemed fit enough to rejoin his brigade in Salonika in March 1917. Five weeks later, on 24th and 25th April 1917, the brigade was involved in the Battle of Doiran. During the action Tom was injured and was once again transported to hospital in Malta. Tom did not recover from his injuries and died in St George's Hospital on 1st May 1917, aged 29.

Thomas is buried in Addolorata Cemetery, Malta (grave E. EA. A. 612). The cemetery lies on the outskirts of the village of Paola and contains 250 Commonwealth burials of the First World War. Tom is also commemorated on the Broadway Council School Memorial Board (see page 128).

The grave of Pte Tom Daffurn, Addolorata Cemetery, Malta.
(Eman Bonnici)

Tom had completed a will in his army pay book on 3rd March 1915 whilst stationed at the headquarters of the Royal Artillery at Woolwich but it is not known whether or not his wishes were carried out. His will reads:

In the event of my death I give half my property and effects to my mother Mrs C. Daffurn, High Street, Broadway, Worcs. The other half to Miss G.C. Britnell, Rose Cottage, St George's Rd, Weybridge, Surrey.

---

48   From the spring of 1915, hospitals and convalescent camps established on Malta and Gozo dealt with over 135,000 sick and wounded mainly from Gallipoli and Salonika. Malaria was the main cause of sickness followed by dysentery and then enteritis. From April 1917 increased submarine activity in the Mediterranean meant that fewer hospital ships were sent to the islands.

Tom's will was filed by the War Office on 19th September 1917. The accompanying form filed with Tom's will states that Tom died of drowning[49] but gives no further details. His beneficiary Gertrude Cecilia Britnell had worked as a servant at Alchester House, Sheep Street, Bicester, near to where Tom had worked as a groom.

The following in memoriam announcement, was printed in the Evesham Journal on 26th April 1919:

In loving memory of Tom Daffurn, of Broadway, Worcestershire, who died at Malta, May 1st 1917. Also of Frank Ingles, of the West Kents, who was reported missing March 21st, 1918, beloved sons of Charles and Elizabeth Daffurn. Their warfare o'er from earthly strife they're gone to hear their Lord's sweet gracious word. Well done.

Tom Daffurn and Francis H. Ingles.
(Peggy Hancock)

---

49   At the time it was reported that Tom died of his injuries in hospital. Drowning, however, was fairly common, men fell into the sea (or were casualties of a sinking at sea), lakes, canals and many slipped into mud or deep shell holes on the battlefields and sank before they could be rescued.

John William Earp
Sergeant 88389, 'C' Battery 84th Brigade Royal Field Artillery

John William Earp was born in the summer of 1879 in Keyham, a small village in the parish of Rothley, Leicestershire, the only son of John Earp, a gardener, and Sarah Earp. After leaving school John entered service and worked as a footman and then as butler for the family of Joseph Crisp Clarke, a thread manufacturer, at Birstall Hall, Birstall, near Barrow-upon-Soar.

In 1909, George Hodges Crisp Clarke, the eldest son of Joseph Crisp Clarke, married Nellie Eileen Game, the daughter of George Game and the sister of Hubert John Game (see page 53) at St Michael's Church, Broadway. Joseph and Eileen moved to The Elms, Bitteswell near Lutterworth, and John moved with them to The Elms to be their butler.

John W. Earp.
(Evesham Journal)

John married Mary Elizabeth James, the cook at The Elms, in 1910 and shortly after they married, John and Mary moved to Broadway where John served as butler to the Game family at Barn House and also for Richard Peirse-Duncombe. On 7th March 1914, John and Mary's daughter, Evelyn Mary, was born in Broadway.

John enlisted in early 1915, and in February 1915 he joined the 84th Brigade of the Royal Field Artillery, part of the 18th (Eastern) Division. The brigade trained at Colchester and then on Salisbury Plain. Whilst on Salisbury Plain the division was inspected by HM King George V on 24th June before mobilization to the Western Front. John was posted to France on 25th July 1915 in the rank of bombardier, and by the end of July 1915 the 18th Division had assembled near Fleselles on the Somme in France where it remained on the Western Front for the duration of the war. During 1916 the 84th Brigade was involved in the many battles and actions of the Somme.

On 25th January 1917, the brigade left the 18th Division and on 8th February 1917 formed a new type of artillery unit, the 84th Army Brigade RFA, which could be attached to any division, corps or army, needing artillery reinforcement. The 84th Army Brigade served with 22 different divisions between February 1917 and the end of the war. In 1917 the brigade took part in the Battles of Vimy Ridge and Messines. John served with 'C' Battery and in March 1917 was promoted to Corporal.

During the war John corresponded with Captain Henry Clement Game (see page 55), the brother of Hubert Game. Henry had also joined the RFA but was injured in 1916 during the Battle of the Somme and had returned home to 3 Primrose Hill Studios, London.

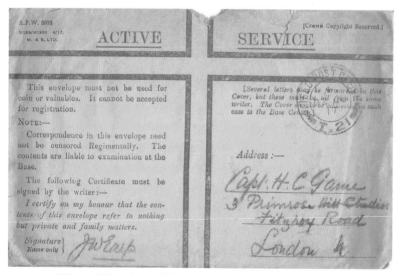

'Honour' Envelope addressed to Captain Henry C. Game
from John W. Earp. (Perran Newman)

John wrote the following letters to Captain Henry Game from the Western Front:

12th April 1917

Sir,

Just a line to thank you for the parcel you so kindly sent me this week. It came very acceptable especially this week. Everything travelled well and did not get a bit broken. I was made Corporal about a month ago. You addressed the parcel to no. 3 Section, but I got it alright my address is (Army F.A.) 84th B.A.C. We have been having some very wintry weather here lately snowstorms and rain and bitterly cold. I have been sick for this last week with a sprained ankle. I am back on duty again, but it is still very painful when I get on it too much and the mud makes it worse. It happened through the trail of a Ammunition Waggon falling on it and they had to move it before I could get it out. I am glad to hear that you are getting to like your new job. But I expect you would rather have kept on with the Artillery. I hope you are quite well and Mrs Game. I am very well in health myself. I think this is all this time.

I am Sir

Yours respectfully

J.W. Earp

12th May 1917

Sir,

Just a few lines in answer to your letter I would have written before, but I am rather busy now all this busy fighting going on as I am working on an Ammunition Dump and am in charge of our part as Issuer so someone is always coming for something. It is quite a change and it is not heavy work for an N.C.O. I am attached to the 2nd Division I am sorry I have not been able to get to know definitely about Truco[50] yet as I am a good way from the Waggon Lines[51] but I understood from Caig[52] last time I saw him that the Capt. in A/84[53] claimed her after Capt. Crumplin[54] left. Caig's address is B/84[55] (Army F.A.). I hope you will be lucky and get her back alright. I was pleased to hear that your health was better and to hear that there were signs of you joining the Army again which by reading shows you must be stronger. I was sorry to hear about Mr McKenzie I did not know he was in England as we have left their Division a good time now. Will you please tell him when you see him again I was sorry to hear about him being ill. I hope he will soon get the time now. We are having lovely weather here now I hope it will continue. We are in a warm part of the line now. We seem to be doing pretty well by the papers. I hope Mrs Game is well. I think this is all this time so will close.

I Remain

Yours Respectfully

J.W. Earp

---

50   Truco was Captain Henry C. Game's horse.
51   The artillery guns were horse drawn (siege batteries were mechanically drawn by motor vehicles or tractors) and once in position the horses and supporting waggons were withdrawn to the rear out of range of enemy fire to the waggon lines. Every night the guns and men at the battery position (behind the front line but within range of enemy fire) would be re-supplied with ammunition and rations by waggons from the waggon lines.
52   Driver 93118, Robert Caig Royal Field Artillery.
53   'A' Battery 84th Army Brigade Royal Field Artillery.
54   Captain Cecil Walter Crumplin Royal Field Artillery.
55   'B' Battery 84th Army Brigade Royal Field Artillery.

20ᵗʰ June 1917

Sir,

Just a few lines to thank you very much for the parcel of food & socks I received quite safely. It was very kind of you to think of me, and it came in very useful. We have been kept very busy lately taking ammunition up during these big strafes[56] and had a lot of night work but we get a good rest in the day time. Leave has started fairly brisk so I hope if it keeps on to get one in about two months time. I hope that you are quite well now, also Mrs Game. I am keeping very fit & well. I was very sorry to hear about Mr John[57] I am sure it must have upset you all very much. We have been having some very hot weather lately, but these last few days we have had thunderstorms and the weather is very unsettled since. I have seen Caig and says that your black mare is alright and that the Capt. in A/84 has got her. Cpl. Atkins is a Sergeant in the Colours now. I have been granted proficiency pay dating from Feb. 14 which makes my pay better. I get plenty of riding now which keeps me fit I think and have got a rather good horse. I think this is all the news for this time so I will close.

I am Sir

Yours respectfully

J.W. Earp

16ᵗʰ October 1917

Sir,

You would think me a long time not writing to you, but I thought I should see you when I was home on leave which I had last month from the 22nd till Oct. 2nd. I should have come to see you but I was only in London in the early morning and at night, and Mrs Game told me that you was expected down to Broadway when Mr Peter[58] came on leave which he was expected to do any time then. I was sorry not to have done so. I was very glad to get my leave as it was 20 months since I had my last one, and I feel very much better for going home and seeing my wife & child but I ought not to grumble as I enjoy very good health out here. We are having wretched weather out here lately rain, hail & wind and the mud is awful but I suppose we must expect it at this time of year. We are pretty busy now I am out about every other day for 7 or 8 hours. Do you think you will be fit enough to come out here again? I hope you have got right again now also that Mrs Game is quite well.

I am Sir

Respectfully

J.W. Earp

During his time on the Western Front, John was promoted to Sergeant and he was killed in action, aged 28, on 17ᵗʰ November 1917 whilst in the area near St Julien. John was buried the following day in German Cemetery West, Zonnebeke Road (reference AA/4/1630) now known as Tyne Cot Cemetery, Zonnebeke, Belgium (grave X. A. 19). The Evesham Journal reported on 8ᵗʰ December 1917:

The news reached Broadway this week that Sergt. J.W. Earp, of the Royal Artillery, was killed in action on November 18 (sic). The Chaplain attached to his battery, in a letter to Mrs. Earp, dated 18th ult., said: - "I write to express my deepest sympathy with you in your sorrow. I was called upon to conduct the funeral service, which took place about 3.30pm on Saturday, November 18th, in the presence of his officers and a number of his comrades. It was obvious that Sergt. Earp was greatly respected and loved both by his officers and the lads under him. He is buried in a military cemetery, and full details will be forwarded to you." His officer, Capt. F.B. Bennett, wrote:- "It is with feelings of pain and deep regret that I write to express my deepest sympathy with you and your family in the death of your husband, Sergt. Earp. He was killed

---

56   Strafe was an attack by low-flying aircraft dropping bombs or using machine guns, but it became a general term for a large fierce attack by small arms or artillery fire. The word is of German origin and a popular slogan amongst the German Army during the war was 'Gott strafe England' or 'God punish England'.

57   Hubert John Game, see page 53, younger brother of Henry Clement Game, who died on 8ᵗʰ June 1917.

58   George Geoffrey Game, brother of Hubert John Game, see page 55.

instantly yesterday afternoon, whilst in the execution of his duty. We buried him quietly this afternoon with the full rites of the Church. My brother officers and the non-commissioned officers and men send their deepest sympathy with you in your irreparable loss. May God comfort you."

Tyne Cot, designed by Sir Herbert Baker, is the largest Commonwealth cemetery in the world in terms of burials. There are now 11,956 Commonwealth servicemen of the First World War buried or commemorated in the cemetery. Following John's death probate was granted in London on 6th June 1918 to his widow Mary, total effects £230 7s 10d. John is recorded in the Roll of Honour 1914-1918 in St Michael's Church as 'Thomas Earpe' (see page 3).

The Cross of Sacrifice, which was built on top of a large pill-box, Tyne Cot Cemetery, c1922.
(Commonwealth War Graves Commission)

The grave of Pte John W. Earp,
Tyne Cot Cemetery.
(Sarah Huxford)

Tyne Cot Cemetery, Zonnebeke, Belgium.
(Commonwealth War Graves Commission)

Henry Harold Edwards

Pioneer 37053, 3rd Indian Divisional Signal Company Royal Engineers

Henry Harold Edwards, known as Harry, was born in Kidderminster in 1886, the eldest son of Thomas James Edwards, a carpet weaver from Kidderminster, and Annie Susan Edwards (née Berry). Harry's parents had married in Kidderminster in 1881. Harry's mother died, aged 27, in 1889 and his father secondly married Julia Perry in Kidderminster in 1890.

Kidderminster is renowned for its manufacture of carpets and in the early 1900s around 15 factories were producing carpets in the town. In the 1901 census, Harry, his father, step-mother and step-brother Thomas are recorded as living at 38 Hoo Road, Kidderminster. His father, Thomas and step-mother Julia are recorded as working in a local carpet factory and Harry as a creeler[59] on the carpet looms.

Harry joined the army at the age of 18 and in the 1911 census for Kidderminster he is recorded as being an army reservist having served for seven years before transferring to the Army Reserve. After leaving the army, Harry found work as a postman, and on 30th April 1913 he married Caroline Cropper at St Michael's Church, Cropthorne, Worcestershire, daughter of Alfred Henry Cropper and Rosina Cropper (née Tarplee). After their marriage Harry and Caroline moved to Broadway where Harry worked as the village postman. Harry and Caroline's daughter Joyce Mary was born in Broadway in 1913 and the family moved to 48 Council Cottages.

As a reservist, Harry would have been called up following the outbreak of war. He joined the Worcestershire Regiment, regimental number 7577, and was posted to the Western Front on 12th August 1914. Harry transferred to the Royal Engineers (Pioneer 37053) and whilst at the front was involved in postal work. In June 1915, Harry came across a postcard addressed to Broadway from fellow Broadway man Wilford Figgitt (see page 42) and he added a note to the card stating that he was well.

Later that year, Harry was posted to Mesopotamia with the 3rd Indian Division, also known as the 3rd (Lahore) Division, a division of the British Indian Army. Orders were received on 31st October 1915 for the division to embark at Marseilles for Mesopotamia but their departure was delayed for a fear of submarine attacks and the division did not arrive in Mesopotamia until April 1916 where it joined the Tigris Corps (the Indian III Corps). Following the earlier disaster at Kut-Al-Amara in April 1916 when the British Army surrendered following the Siege of Kut, a new campaign against the Ottoman forces in Mesopotamia which involved the division was launched on 13th December 1916 led by Lieutenant General Sir Frederick Stanley Maude. The division advanced across Mesopotamia on both sides of the River Tigris and was involved on 24th February 1917 in the re-capture of Kut and later in the fall of Baghdad when the British forces took control of the city from the Ottoman troops on 11th March 1917.

Following their success at Baghdad, the division moved north to consolidate their position at Baghdad and to capture the railway at Samarrah. The division was involved in the seizure of Falluja west of Baghdad on 19th March and the Battle of Jebel which started on 25th March 1917. Harry Edwards died, aged 30, on 25th March 1917 and he is commemorated on the Basra Memorial in Iraq (Panels 5 and 61). Until 1997 the Basra Memorial was located on the main quay of the naval dockyard at Maqil, on the west bank of the Shatt-al-Arab to the north of Basra. The memorial was moved to a position along the road to Nasiriyah which was the centre of a major battleground during the Gulf War.

Harry is also commemorated on the Kidderminster War Memorial which was unveiled on 22nd October 1922 by The Earl of Coventry, the Lord Lieutenant of Worcestershire. At the time of his death, Harry's widow, Caroline and young daughter Joyce, were living at 48 Council Cottages, and his father at 7 Jerusalem Walk, Kidderminster.

---

59   Creelers were responsible for maintaining a full supply yarn on the rack (creel) from which the yarn was drawn by the carpet tufting machine.

Due to the political situation in Iraq, a two volume Roll of Honour listing all casualties buried and commemorated in Iraq, has been produced which are on display at the Commission's Head Office in Maidenhead.
(Commonwealth War Graves Commission)

The Kidderminster War Memorial is in two parts, a statue by Alfred Drury and a crescent shaped wall designed by G.H. Goodwin and built by George Brown & Sons of Kidderminster. The memorial was unveiled by the 9th Earl of Coventry, Lord Lieutenant of Worcestershire, and dedicated by the Bishop of Worcester on 22nd October 1922. (Robin Cartwright)

Ebenezer Evelyn Emms
Private 32962, Royal Berkshire Regiment and 146497, 424th Agricultural Company Labour Corps

Ebenezer Evelyn[60] Emms was the second son of George William Emms, a groom from Broadway, and Elizabeth Emms (née Hopkins). Ebenezer was born in Broadway on 24th May 1884 and grew up in the village where the family lived at Tan Yard. Ebenezer was a pupil at Broadway Council School and after leaving school worked as a butcher's assistant. Ebenezer is recorded in the 1901 census as living with John Roberts and his family at West End, Broadway, whilst working as a butcher.

The following year, on 17th February 1902, Ebenezer enlisted with the Royal Artillery (Royal Horse Artillery and Royal Field Artillery) in Worcester. His enlistment papers record that Ebenezer, service number 22342, was 5' 5¾" tall, weighed 127lbs and had brown hair, a fresh complexion with blue eyes. Ebenezer trained and served as a gunner, initially serving at home from 29th April 1902 in Coventry, Trowbridge, Okehampton, and later at Bulford having been posted to the 118th Battery of the RFA. At the end of March 1904, Ebenezer requested the extension of his army service to 8 years and he was posted to the 10th Battery RFA on 17th August 1907. A month later Ebenezer was posted to South Africa with the 10th Battery. Whilst in Pretoria, on 14th November 1909, he was transferred to the 95th Battery and served as a gunner until he was posted back to England on 21st March 1910. On his return Ebenezer was transferred to the Army Reserve and he returned to Broadway.

In the 1911 census Ebenezer is recorded as lodging with Frederick and Ursula Roberts and their family along Back Way, Broadway. At the time Ebenezer was working as a builder's labourer with their son Fred Roberts[61]. Ebenezer married Marion Jane Tebby, sister of Walter Tebby (see page 109) on 26th October 1912 in Lyonshall, Herefordshire, and they moved to the cottages at the bottom of the High Street, Broadway, near Russell House, where their eldest son, George Thomas, was born on 20th April 1913. On 16th February 1914, Ebenezer was discharged from the army having served a total of 12 years, eight years with the Colours and four in the Reserve. The same year the family moved to 18 Church Cottages where their second son Francis William was born.

Ebenezer re-enlisted after conscription was introduced in 1916[62]. At the time of his enlistment Ebenezer was employed as a kennelman by the North Cotswold Hunt. Ebenezer was posted to the Royal Berkshire Regiment (Private 32962) but it is not known how long he served with the regiment before he was transferred to the Labour Corps. Ebenezer subsequently served with the 424th Agricultural Company (Private 146497) whose headquarters were at Worcester. Agricultural companies were formed in February 1917 with soldiers classed as unsuitable or unfit for overseas duties to work on the land replacing the agricultural labourers who had been called up for service. In June 1917 the companies became part of the Labour Corps and by the end of the war over 75,000 soldiers were working on farms across the United Kingdom.

In late 1918 both Ebenezer and Marion contracted influenza. Ebenezer died at home of pneumonia, aged 34, on 6th November 1918. Marion made a full recovery but was not well enough to attend Ebenezer's funeral which was held at St Eadburgha's Church on 9th November 1918 and he is buried in the churchyard (grave N1. 4. 19). Ebenezer is commemorated on the Broadway Council School Memorial Board (see page 128). After Ebenezer's death, his widow Marion worked at The Lygon Arms Hotel. Marion died at 18 Church Cottages, Broadway, in 1978.

---

60 His middle name was often spelt 'Eucling' or 'Eveling' and he is recorded as Pte Ebenezer Eveling Emms in the Commonwealth War Graves Commission's records.
61 Fred or Frederick Roberts also served with the Royal Berkshire Regiment, see page 139.
62 On 27th January 1916, the Military Service Act 1916 became law. Every man between the ages of 18 and 41, if unmarried, was 'deemed to have enlisted'. On 16th May 1916 the Second Military Service Bill extended conscription to married men.

The grave of Pte Ebenezer E. Emms,
St Eadburgha's Churchyard, Broadway.

Marion Emms (née Tebby), Ebenezer Emms and George
Thomas Emms c1913. (Robert Emms)

Church Row (Church Cottages), Broadway.
(J. Jacques Junr., Broadway)

Wilford Charles Figgitt
Private 10503, 2nd Battalion Royal Warwickshire Regiment

Pte Wilford C. Figgitt.
(Evesham Journal)

Wilford Charles Figgitt (also spelt Figgett), the eldest son of Wilford John Figgitt and Hannah Figgitt (née Lambley), was born in Broadway and baptised at St Michael's Church on 19th February 1893. Wilford's parents had married in Broadway on 26th December 1891. His father, a shepherd and agricultural labourer, had been born in Broadway and lived at Pye Corner on the edge of the village. His mother, Anna (also known as Hannah), had been born in nearby Childswickham and by 1891 had moved with her father and two brothers and two sisters to Bury End, a few houses away from the Figgitt family. Anna was employed as an outworker making gloves most likely for one of the glove factories in Worcester[63].

Wilford had a younger sister, Sarah born in 1894, and a brother, Walter born in 1896. His mother died in 1900 and his father remarried in 1904 and had five children with his second wife, Annie Maria (née Kyte). Wilford attended Broadway Council School and by 1911 the family had moved to Chapel Row and Wilford had left school and was working as a market gardener.

The following year, in Cardiff, Wilford married Tryphena Jane Cooke, the daughter of a beerhouse keeper from Avenbury, Herefordshire. Tryphena had moved to Broadway and worked as a servant for Mr and Mrs Austin Read Williams at West End Farm. Wilford and Tryphena had one daughter, Mabel, born in 1912 in Avenbury.

In November 1914, Wilford enlisted with the Royal Warwickshire Regiment in Stratford-upon-Avon and was posted to France with the 2nd Battalion on 27th May 1915. During his time on the Western Front, in the trenches between La Bassée-Béthune Road and Souchez, Wilford wrote[64] to The Evesham Journal. On 19th June, the newspaper published a postcard from Wilford dated 12th June 1915:

I am all right and am just come out of the trenches for a rest. I saw Jack Glover, Harvey Carter[65], and Gloster Ingles going up to the trenches, but they are in a different company to me. Jack Glover is a bomb thrower. Gloster Ingles has been wounded slightly, but all is well again. We see some sights here; hardly any houses or anything else standing. Trees are knocked down like match sticks. I should like you to see a 'Jack Johnson' hole[66], it would surprise you. Best of luck to all.

The same article also reported:

This card, in passing through the Field Post Office, evidently went through the hands of Pte. H.E. Edwards[67], a Broadway postman, who as a reservist was called to the colours, and he noting that the card was from and to Broadway people wrote his name across the postmark to show that all was well, and though at the front, engaged in his old occupation of postal work.

Published by The Evesham Journal on 3rd July 1915:

We have had a pretty rough time during the last week and lost a few men: sixty out of one company were killed or wounded. Last Wednesday I had a job carrying rations up to the Royal Scots in the middle of an attack, and shall not forget it in

---

63   Dent Allcroft and Co. Ltd and Fownes Gloves Ltd were large employers of outworkers at the time.

64   At the beginning of the war every letter home was opened and read by a junior officer. It was then opened and read again at the Home Depot to ensure that it contained no classified information about troop movements or casualties. Eventually men could opt for an 'Honour Envelope' which meant the letter would only be read in London, saving the embarrassment of having their deeply personal endearments read by a censor they knew. When the letters reached the Evesham Journal they were also submitted to the Press Bureau for censorship before publishing. At the peak 12 million letters and a million parcels were sent to soldiers every week.

65   See footnote 20 at the bottom of page 9.

66   A Jack Johnson hole was the British nickname used to describe the impact of a heavy, black German 15cm artillery shell. Jack (John Arthur) Johnson (1878-1946) was the popular U.S. world heavyweight boxing champion who held the title from 1908-15.

67   This is a reference to Broadway postman, Henry Harold Edwards, see page 38.

a hurry. The shells fell like hail and bullets whistled like hell. The sights I shall never forget, for there were piles of dead and wounded to walk over, some with their heads blown off. We had a bit of amusement on Saturday. Our artillery and the French started shelling the German trenches and you could see nothing but smoke and sandbags flying up in the air. It just pleased the Canadians, and they started throwing ladders over the top of their trenches to make believe they were going to attack, and as soon as the Germans showed their heads over theirs they opened on them with machine guns and yelled themselves hoarse. The time before when we got in their trenches we found a German boy, not more than thirteen years old, red-haired and wearing big jack-boots. He had probably been sent to throw bombs at us and got shot. I could tell you heaps more, but haven't any paper to write on.

On 31ˢᵗ July 1915:

I am in the pink again now, after having a slight touch of fever a fortnight ago. It made me feel a bit queer, I can tell you. We have been in the trenches for five days after having a rest for ten, but we have had it pretty quiet this time for once. We relieved the Indians in a fresh quarter altogether to what we have been in before. We are living like toffs now, our only shortage being bread, of which we only get half a pound a day. We get suppers when we are out of the trenches – young 'spuds' and green peas, quite a treat. We have had several long marches – about 20 mile jobs. I can stick it all right, but it knocks some out. I saw Lord Kitchener the other day when he passed on the road to Lillers[68].

On 21ˢᵗ August 1915:

We are fifteen miles from the firing line for a rest this week and having a good time. We were in the trenches all last week, went in on the Monday and came out on the Sunday, and marched here straight out of the trenches. It nearly knocked me up. No one knows what a difference it makes not having your boots off for a week. It has been pretty quiet lately, but one night the Germans had a large working party out and we gave them thirty rounds rapid just to brace them up a bit. We are having an enjoyable time here, sports in the day and concerts at night. The best time I have had out here. I hope by the next time I write we shall have shifted the Germans a little bit further, for its nearly time they got stirred for a bit. I saw a Zeppelin last Monday and hear that it was brought down by our naval guns. We had a few successes this week and I hope it will continue.

The following month, Wilford was killed in action on Saturday 25ᵗʰ September 1915, the first day of the Battle of Loos. The battle which lasted until 18ᵗʰ October 1915 was the first major British offensive on the Western Front and the first time the British used chlorine gas in the war. The initial attacks were from the La Bassée Canal at Givenchy in the north to the village of Grenay in the south, near the Double Crassier slag heap, a front of about 7 miles. Upon receiving the word to advance 'Over the top and the best of luck!' the 2ⁿᵈ Royal Warwicks, part of the 22ⁿᵈ Brigade of the 7ᵗʰ Division, donned their gas helmets and left the safety of the fire trenches and advanced eastwards across No Man's Land towards the German trenches and the Hulluch Quarries.

The distance of No Man's Land between the British and German Front Lines in the Loos sector up to 25ᵗʰ September 1915 varied from as little as 200 metres to as wide as 900 metres in places and there were many hundreds of casualties as the men made their way across to the other side through the gas and barbed wire.

The Hulluch Quarries were captured by the 22ⁿᵈ Brigade by 9.30am on the 25ᵗʰ but the 2ⁿᵈ Royal Warwicks had suffered heavy losses. On that first day there had been 527 casualties, nearly half the battalion had been lost.

The Evesham Journal reported

British infantry of the 47ᵗʰ (2ⁿᵈ London) Division advancing through the gas cloud during the Battle of Loos on 25ᵗʰ September 1915. It is believed that the photograph was taken by a soldier of the 1/5ᵗʰ London Regiment.

---

68   Lillers in the Pas-de-Calais was used for billets and headquarter offices from the autumn of 1914 to April 1918.

three weeks later on 16th October 1915:

We are sorry to learn that Pte. W. Figgitt, of the 2nd Royal Warwicks, several of whose cheery letters have been published in this column, has been wounded in France. No particulars of the nature of this casualty have been received, but a letter sent to him by his wife has been returned and endorsed: "Wounded: present location not known." We sympathise with the wife and family in their suspense and hope that injury may prove not to have been serious.

On 23rd October 1915 the following report was published:

Pte. W. Figgitt, previously reported wounded, is now officially reported to have been killed at the great battle of Loos on September 25. Pte. Figgitt was the elder son of Mr. W.J. Figgitt, of Church-row, Broadway, and was twenty-three years of age, and had been married three years. He was a market gardener, and besides working his own land used to put in part of his time assisting his neighbours. He joined the Royal Warwicks in November last, and after three months' training volunteered for the front, and had been six months in France. Pte. Figgitt bore a good character both in and out of the army, and was liked and respected by all who knew him. He leaves a young widow and a little daughter of two years old, with whom and the other members of his family general sympathy is felt.

After the Battle of Loos the front lines changed very little and it was not possible to recover or bury many of the fallen until the battlefields were cleared from 1919. Wilford has no known grave and is commemorated on Loos Memorial, France (Panel 22 to 25). This memorial, at Dud Corner Cemetery, commemorates 20,633 soldiers who were killed in the Loos sector from September 1915 until October 1918. The majority of the names are men who fell in the Battle of Loos in 1915 and every regiment of the British army is represented. Wilford is also commemorated on Broadway Council School Memorial Board as 'Wilfred Figgett' (see page 128).

Loos Memorial, Dud Corner Cemetery, France. (Commonwealth War Graves Commission)

At the time of Wilford's death, his widow Tryphena and daughter Mabel were living at 55 Council Cottages. Tryphena later remarried Alfred Charles Hill, the older brother of Reginald Hill (see page 71) in 1919.

Wilford's younger brother Walter, a farm labourer, emigrated to Australia in February 1913 where he worked as a labourer at Lake Marmal near Boort, Victoria. Walter enlisted with the Australian Imperial Force in Bendigo, Victoria, on 31st March 1916 and served with the 6th Infantry Battalion, 17th Reinforcements, of the Australian Imperial Force in France. Private 5379 Walter Figgitt was wounded in the thigh and shoulder in March 1917 and returned to live with his father in Church Street, Broadway. Walter married Elsie Jane Newbury from Childswickham in 1918 and they had five children. The family emigrated to Boort, Victoria, Australia, in 1920 before moving permanently to Canada in June 1927.

Lieutenant Colonel Oswald Swift Flower
13th (Service) Battalion (1st North Wales) Royal Welsh Fusiliers

Born in 1871 at his parents' home, The Firs, 1 Rother Street, Stratford-upon-Avon, Warwickshire, Oswald Swift Flower was the third son of ten children of Edgar Flower, JP from Stratford-upon-Avon, and Isabella Sophia Flower (née Dennis) from Union Hill, County Westmeath, Ireland. Oswald was christened at Holy Trinity Church in Stratford-upon-Avon on 7th June 1871.

Oswald's grandfather, Edward Flower, had founded the Flower brewery in Stratford-upon-Avon in 1831 and Oswald's father and his uncle Charles Edward Flower, later entered the partnership. In 1870 larger premises were opened on the Birmingham Road and a number of inns and public houses were added to the family business which was incorporated as Flower and Sons Limited[69] in 1888.

Lieutenant Colonel Oswald S. Flower. (Graham Knight)

Shortly after Oswald was born, the family moved to The Hill, Warwick Road, and later purchased Middle Hill House[70] in parkland on the hillside above Broadway. In October 1885, at the age of 14, Oswald was sent to boarding school and he was educated at Wellington College, Crowthorne, Berkshire, where he was in Penny's House (now Picton House). Oswald left Wellington in 1888 and he enlisted with the army and joined the Royal Warwickshire Regiment.

In October 1890 Oswald followed his older brothers Archibald Dennis[71] and Richard Fordham[72] to Cambridge University where he joined Jesus College. In the 1891 census, taken during the night of 5th April, Oswald, a Second Lieutenant with the 4th Battalion Royal Warwickshire Regiment, is recorded as staying with his friend and fellow Cambridge student, Charles Herbert Isaacson[73] at The Rectory, Hardingham, Norfolk.

Oswald was reportedly a good amateur actor and when in Broadway often took comic parts in plays put on in the village and at Stratford-upon-Avon by Richard Peirse-Duncombe[74]. He was also a keen sportsman: he played tennis at Broadway Lawn Tennis Club, enjoyed horse riding, polo, and was a member of the North Cotswold and Warwickshire Hunts taking part in point-to-point races. Whilst in the army Oswald rode in steeplechases and in Bhamo, Burma, won the Regimental polo cup in 1909.

Oswald left Cambridge in 1892 and his transfer to the Royal Welsh Fusiliers was announced in the London Gazette:

The Royal Welsh Fusiliers, Lieutenant Oswald Swift Flower, from the 4th Battalion, the Royal Warwickshire Regiment, to be Second Lieutenant, in succession to Lieutenant P.R. Mantell, promoted. Dated 19th October 1892.

Oswald was posted to Crete in 1897 at the time of the international occupation where he almost

---

69   Members of the Flower family continued to control the brewery until its takeover and subsequent closure by Whitbread in the 1970s. Charles Edward Flower played a major role in the development of the Shakespeare Memorial (later Royal Shakespeare) Theatre in Stratford.

70   Walter's sister, Marion Jane Tebby, wife of Ebenezer Ernest Emms (see page 40) and sister of Walter John Tebby (see page 109) worked as a servant for the Flower family at Middle Hill.

71   Sir Archibald Dennis Flower (1865-1950) was educated at Clifton College, Somerset, Bedford Modern, Bedford, and Clare College, Cambridge University.(BA 1887 and MA 1892).

72   Richard Fordham Flower (1867-1900) was educated at Eton College and Jesus College, Cambridge University.

73   Charles Herbert Isaacson (1872-1965) was born in Australia, the eldest son of English parents. He studied for a BA at Queen's College, Cambridge University, and became a Church of England Minister. Charles emigrated to New Zealand and served as a Chaplain (4th Class) with the 11th Reinforcements, New Zealand Expeditionary Force, during the First World War.

74   The cast of Richard Peirse-Duncombe's plays and pantomimes often included Henry Clement Game, see page 55.

died of a fever. From Crete he was posted to Malta. In January 1899 with the 2nd Battalion, Oswald was posted to Hong Kong. From there, in the middle of June 1900, the battalion set sail on HMS Terrible for Tientsin in northern China where Oswald took an active part in the suppression of the Boxer Rebellion. Oswald's regiment was the only British regiment present at the taking of Tientsin and Peking. Oswald was twice mentioned in despatches and was subsequently awarded the silver China War Medal on 1st April 1902. Following his return from China, Oswald returned to battalion headquarters in Wrexham and was promoted to the rank of Captain in July 1900 and was seconded for service in the Army Pay Department.

The following month, on 20th August 1900, Oswald's older brother Lieutenant Richard Fordham Flower[75] of the Warwickshire Imperial Yeomanry, who was serving in the Boer War, died in battle at Haman's Kraal, South Africa. Three years later, Oswald's father Edgar[76] died, aged 70, in Broadway on 29th July 1903.

In the November of that year, Oswald was seconded for service as an Adjutant of Volunteers and in the reorganisation of the Army in 1908, the London Gazette announced:

4th (Denbighshire) Battalion, Royal Welsh Fusiliers; Captain Oswald Swift Flower, The Royal Welsh Fusiliers, from the Adjutancy of the 1st Battalion, The Royal Welsh Fusiliers, to be Adjutant for the residue unexpired of his tenure. Dated 1st April 1908.

Oswald served in Burma from January 1908 to December 1910 and was serving in India at the time of the 1911 census. On 4th May 1912, Oswald was promoted to the rank of Major and later that year, on 19th October 1912, he retired from the army due to poor health attributed to his time in India. Oswald returned home to Broadway, and with his brother, Archibald, toured Canada and the United States.

In November 1914, following the outbreak of the First World War, Oswald rejoined his old regiment at the headquarters at Wrexham and as Brigade Major trained and organised the service battalions of the Royal Welsh Fusiliers.

In September 1915 Oswald was appointed temporary Lieutenant Colonel and placed in command of one of the battalions he had raised, the 13th (Service) Battalion Royal Welsh Fusiliers, the North Wales Pals, and he took them to the Western Front on 1st December 1915. In June 1916, following a period of ill health, Oswald returned home to Broadway on leave for ten days for rest and recuperation.

Despite his failing health, Oswald returned to the Western Front and the following month, on 10th July 1916, during the First Battle of the Somme, his battalion, part of the 113th Brigade of the 38th (Welsh) Division (sometimes referred to as Lloyd George's Division) attacked Mametz Wood, the largest wooded area on the Somme. Oswald was seriously wounded during the 11th July. He was at battalion headquarters when tragically a British 18 pounder artillery shell hit a tree, deflected, and wounded him[77] and his adjutant. Oswald died of his wounds the following day, 12th July 1916. Oswald's mother, who had moved from Middle Hill to Dor Knap, Broadway, received a telegram from the War Office informing her of Oswald's death on Sunday 16th July 1916. Brigadier-General Llewelyn A.E. Price-Davies[78] commanding the 113th Brigade later wrote:

In particular the names of Lieutenant-Colonel Flower, Lieutenant-Colonel Carden[79], and Major R. H. Mills[80] should ever be remembered by us as officers who have set a glorious example, an example we should all endeavour to copy. Such officers can never be replaced, but it is hoped that their courage and self-sacrifice may long act as an inspiration to those who witnessed their gallant conduct.

---

75   There is a bronze memorial plaque commemorating Lieutenant Richard F. Flower (1867-1900) on the north wall of St Eadburgha's Church and at Holy Trinity Church, Stratford-upon-Avon, a stained glass window in his memory.

76   There is a marble memorial plaque commemorating Edgar Flower (1833-1903) on the north wall of St Eadburgha's Church.

77   It was initially reported in the North Wales Chronicle and Advertiser for the Principality on 21st July 1916 that Colonel Oswald Flower had died from the effects of a bayonet wound.

78   Major General Llewelyn Alberic Price-Davies, VC, CB, CMG, DSO (1878-1965).

79   Lieutenant Colonel Ronald James Walter Carden, 17th Lancers (Duke of Cambridge's Own) attached 16th Battalion Royal Welsh Fusiliers, was killed in action at Mametz Wood on 10th July 1916.

80   Major Robert Henry Mills, 14th Battalion Royal Welsh Fusiliers, was killed in action at Mametz Wood on 10th July 1916.

Oswald is buried in Morlancourt British Cemetery No. 1, Morlancourt, Somme, France (grave B. 21). His epitaph reads: BLESSED ARE THE PURE IN HEART. The cemetery was created in June and July 1916 by Field Ambulance units operating in the nearby village of Morlancourt. On 21st October 1916 probate was granted to his brother Sir Archibald Dennis Flower, brewer, total effects £10721 2s 2d (resworn £12044 2s 9d).

Oswald is also commemorated on the Wrexham War Memorial (a bronze plaque inside the Memorial Hall at Bodhyfryd), on a marble memorial plaque on the north wall inside St Eadburgha's Church and on a memorial brass in Holy Trinity Church, Stratford-upon-Avon. A memorial to the 38th (Welsh) Division was erected on the edge of Mametz Wood in 1987 (see page 110).

Morlancourt British Cemetery No. 1. Lieutenant Colonel Oswald S. Flower, Royal Welsh Fusiliers
is buried in the front row near the Great Cross (17th grave from the right).
(Commonwealth War Graves Commission)

The grave of Lieutenant Colonel Oswald S.
Flower, Royal Welsh Fusiliers, Morlancourt
British Cemetery No 1.
(Sybilla Flower)

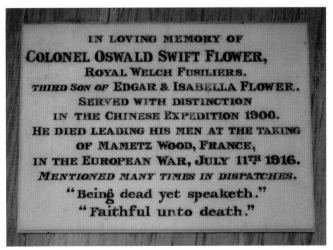

IN LOVING MEMORY OF
COLONEL OSWALD SWIFT FLOWER,
ROYAL WELCH FUSILIERS.
THIRD SON OF EDGAR & ISABELLA FLOWER.
SERVED WITH DISTINCTION
IN THE CHINESE EXPEDITION 1900.
HE DIED LEADING HIS MEN AT THE TAKING
OF MAMETZ WOOD, FRANCE,
IN THE EUROPEAN WAR, JULY 11TH 1916.
MENTIONED MANY TIMES IN DISPATCHES.
"Being dead yet speaketh."
"Faithful unto death."

Marble plaque commemorating Lieutenant Colonel Oswald S.
Flower, St Eadburgha's Church, Broadway.

Alfred Folkes
Guardsman 23203, King's Company, 1st Battalion Grenadier Guards

Guardsman Alfred Folkes.
(Berrows Worcester Journal)

Alfred Folkes was born in Broadway in 1887, the seventh son of William Smith Folkes from Broadway, and Alice Folkes (née Parker) from Mickleton. Alfred was baptised at St Michael's Church on 26th March 1887. Alfred's parents had married on 16th February 1871 in the parish church of St Peter and St Paul, Witton Lane, Aston, near Birmingham, and they had moved to live on the High Street, Broadway, shortly after their marriage. Alfred's father initially worked as a baker but by 1887 was working as a painter and decorator joining the family's painting and decorating business in the village.

By 1911 the family had moved to Leamington Road. After leaving school Alfred worked as a general labourer but he later joined the Gloucestershire Constabulary and moved away from Broadway. In early 1915, Alfred married Millicent Annie Dixon and shortly afterwards enlisted as a Private[81] with the 1st Battalion Grenadier Guards. Alfred was posted to the Western Front on 23rd October 1915 where he served with his battalion, part of the 3rd Guards Brigade.

During the autumn of 1918 Alfred was honourably discharged from the Army with the Silver War Badge[82]. Alfred returned home to Gloucestershire but was one of the many who contracted influenza during the 1918-19 flu pandemic. He died a couple of weeks later from pneumonia, aged 31, on 29th October 1918, at Frampton-on-Severn. His funeral was held at St Eadburgha's Church on Saturday 2nd November 1918 and Alfred is buried in the churchyard (grave N2. 4. 4). His epitaph reads: THY WILL BE DONE. The Evesham Journal published the following report of Alfred's funeral on 9th November 1918:

We record with great regret the death of Pte Alfred Folkes, of Broadway, of the Grenadier Guards, which occurred at Frampton-on-Severn on October 29, in his 31st year, from pneumonia, following an attack of influenza, after an illness of fourteen days. The Military funeral took place on Saturday at St. Eadburgha's Church, Broadway. The coffin was covered with a Union Jack, and four soldiers from Farncombe Hospital acted as bearers, a bugler sounding the Last Post at the conclusion of the service, which was conducted by the Rev. Nason[83] of Saintbury. There followed as mourners Mr. and Mrs. W.S. Folkes (father and mother), Mrs. A. Folkes (widow), Mr. and Mrs. J.A. Folkes[84] (brother and sister-in-law), Mr. H.L. Folkes[85] and Pte. C. Folkes[86], M.T.C. (brothers), Miss D. Folkes[87] (sister), Miss Butler (sister-in-law), Miss G. Folkes[88] (niece), Inspector Hall (representing the police force in which Pte. A. Folkes formerly served). Dr. C.T. Standring, and a number of men from Farncombe Hospital under Commandant Mrs. Walsh. Wreaths were contributed by many relatives and friends.

Alfred's older brother Reginald Duncan Folkes served with the 3rd Battalion Worcestershire

---

81 In 1919 HM King George V commanded that the rank of Guardsman replace that of Private in recognition of the regiment's efforts during the war.

82 The Silver War Badge (see page 49) was issued to those who had been honourably discharged due to wounds or sickness. The badge could be worn on the right breast or right lapel of a jacket but not on Naval or Military uniform. Each badge was uniquely numbered on the reverse. Approximately 1,150,000 badges were issued.

83 Second Lieutenant Richard Philip Nason Nottinghamshire Yeomanry (Sherwood Rangers), youngest son of Reverend Richard Muriel Nason and Alice Nason of Rex House, Willersey, died, aged 20, on 16th April 1918 and is commemorated on Ploegsteert Memorial (Panel 1).

84 John Arnold Folkes (1875-1942) and Minnie Elizabeth Folkes (née Spiers, 1876-1968) who lived off North Street, Broadway.

85 Alfred's older brother Henry Lambert Folkes (born 1884) served with the Army Service Corps.

86 Alfred's older brother Charles Folkes (born 1886) served with the Army Service Corps.

87 This appears to be a typographical error, Alfred's younger sister was Gertrude Adelaide Folkes. Gertrude was unmarried at the time of Alfred's death.

88 Annie Gertrude (known as Gertrude) Folkes, eldest daughter of John Arnold and Minnie Elizabeth Folkes.

Regiment in France from 20th January 1915 for the duration of the war. Alfred's widow Millicent secondly married Allen Sysum in 1924 and moved to Lydney, Gloucestershire.

Farncombe Voluntary Aid Detachment Hospital, Broadway (Red Cross Society, Worcestershire Branch VAD No. 96), which was opened as a hospital for convalescent soldiers in 1917.

Silver War Badge (SWB).
In September 1916, HM King George V authorised the issue of the SWB, also known as the silver wounds badge, to all military personnel who had served at home or overseas and who had been discharged because of wounds or illness.

The grave of Pte Alfred Folkes,
St Eadburgha's Churchyard, Broadway.

Francis Alfred Folkes

Private 2414, 1/1st Worcestershire Yeomanry (Queen's Own Worcestershire Hussars)

Pte Francis A. Folkes.
(Evesham Journal)

Francis Alfred Folkes, known as Frank, was the eldest son of William James Folkes, a stonemason and bricklayer from Broadway, and Alice Folkes (née Groves) from Chipping Campden. Frank was born in 1889 and baptised at St Michael's Church on 29th July 1889. Frank's parents had married in Broadway in 1888 and lived on the High Street where they raised their six children. Frank attended Broadway Council School and after leaving school was apprenticed as a butcher.

By 1911 the family had moved to live at The Baker's Arms, Church Street, and shortly afterwards Frank moved to South Wales to work for the London Central Meat Company.

Following the outbreak of war, Frank returned to Broadway and in September 1914 enlisted with the 4th draft of the 1/1st Worcestershire Yeomanry, the Queen's Own Worcestershire Hussars. The Yeomanry was divided into four squadrons: 'A' was based at Kidderminster, 'B' at Birmingham, 'C' at Malvern and 'D' at Worcester. Frank was in 'D' squadron and trained at the regimental headquarters in Worcester before moving to Newbury where the regiment transferred from the 1st Mounted Division to the 2nd Mounted Division. In November 1914, the regiment moved to King's Lynn, Norfolk, where on 15th January 1915 they were called upon to assist following a Zeppelin raid where bombs were dropped on the town during the night. On 8th April the regiment entrained for Avonmouth and arrived at Avonmouth Docks the following day. Over the next couple of days the regiment and other units embarked for Egypt via Malta on the SS Saturnia. The Yeomanry's 530 horses were transported on SS Eloby and on the way they passed the SS Wayfarer that had been transporting the horses of the 1/1st Warwickshire Yeomanry before being damaged by an explosion off the Scilly Isles.

From 20th April 1915, the regiment disembarked at Alexandria and with the rest of the 1st Brigade moved into camp on the beach at Chatby, about a mile outside Alexandria where for the next couple of months they carried out garrison duties. In July they moved out of camp to Aboukir Bay for training and at the beginning of August received orders to proceed to Gallipoli unmounted as infantry rather than as cavalry. The regiment's horses were left behind along with 100 men and four officers to look after them. In the second week of August the regiment was inspected and left Alexandria on HMT Ascania for Mudros on the island of Lemnos where they changed ship before sailing on to Suvla Bay, Gallipoli (see map on page 108).

The regiment landed at 'A' Beach, Suvla Bay on 18th August 1915 and Frank was wounded shortly afterwards. It is likely that he was wounded during the attacks on Chocolate Hill[89] and Hill 112 on 21st August 1915 or during an Ottoman gun attack on the brigade after they had captured Chocolate Hill. During the afternoon of 21st August, the 1/1st Worcestershire Yeomanry, part of the 1st Brigade, alongside the Warwickshire and Gloucestershire Yeomanry (Royal Gloucestershire Hussars), commenced attack on the Ottoman positions. The brigade marched across the salt lake plain towards the hill in full view of the enemy and into a hail of shrapnel and high explosive cannon shells. There were several hundred casualties and many men died before even firing a single shot. Commander of the Mediterranean Expeditionary Force, Sir Ian Hamilton's despatch, reported in The Times on 7th January 1916 reads:

The advance of these English yeomen was a sight calculated to send a thrill of pride through anyone with a drop of English blood running in their veins. Such superb martial spectacles are rare in modern war. Ordinarily it should always be possible to bring up reserves under some sort of cover from shrapnel fire. Here for a mile and a half, there was nothing to conceal a mouse, much less some of the most stalwart soldiers England has ever sent from her shores. Despite the critical events in

---

89   Chocolate Hill was given its name due to the very dark rich soil and to distinguish it from Green Hill nearby.

other parts of the field, I could hardly take my glasses from the yeoman; they moved like men marching on parade. Here and there a shell would take a cluster; there they would lay; there was no straggling; the others moved steadily on; not a man was there who hung back or hurried.

The 1ˢᵗ Brigade suffered further casualties during the early hours of 28ᵗʰ August when the Ottoman forces took up a new gun position and bombarded the hill with shrapnel. After Frank had been wounded he would have been transferred to a casualty clearing centre on the coast where he would have been loaded onto a barge and transferred to a hospital ship[90] anchored in Suvla Bay before being transported back to England to a military hospital.

Frank recovered from his wounds and was able to rejoin his regiment, and with the Corps of Hussars, part of the 5ᵗʰ Mounted Brigade, sailed from Devonport on 1ˢᵗ February 1916, arriving in Alexandria, Egypt, on 13ᵗʰ February 1916 where he served with the 5ᵗʰ Mounted Brigade of the Egyptian Expeditionary Force stationed in the Sinai Peninsula to defend the eastern side of the Suez Canal.

During April 1916 the Worcestershire, Warwickshire and Gloucestershire Yeomanry, were engaged in Battle of Katia, also known as the Affair of Qatiya, against the Ottoman forces[91] that were advancing towards the Suez Canal. The Worcester Yeomanry were able to capture the village of Katia, to the south east of Port Said, but Ottoman and German forces held the high ground overlooking the village. On Easter Sunday, 23ʳᵈ April 1916 , the British forces had not had time to reinforce their positions before the Ottoman army attacked again. In the hot desert sands, they faced 2,000 Ottoman troops, 1,000 German and Austrian troops and some Arabic troops mounted on camels, all supported by mountain guns and several machine guns. The brigade suffered heavily from the shell fire and the mountain guns destroyed most of their horses, which forced the men to retreat on foot while the mounted Germans and Ottomans continued to overwhelm them. The Worcester Yeomanry lost all of their officers except one in the fighting. 102 men were killed and many more were wounded and taken prisoner. Despite the heavy losses, the Ottoman attack was defended long enough for a proper defence of Suez to be organised in conjunction with Australian and New Zealand forces and the Suez Canal, Britain's supply route to India and the rest of the Empire, was kept open.

Frank Folkes was initially reported missing after the battle and the Evesham Journal reported on 13ᵗʰ May 1916:

Official reports were received last week that Trooper[92] Frank Folkes, son of Mr. and Mrs. James Folkes, of Chapel-street, Broadway, and Trooper Sidney Halford[93], second son of Mr. and Mrs. Walter Halford, of Evesham-road, Broadway, and both of the 1st Worcester Yeomanry, were missing after the action east of the Suez Canal on Easter Sunday. No further news has yet been received; it is hoped that both are only prisoners and general sympathy is expressed with the parents in their uncertainty and anxiety.

A couple of weeks later the Evesham Journal reported that Colonel the Honourable Charles Coventry, 20 officers and 207 men of the Worcester Yeomanry had been taken prisoner at Damascus and a list of 37 casualties from the local area including Frank was printed. It was later confirmed that Frank was killed in action on 23ʳᵈ April 1916 and on 13ᵗʰ January 1917 the Evesham Journal reported:

There is now unfortunately no room for doubt that Trooper Frank Folkes, of the Worcestershire Yeomanry, who was posted as missing after the affair at Katia on April 23 last, was killed in the fighting at that place and date. A letter has been received from Trooper Sidney Halford, also of Broadway, who was taken prisoner at the same time, in which he states that Trooper Folkes was shot twice and died instantly.

---

90   HMHS Rewa transported a number of the casualties from the August attacks home to Devonport arriving 9ᵗʰ September 1915.

91   In August 1914, the Ottoman Turks ruled an empire that covered much of the Middle East and they entered the war on the side of Germany and Austria against Britain, France and Russia.

92   The rank of Trooper was widely used instead of Private but was not officially recognised until 1922.

93   Sidney Halford of Station Road, Broadway, enlisted with the Worcestershire Yeomanry in October 1914. He was taken prisoner on 23ʳᵈ April 1916 and imprisoned in Turkey for the duration of the war. Sidney returned home to Broadway on 8ᵗʰ December 1918.

Frank is commemorated on Jerusalem Memorial, Israel (Panel 3 and 5). The memorial, in Jerusalem War Cemetery, commemorates 3,300 Commonwealth servicemen who died during the First World War in Egypt or Palestine who have no known grave. Frank is also commemorated on the Broadway Council School Memorial Board (see page 128).

Jerusalem Memorial, Jerusalem War Cemetery. (Commonwealth War Graves Commission)

Frank's youngest brother Charles (1897-1980) enlisted with the 11th (Reserve) Battalion Gloucestershire Regiment in Chipping Campden on 27th August 1915 at the age of 18[94]. Prior to his enlistment Charles was living in Church Street working as a yardman at The Lygon Arms Hotel. Charles trained at Seaforth, Lancashire, and was posted to the 8th (Service) Battalion on the Western Front on 9th March 1916. On 18th November 1916, during the Battle of the Somme, he was wounded in the field receiving a compound fracture of the arm and was transferred to the 2nd Southern General Hospital, Southmead, Bristol. Charles was discharged from Southmead on 22nd June 1917 and he appeared before a medical board on 21st May 1918 to assess his fitness for service. Charles was subsequently discharged as being no longer fit for war service on 11th June 1918 and was awarded the Silver War Badge. His war service records also state that he was entitled to wear one gold wound stripe.

Frank's brother Jim (1892-1973) enlisted in Evesham on 2nd November 1915, aged 23, with the Army Service Corps Remounts Service[95]. Prior to his enlistment he had worked as a groom for Henry Gordon Clegg[96] and Maud Clegg (née Field) at Bibsworth House. Jim married Rose May Irish from Fladbury at the Register Office, Evesham, on 17th June 1914 and they moved to 49 Council Cottages, Broadway. Jim was posted to the Remounts Depot in Romsey[97] before being posted to France on 27th September 1916 where he served with the No. 2 Advanced Remounts Depot in Abbeville. Jim was discharged from the army on 25th May 1919.

Frank's father, William, joined the Broadway War Memorial Committee in 1919 (see page 4) and he contributed towards the memorial in memory of his son.

---

94 Charles Folkes's service record states that he was 19 years and 111 days old when he enlisted.

95 The Royal Army Service Remounts Service was responsible for the provisioning of horses and mules to all other army units.

96 Henry Gordon Clegg (1868-1927) was a silk dyer from Altrincham, Cheshire, who retired to live at Bibsworth House, Broadway with his family. At the time of his death in 1927, Henry Clegg was living at Wormington Grange, Wormington.

97 The Romsey camp, one of the four depots set up, was established at the summit of Pauncefoot Hill, in the vicinity of Ranvilles Farm. It received its first horses in March 1915. By the end of the war it had processed about 120,000 horses, around 10% of the animals acquired by the Remounts Service.

Lieutenant Hubert John Game
Royal Field Artillery attached Royal Flying Corps

Born in Harrow in Middlesex, on 13th December 1890, Hubert John Game, known as John, was the youngest son of George Beale Game, JP from Stoke Newington, and Clara Game (née Vincent) from Falmouth. John was christened on 24th June 1891 at All Saints' Church, Harrow Weald, Middlesex.

Hubert John Game. (Malvern College)

John's father, George, was a Member of the Baltic Exchange, a produce and oil broker who owned a number of companies (he was Chairman of Messrs. Palmer & Company and Corticine Floor Covering Limited) and had offices at 38 Threadneedle Street in the City of London. George had married Clara Vincent, the youngest daughter of Royal Navy officer Staff Commander William Vincent and Louisa Vincent (née Saxon), in South Stoneham, Hampshire, in 1874.

As a young boy, John lived at Waldoes, Harrow Weald, a large family house with stables, coach houses, gardens and land, which his parents had rented from Thomas Francis Blackwell, the co-founder, along with Edmund Crosse, of Crosse and Blackwell. In the 1901 census, the family are recorded as living at 3 Park Crescent, Marylebone, London, and by 1906 they had moved out of London to Broadway. The family firstly rented Cotswold House, Springfield House and Russell House before purchasing Barn House on the High Street. John's parents became very involved in Broadway life but shortly after they had settled into the village his mother was taken ill and her health never fully recovered. His father George, having shown an interest in local affairs whilst living in Harrow Weald, joined Broadway Parish Council and was elected Chairman of Broadway Parish Council in 1913. George was a local Justice of the Peace, he hunted with the North Cotswold Hunt and was a member of the Broadway War Memorial Committee (see page 4).

John was firstly educated at Aldro School, Eastbourne, and in 1904 John went on to Malvern College. On leaving school in 1910, John joined the Royal Military Academy Sandhurst.

Following the outbreak of war, on 14th September 1914, John received a commission to the Royal Field Artillery and he was posted to the Western Front that November. The following year, on 25th April 1915, John was wounded in the Second Battle of Ypres and returned to Broadway to recuperate. The Evesham Journal reported on 1st May 1915:

Lieut. John Game, the youngest son of Mr. G.B. Game of Barn House, Broadway, who joined the Royal Field Artillery at the commencement of the war, was in the midst of fighting near St Julien on Sunday. The Germans had got the exact range, and rendered the position of his battery untenable. The Captain in command had moved off with two guns to take up a fresh position, and left Lieut. Game with orders to remove the remaining three guns as soon as that operation was feasible. One of these guns was already out of action, and another had a wheel smashed, while having located their objective the enemy simply rained shells on the battery. It was under these circumstances, and whilst directing the affixing of a new wheel to the disabled gun that Lieut. Game was struck on the right arm with a fragment of a German shell. He however, continued to command his portion of the battery till a second heavy shell exploded in his immediate vicinity. Most fortunately no fragment of this touched Lieut. Game, but the concussion was so great that he was immediately rendered insensible, and though got away by his men did not regain consciousness till the next day, when he woke up in the base hospital. Lieut. Game has since been removed to the Royal Military Hospital, Osborne, and the many friends of the Lieutenant and his family will be pleased to learn that he is there making satisfactory progress. It is not anticipated that there will be any permanent injury to the arm, and Lieut. Game hopes to be out again in a week or two.

John returned to the Western Front but in December 1916 he returned home to Broadway on sick leave. John was unable to return to the RFA and in March 1917 he transferred to the Royal Flying Corps. John was posted to Narborough, Norfolk, where he trained with 53 Squadron. John passed as a fast scout and also qualified in technical construction but died whilst on a training flight on 8th June 1917. His BE2e aircraft, serial number A2794, suffered a technical fault at 5,000ft whilst he was practising a nosedive manoeuvre and although he recovered the aeroplane, he crash landed and died on impact.

John's funeral was held on Monday 11th June 1917 at All Saints' Church, Narborough, and he is buried in the churchyard. On the day of his funeral, Broadway Lawn Tennis Club and Broadway Croquet Club closed out of respect. John had been a member of both clubs and had won several cups for the Croquet Club. John left the effects of his will, £3959 0s 1d to his father, George. He is recorded in the Roll of Honour 1914-1918 in St Michael's Church as 'John Game'.

Grave of Lieutenant Hubert J. Game,
All Saints' Churchyard, Narborough.

Narborough Aerodrome Memorial Plaque
All Saints' Churchyard, Narborough.

A BE2e, as piloted by Hubert Game, with a BE12a behind.
(Mark Porter)

John's mother Clara, who had been taken ill in 1906, died on 28th December 1917. Her funeral took place at St Eadburgha's Church on 2nd January 1918 and she is buried in the churchyard. His father, George died whilst on holiday at the Imperial Palace Hotel, Santa Margherita, Italy, on 15th March 1925 and he is buried with Clara at St Eadburgha's.

John had four older brothers and two older sisters. His eldest brother William (1875-1922), was educated at Sherborne School. William married Mary Beit, from Sydney, Australia, at St Michael's Church on 4th October 1909 and they set up home at Ballybroust in the village. William died, aged 47, on 25th October 1922. Mary, died the following year and they are both buried in St Eadburgha's churchyard alongside William's parents.

John's brother, Philip Woolcott (1876-1961), was educated at Charterhouse School and entered the Royal Military Academy Woolwich in 1893 gaining a commission with the Royal Artillery on 2nd November 1895. Philip saw action in the Boer War and was mentioned in despatches. On 11th August 1908 he married Gwendoline Margaret Hughes-Gibb and they had three children. Following the outbreak of the First World War, Philip served on the Western Front from 1st December 1914 and was awarded the DSO, the Légion d'honneur, the Order of the Crown of Italy and was five times mentioned in despatches. Philip transferred to the Royal Flying Corps in 1916 and by the end of the war was Acting Major General. He remained in the Royal Air Force and served as Air Officer Commanding RAF India and Air Member for Personnel. He was appointed KCB in 1924 and retired in 1929 having reached the rank of Air Vice-Marshal. Later that year he was promoted to GBE and in March 1930, Philip was appointed Governor of New South Wales. At the end of his term in January 1935 he was made KCMG, returned to London and was appointed Commissioner of the Metropolitan Police retiring at the end of the Second World War having been appointed GCVO for his work in organising the 1937 coronation of HM George VI and promoted to GCB.

John's brother George Geoffrey (1881-1957), known as Peter, was also educated at Charterhouse School. He was gazetted to the Royal Field Artillery as a Second Lieutenant from the Inns of Court Officer Training Corps in December 1915. George was promoted to the rank of Lieutenant during the war and served with 'C' Battery 174th Brigade with the 39th Divisional Artillery on the Western Front. George was awarded the Military Cross in 1919. Supplement to the London Gazette 29th July 1919:

On September 7th and 15th, 1918, at Buissy, the battery position was heavily shelled with Yellow Cross[98]. On each occasion he went round the position through the shelling and made sure that all men had their masks on. On 26th and 27th it was necessary to dump large amounts of ammunition east of Baralle for future operations. The whole area under constant shell and machine-gun fire, he volunteered to lead all teams through to the position and performed the task without a casualty. He has in all times of danger invariably set an example of absolute fearlessness and devotion to duty.

His brother Henry Clement Game (1883-1966) was also educated at Charterhouse School and is recorded in the 1901 census as a student studying engineering but by the 1911 census Henry was studying art. Henry lived with the artist George Lawrence Kennedy at 8 Primrose Hill Studios[99], a development of twelve artists' mews houses off Fitzroy Road, London, and he attended the Slade School of Fine Art. Henry was also a good amateur actor and whilst in Broadway often appeared in plays and pantomimes put on by Richard Peirse-Duncombe in the village and at

Henry C. Game outside Barn House, Broadway.
(Perran Newman)

---

98   Yellow Cross, Gelbkreuz, or Mustard Gas. Mustard Gas was first used on 12th and 13th July 1917 and was intense during the period of withdrawal in September to October 1918 when the British Army suffered 3,000-4,000 casualties per week.
99   In the 1911 census, the landscape and animal painter Edmund G. Caldwell (1852-1930) is recorded as living at 2 Primrose Hill Studios, the portrait figure and rustic painter Collier Twentyman Smithers (1867-1943) at 10 Primrose Hill Studios and the landscape and miniature portrait painter Cyrus Johnson (1848-1925) at 11 Primrose Hill Studios.

Stratford-upon-Avon.

Henry married Annie Appleyard in London in 1913 and they moved to 3 Primrose Hill Studios. Henry enlisted in 1914 and served on the Western Front with the Royal Field Artillery from 25th July 1915 and was promoted to Captain of 'D' Battery, 82nd Brigade. Henry was wounded at Trones Wood, during the Battle of Bazentin Ridge on 17th July 1916. His battery was heavily shelled and Henry received shrapnel injuries to his leg and arm. Henry returned to England and was subsequently honourably discharged. During the war Henry corresponded with John Earp (see page 34) who had been butler to the Game family at Barn House.

After the war Henry was awarded the OBE. In 1930 Henry was appointed Assistant Examiners of Plays to the Lord Chamberlain and on 20th July 1936 was appointed Senior Examiner, a position he held until 1952. Henry was awarded the MVO on 1st January 1941 and CVO in 1952.

John's eldest sister, Nellie Eileen (1878-1963), married George Hodges Crisp Clarke at St Michael's Church, Broadway, on 16th November 1909. John Earp had worked for the Crisp Clarke family in Leicestershire (see page 34) before he moved to Broadway to work for the family at Barn House. Nellie and her husband spent a lot of time in Broadway and their son John Anthony was born in Broadway in 1913. Both Nellie and George were also involved in Richard Peirse-Duncombe's theatrical productions.

John's sister Mary Beatrice Game married Percy Alexander Maxwell, a Lieutenant in the Indian Army, at St Michael's Church on 31st August 1909. Percy had been born in Darjeeling, India, in 1883, and after attending the Royal Military Academy Sandhurst in 1901 was gazetted to the Indian Army. He was promoted to the rank of Captain in January 1911. During the war Percy served with the 1st Battalion 3rd Brahmans Infantry Regiment in Mesopotamia and India and was promoted to the rank of Major in January 1917.

Barn House, High Street, Broadway.
(Valentine)

William Gardner
Private M2/153742, Mechanical Transport Company, Army Service Corps

The Commonwealth War Graves Commission does not have a record of a soldier named William Gardner[100] from Broadway being killed during the First World War nor has William been found in the UK, Soldiers Died in the Great War, 1914-1919 database. It has not been possible, therefore, to find out when and/or where William died or provide much detail about his army service.

The Absent Voters List 1918 for the parish of Broadway lists William Gardner of Chapel Street as serving with the Caterpillar Section of the Army Service Corps attached to the 2nd Australian Siege Battery. The following earlier report mentioning William was published in the Evesham Journal of 18th March 1916:

Mr. and Mrs. John Gardner, of Chapel-street, Broadway, are to be congratulated on being the parents of four sons who have put on khaki. Pte. John Gardner, of the Duke of Cornwall's Light Infantry, was wounded in the Boer War, and died in hospital in 1901; Pte. W. Gardner is in the Motor Transport of the Army Service Corps; Pte. Joe Gardner is serving in the 11th Batt. Glos. Regt.; and Pte. Harry Gardner, who has been to the French front, is now in hospital at Birmingham.

Private W. Gardner referred to in the above article was William Gardner born in Broadway in 1892, the son of John Gardner, a labourer, and Emma Gardner (née Keyte). William was baptised at St Michael's Church, on 10th April 1892. William's parents had both been born in Broadway and had married in the village in 1878 and they had nine children of which three died in infancy. In the 1891 census the family are recorded as living at Bury End and at West End in the 1901 census. By 1911 William, aged 19, was working as a farm labourer living with his parents on Church Street in the village.

William enlisted with a Mechanical Transport Company of the Army Service Corps and at some stage during the war, was posted to a Caterpillar Tractor Company attached to the 2nd Australian Siege Battery Ammunition Column. The battery used 9.2" BL Howitzer Mark 1 guns, manufactured by Vickers, Son & Maxim, which were drawn by Holt Caterpillar Tractors. The battery served in France from Cambrai to St Jean near Passchendaele, Belgium, from March 1916 until the end of the war, a total of 860 days in action.

At some stage during the war William Gardner of Broadway died and the Broadway War Memorial Committee agreed to inscribe his name on the war memorial.

Pte John Gardner, born
Broadway c1881, who died
in 1901 during the Boer War.
(Evesham Journal)

Australian Battery of 9.2 inch Mark I Howitzers
in action at Fricourt during the Battle of the Somme,
August 1916.

---

100   Including various spellings of the surname 'Gardner'.

Left to Right: Pte William Gardner, Pte Joseph Gardner and Pte Harry Gardner.
(Evesham Journal)

William's younger brothers, Joseph, aged 21 and Harry aged 19, enlisted in Chipping Campden on the same day, 27th August 1915 and were both posted to the 11th (Reserve) Battalion Gloucestershire Regiment. Joseph (Private 24386), who worked as a butcher's assistant before the war, transferred to the 9th Battalion and served with the regiment throughout the war.

Harry (Private 24381) trained with the 11th Battalion at Belhus Park, Essex. He was transferred to the 10th (Service) Battalion and was posted to the Western Front with the British Expeditionary Force on Boxing Day, 26th December 1915, arriving at Le Havre, France, the following day. Harry served for only a few days before being admitted to the No. 6 Stationary Hospital, Le Havre, on 6th January 1916. Harry was transported back to England on 15th January 1916 on Hospital Ship Copenhagen and was transferred to the 1st Military Hospital, Rubery Hill, Rednal, Birmingham, where he spent four months. Less than a year after enlisting, on 11th July 1916, Harry was discharged from the army under paragraph 392(xvi) of the King's Regulations 1912, as he was deemed to be no longer physically fit for war service due to a goitre that he had suffered with for many years prior to enlistment.

William's older brother George, a farm labourer, worked for Mary Keyte[101] of Cowley House, Church Street. When George's conscription papers arrived in early 1916, Mrs Keyte appealed against George's enlistment at the Evesham Military Service Tribunal held in March. The Evesham Journal of 25th March 1916 reported:

Mrs. Mary Keyte, of Cowley House, Broadway, appealed on behalf of George Gardner, her bailiff, stating that he was the only man she had on her farm of 10½ acres. He looked after the cows, pigs and poultry, and also did the gardening. Gardner had been in her employ for 10½ years. She had no relation or anyone to help her. Gardner was single. - Exemption refused.

George subsequently enlisted with the 11th Battalion Royal Berkshire Regiment at Worcester on 1st June 1916. His medical classification on joining was 'Class B2 Labour' meaning that he was fit for labour service abroad. However, after four weeks of training, George (Private 25188) was discharged on 29th June 1916 as he was 'not likely to become an efficient soldier' under paragraph 392(iii) of the King's Regulations 1912.

William's brother Arthur was also called up for service in 1916 and enlisted in Worcester on 1st July 1916. At the time of his enlistment Arthur was living at Belle Vue Cottage, working as a bricklayer. Arthur served at home for the duration of the war and was posted to the 13th (Works) Battalion Devonshire Regiment and later transferred to 627th Agricultural Company Labour Corps and Southern Command Labour Centre, Fovant, before his demobilization in 1919.

---

101   Mary Keyte (née Keitly, 1853-1922) was the widow of Samuel Keyte (1852-1915), farmer of Cowley House, Broadway.

Arthur Harold Goddard

Private 37889, 1/5th Battalion Duke of Cornwall's Light Infantry

Pte Arthur H. Goddard.
(Evesham Journal)

Arthur Harold Goddard, known as Harold, was born in 1899 in Cow Honeybourne, the second son of George Goddard from North Piddle, and Ruth Elizabeth Goddard (née Nason) from Packwood, Warwickshire. Harold's parents married in 1896 but they do not appear to have settled in one particular place for long as Harold's father worked as a farm labourer and frequently moved from farm to farm. Harold's older brother Frederick was born in South Littleton in 1897, and by the time of the 1901 census the family had moved to live with Harold's paternal grandparents in Church Honeybourne. Harold's younger brother Sydney Leonard was born in Long Marston in 1903 and brothers Leslie and Raymond were born in Pebworth in 1906 and 1908. Harold had one sister, Dorothy who was born in Church Honeybourne in 1910. The following year the family moved to Murcot before settling in Broadway a couple of years later at Council Cottages.

As a boy Harold was a member of the Broadway Scouts and after leaving school worked as a labourer for Mr H. Roberts at Little Buckland. Aged 18, Harold enlisted in Worcester in August 1917 and he joined the 1/5th Battalion Duke of Cornwall's Light Infantry.

Harold was posted to the Western Front on 3rd April 1918 joining the battalion, part of the 61st (2nd Midland) Division, just before they took part in the Battle of Estaires, from 9th to 11th April 1918, one of the opening phases of the Battle of Lys. From the 12th April the battalion was involved in the Battle of Hazebrouck which lasted four days and it was on the first day of the battle that Harold was reported as missing in action.

Harold's parents received the following letter from Harold's commanding officer the following month:

Dear Mr Goddard, - By this time you will have heard officially that your son, Pte. H. Goddard, was reported missing on April 12. At present this is all we know, but should any further particulars come to light at any time we will let you know immediately. So far as I can gather I think there is every possible hope of his being a prisoner and unwounded, and I sincerely trust that is the case. You have my sincerest sympathy in your troubles.

Sir Douglas Haig's sixth despatch of 20th July 1918 mentions the 61st Division and the operations on the 12th April 1918:

On the left of the 51st, the 61st Division was coming into action about the Clarence River. Both the 3rd and 61st Divisions had been engaged in many days of continuous fighting south of Arras; but with the arrival of these troops, battle-weary though they were, the enemy's progress in this sector was definitely checked.

The Evesham Journal later reported on 12th October 1918:

Mrs. Goddard, of Council Cottages, Broadway, received a report from Geneva last Friday in reference to the fate of her son Pte. H. Goddard, of the Duke of Cornwall's Light Infantry. The report is as follows:

"Dear Madam, - We are much grieved to inform you that the following report appears on lists despatched from Berlin: 'Pte. H. Goddard, 37889 D.C.L.I., killed 12 or 14-4-1918, and buried between Estaires and Le Gd Pacand[102] (south of the railway Estaires Merville)'. Should we receive further particulars at a later date we shall let you know. We trust you will accept our deep sympathy with you in your great loss."

Harold was later officially reported as being killed in action on 14th April 1918 and he is commemorated on Ploegsteert Memorial, Belgium, (Panel 6). The Memorial (see page 22) is about 15 miles away from where he was reported to have been buried in 1918.

---

102   Le Grand Pacault, south of Merville, Pas de Calais, France.

Harold's brother Frederick, who survived the war, worked as a plough boy after leaving school, and then as a yardman at The Lygon Arms Hotel. Frederick enlisted, aged 19, in Stratford-upon-Avon on 4th December 1914 with George Barnett (see page 8) and Reginald Hill (see page 71). He was initially posted to and trained with the 3rd Battalion Royal Warwickshire Regiment. On 2nd May 1915 Frederick, was posted to the Western Front with the 1st Battalion Royal Warwickshire Regiment, part of the British Expeditionary Force.

Frederick often wrote home to his mother from 'somewhere in France' recounting his experiences of being in the trenches including surviving a gas attack on 24th May 1915. Some of Frederick's letters were published in the Evesham Journal:

5th June 1915:

I am quite well, and hope you are the same. Badger[103] has got wounded, poor chap, through the head. I have not had a letter since I have been here; have you written to me? Don't worry, I am trusting in God to bring me back safe to my dear home again. Give my love to all, especially to Winnie. Answer as soon as possible. The Germans are hot stuff, but we will conquer them.

19th June 1915:

I received the 'Journal' too the other week and was glad to read a bit of news from home. It makes us hold our breath and crouch up in our dugouts when we hear the 'Jack Johnsons' come whizzing over, but I have got used to them now, and don't take much notice of them. We had a rotten day in the trenches yesterday; it was wet and miserable; but never mind, we got a fire on the go, tea and a fag and we were all 'kiff'[104]. It is nothing to see aeroplanes out here, they are as numerous as birds. They are the worst thing that could ever have come out. The Germans are like rabbits; they keep in all day, and come creeping out at night. Oh I should like to have a go at old grey-bearded Kaiser Bill. Last night F. Lambley[105] and I went out and enjoyed ourselves with a Belgian soldier.

21st August 1915:

I am still in the land of the living and quite well. I have been out here now three months, and have seen a bit of rough fighting. We are having it rather quiet just now; they say the Russians have had a large victory, and I hope they have: the Germans think they can do just as they like with the Allies but 'I don't think'. I have had a few narrow escapes out here. One day in the trenches, about twelve o'clock, I was just going to make a can of tea, when all at once, biff, came a whizz and a bang[106] and burst about five yards from me; a piece hit my trousers, and exploded the cap of a cartridge, but lucky for me it never forced the bullet out or else I should have been hit in the thigh. I am now a bomb thrower, and we go out at night and don't half give them beans. Up comes a light, and down we go and get ready for them again. Some of our officers think we can do more good work with a bomb than with a bayonet, and I think so myself. Well, roll on the day that I shall return, which I hope to do, trusting to God to keep me safe.

18th September 1915:

Just a line to let you know that I am quite well. I have not received a letter from you lately, as we are away from the company and regiment, going through a course of grenade throwing. The regiment is in the trenches at present; five of our company are not. When we get a letter I expect we shall get four or five together. We are going to have more money for bomb throwing now, and also wear badges on our arm. We have just been to church. I am glad to tell you. Will you please send me a parcel of cigarettes, also a book or two? We have not had a smoke for a long time. It is getting rather cold at night now. Please send a few envelopes and writing paper, as I cannot write until you do, as I haven't any.

30th October 1915:

Just a line to say I am quite well at present, and hoping all at home are the same. It is getting very late in the year now, and is very much like winter out here now. We have had it foggy this last three days. How is the weather at home? I have been

---

103   Joseph Lawrence Badger suffered a gunshot wound to the head at Ypres in May 1915 (see page 137).
104   'Kiff' is a South African word meaning great. It is likely that the word was picked up by men serving in the Boer War.
105   Felix Wilfred Lambley of Childswickham who enlisted with Frederick Goddard (see footnote on page 8).
106   'Whizz bang' was the slang term for a light shell fired from one of the smaller calibre field guns, referring to the sound as the shell came to explode.

out on a bomb course again, and passed out this time. We are present in the trenches, but we have had blankets issued out to us, and that is worth a great deal to anyone's comfort; also coke and charcoal to make fires to cook anything we have got. I had a parcel two days ago, cakes, etc. Have you received the silk postcards? I hope you have. I will send some more as soon as I get a chance. Broadway is very dull now is it not? I can just imagine what it looks like. Well, do not worry. Trust to God that I may return, and I will make you happy.

A day later on 31st October 1915, whilst on listening patrol, Frederick was wounded in the shin by an explosive bullet and was transferred to No. 4 Casualty Clearing Station where three days later had his right leg amputated below the knee. On 9th November 1915, Frederick was posted home and admitted to Cambridge Hospital where he spent a further eight weeks before being transferred to a convalescent home. Frederick was fitted with an artificial limb and honourably discharged from the Royal Warwickshire Regiment on 16th December 1916 with the Silver War Badge (see page 49). After leaving the army, Frederick worked as a munitions worker before re-enlisting on 23rd September 1918. He was accepted into the Army Pay Corps and served in Nottingham until he was transferred to the Army Reserve on 9th March 1919 following which he returned home to Broadway.

Royal Warwickshire Regiment
First World War silk embroidered postcard.
(Mary Smith)

Royal Warwickshire Regiment Cap Badge.
(Mary Smith)

Leonard Frank Green
Corporal 240841, 1/8th Battalion Worcestershire Regiment

Corporal Leonard F. Green.
(Evesham Journal)

Leonard Frank Green, known as Len, was born in Birmingham on 2nd September 1896, the second son of Harold Joseph Green, a tailor from Sparkhill, Birmingham, and Mary Ann Green (née Sharp). Len's parents had married in 1886 in Birmingham and he had two brothers and two sisters.

Len and his family are recorded in the 1901 census as living at 110 Durham Road, Sparkhill, Birmingham. The family later moved to Broadway and Len was enrolled at Broadway Council School. By 1911 his father had opened an outfitters on the High Street where Len worked as his assistant. Len was a member of the choir at St Michael's Church (see page 136) and played cricket for the Junior XI at Broadway Cricket Club. He was one of the first members of the Broadway Scouts and prior to his enlistment was Assistant Scout Master to Scout Master William Tracy-Arkell.

On 28th September 1914, in a car lent by Sydney Russell of The Lygon Arms Hotel, Len aged 18, along with fellow St Michael's choristers Albert Henry Box[107], Arthur Edwin Berry, John Oram and Edgar Turner[108], travelled to Worcester to enlist with the Worcester Territorials. Len joined the 1/8th Battalion Worcestershire Regiment as Private 3112 and trained at Maldon, Essex, during the winter months of 1914 before being posted to the Western Front.

1/8th Battalion Worcestershire Regiment, 1915.
(Berrows Worcester Journal Supplement)

The battalion sailed from Folkestone on the SS Invicta and landed at Boulogne on 1st April 1915. After three days training near Armentières in the Pas de Calais the battalion took over the trenches at Ploegsteert Wood where their principal duty was digging trenches as the front line was incomplete and lacking reserve trenches[109]. The battalion joined the 144th Brigade of the 48th (South Midland) Division in May 1915 and moved from Ploegsteert Wood towards Messines Ridge and from there on towards Loos where the battalion dug trenches at Bully Grenay ahead of the Battle of Loos which was to take place later in the year. In July 1915 the battalion took over the trenches at Hébuterne where they remained for many months.

---

107   Sergeant 202847 Albert Henry Box Worcestershire Regiment.
108   Lance Corporal 240817, Edgar Turner was born in Broadway in 1894, the son of James Turner and Agnes Maria Turner (née Keyte). Previous to his enlistment Edgar worked as a carpenter and lived with his family at Church Row, Broadway.
109   The reserve trenches were behind the front line and support trenches and were linked by communication trenches.

The battalion saw little heavy fighting during the harsh winter of 1915/16. The first six months of 1916 were spent in and out of the trenches at Foncquevillers, Auchonvillers and Le Sars before proceeding to the Somme and the Battle of the Somme which started on 1ˢᵗ July 1916. Len returned home to Broadway on leave in October 1916. Afterwards he rejoined his battalion on the Western Front and was subsequently promoted to the rank of Corporal and in March 1917 he was assigned a new regimental number, 240841, following the renumbering of the territorial battalions.

In July 1917 the battalion was involved in the Battle of Passchendaele (Third Battle of Ypres), a battle which lasted more than three months and became infamous not only for the large number of casualties but also for the unusually wet weather which turned the battlefield into a quagmire. The battalion was involved in the attack at Maison du Hibou and during the advance on Springfield Farm on 27ᵗʰ August 1917, Len was killed in action, aged 20, a few days short of his 21ˢᵗ birthday.

On 15ᵗʰ September 1917 the Evesham Journal printed the following letter from his Broadway friend and fellow NCO Lance Corporal Edgar Turner:

29ᵗʰ August 1917: It is with sincere regret that I write to tell you what I can of the circumstances under which Len fell in action on Monday last. We were close chums, and I feel his loss more keenly than I can tell. We were together the night before we went into action, and he was just as happy and confident, as ever. His company was given a very difficult task, and they succeeded in storming the enemy's strongest point by a tremendous assault. It was in this action that Len met his death in front of his section, a bullet followed by instantaneous death and undying honour. Please accept my deepest sympathy with you in your great loss.

A further letter from Second Lieutenant J.R. Willis[110] was also printed:

3ʳᵈ September 1917: You have probably been notified by now of the death of your son, Corpl. L.F. Green, in action on 27ᵗʰ August. He was shot and killed instantaneously by a sniper's bullet, after leading his section gallantly in the attack the company was making on a farm. We shall all miss his cheerful disposition in company very much. He was a very efficient N.C.O. We all sympathise with you in your loss very deeply.

Len is commemorated on Tyne Cot Memorial, Belgium (Panel 75 to 77). The memorial forms the north-east boundary of Tyne Cot Cemetery (see page 37) and bears the names of almost 35,000 officers and men whose graves are not known. Len is also commemorated on the Broadway Council School Memorial Board (see page 128).

Corporal Leonard F. Green's inscription on Tyne Cot Memorial, Belgium.
(Sarah Huxford)

Len's older brother Wilfred Harold, who had been born in 1890, was employed prior to the war as a commercial traveller selling woollens. Wilfred served with the 10ᵗʰ (Service) Battalion Royal Warwickshire Regiment and was injured during the Battle of Messines in June 1917 after which he was honourably discharged from the army and awarded the Silver War Badge.

The Evesham Journal reported Wilfred's injuries on 15ᵗʰ September 1917:

After an advance of four miles he had his jaw fractured in two places by the ring of a "whizz-bang" besides receiving a gunshot wound. A large section of the bronze ring and a large bullet have been removed from Private W. Green's head, and he has recently had a short leave home preliminary to a further operation in a Birmingham hospital. Pte. Green was in good general health, though his recovery from his injuries, will be a matter of several months, and probably mean his discharge from the army.

In 1924, Len's elder sister, Doris May, married Frank Phillips who served with the 1ˢᵗ Battalion Royal Warwickshire Regiment (see page 136).

---

110   Second Lieutenant J.R. Willis 1/8ᵗʰ Battalion Worcestershire Regiment, was awarded the Military Cross on 18ᵗʰ October 1917.

Cecil Frank Haines
Rifleman 4632, 1/12th Battalion London Regiment (The Rangers)

Cecil Frank Haines was born in Broadway in 1888, the eldest son of eight children of Hubert John Haines, a cattle dealer from Buckland, and Annie Sophia Haines (née Crisp) from Bretforton. Cecil's younger brother, Gerald, was born six years later in 1894 and is also commemorated on the Broadway War Memorial (see page 66).

Cecil's parents had married in 1885 and lived on the High Street, Broadway. By 1901 they had moved to Buckland and by 1911 to nearby Aston Somerville. By then, Cecil's eldest sister, Adelina Maud, was working for William Heming the baker in North Littleton near Evesham whom she later married in 1919. Cecil attended Broadway Council School and after leaving school moved to London where he worked as a footman for the stockbroker Viscount Montagu Brabazon Acheson and his wife Viscountess Caroline Mildred Acheson at 15 Chesham Street, Belgravia.

Whilst working in London Cecil enlisted with the 1/12th Battalion London Regiment (The Rangers). The battalion served on the Western Front and from January 1916 was part of the 56th (1st London) Division. From the beginning of July 1916 the battalion was engaged in the battles of the Somme and on 9th September 1916, during the first Battle of Ginchy, Cecil was killed in action. Cecil's body was never recovered and he is commemorated on Thiepval Memorial, France (Pier and Face 9C). Thiepval Memorial, the Memorial to the Missing of the Somme, bears the names of more than 73,000 officers and men of the United Kingdom and South African forces who died in the Somme sector before 20th March 1918 and have no known grave. Over 90% of those commemorated on the Memorial died between July and November 1916. Cecil left a will and probate was granted in Worcester on 1st January 1918 to his sister, Adelina, total effects £20 3s 1d.

Thiepval Memorial, Somme, France. (Commonwealth War Graves Commission)

Cecil is also commemorated with his brother Gerald on the Claines War Memorial in the churchyard at St John Baptist Church and on the marble memorial plaque inside the Claines Institute. Cecil is also commemorated on the Broadway Council School Memorial Board (see page 128).

Cecil's younger brother Percy John was born in Broadway on 27th January 1890. After leaving

The Haines brother pictured left to right: Rifleman Cecil F. Haines, Pte Gerald Haines, Pte Conway Haines and Driver Percy J. Haines. (Berrows Worcester Journal)

school Percy worked as a groom and on 26th February 1916, aged 26, attested under the Derby Scheme[111]. Percy was called up from the reserve and mobilized on 17th April 1916. Nearly eight months later, on 10th November 1916, Percy was posted to the Western Front as a Driver with the Royal Field Artillery and he served with the RFA until his demobilization in early September 1919.

Brothers Conway and Gerald were the first of the brothers to enlist. Conway, born in Broadway in 1892, worked as a farm labourer in the village before finding work as a boot salesman. He enlisted, aged 22, on 20th September 1914 in Cardiff and joined one of the new

Pte Cecil Haines's inscription on Thiepval Memorial. (Sarah Huxford)

battalions of the Welsh Regiment, the 11th (Service) Battalion, the Cardiff Pals Commercial Battalion. Conway trained with the battalion for nearly a year at camps in Hastings, Seaford in Sussex and Aldershot before the battalion embarked at Southampton for France on 4th September 1915 landing at Le Havre the following day. After only a few weeks in and out of the lines serving with 67th Brigade, part of the 22nd Division, the battalion was ordered to proceed to Salonika, setting sail from Marseilles on 30th October arriving on 8th November 1915. The Cardiff Pals fought in Salonika for three years, during which time Conway contracted both dysentery and malaria. Due to ill health, Conway was posted back to England in May 1918. The following month Conway was posted to the 3rd (Reserve) Battalion Welsh Regiment as he was no longer deemed fit for service in a theatre of war where malaria was prevalent. His continuing poor health led to his eventual discharge from the army on medical grounds. On 14th September 1918, having served five days short of four years, Conway was honourably discharged under paragraph 392(xvi) of the King's Regulations 1912 and was awarded the Silver War Badge.

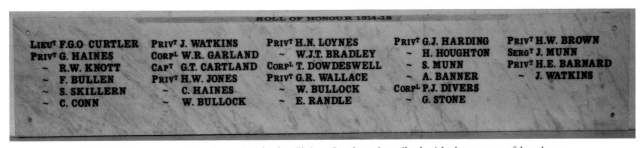

Roll of Honour marble plaque inside the Claines Institute inscribed with the names of brothers Rifleman (Pte) Cecil F. Haines and Pte Gerald Haines.

---

111   Lord Derby's Scheme or Group Scheme was a voluntary recruitment policy created in October 1915 by Edward Stanley, 17th Earl of Derby. Men who voluntarily registered were only called upon when necessary and married men were advised that they would only be called up once the supply of single men was exhausted. Men were classified into groups according to their year of birth and marital status. The scheme was abandoned on 15th December 1915.

Gerald Haines
Private 15024, 2nd Battalion Worcestershire Regiment

Gerald Haines was the younger brother of Cecil Frank Haines (see page 64) and the fourth son of Hubert John Haines and Annie Sophia Haines (née Crisp). Gerald was born in Broadway in 1894, and by 1911 had moved with his parents to Aston Somerville where Gerald worked as a gardener at The Rectory in the village.

Gerald enlisted in 1914 with the 2nd Battalion Worcestershire Regiment and embarked for France on 18th February 1915 where he joined the battalion, part of the 5th Brigade of the 2nd Division, in billets at Les Choquants.

Gerald served on the Western Front and in the middle of May 1915 the battalion was involved in the Battle of Festubert. During the evening of 14th May 1915, two of the battalion's companies, 'B' and 'D' companies, moved to the front line near the village of Richebourg L'Avoué, the other two companies were left in support in billets close by. The plan was for 'B' and 'D' companies to attack the German front line at 11.30pm under the cover of darkness at the same time as the battalions of the Indian Corps and the 2nd Battalion Royal Inniskilling Fusiliers. However, the watches of the 2nd Worcesters were not synchronised with those of the Inniskilling Fusiliers, and the Fusiliers, a few minutes ahead of the Worcesters, *rose to their feet and with a chorus of wild Irish yells, charged forward through the darkness[112]* so that by the time the Worcesters started their advance across the mud towards the German lines all surprise had been lost and there were many casualties brought down by a hail of German bullets. 'C' Company provided reinforcements but the attack had failed and was ordered to withdraw. As morning broke the battalion withdrew into reserve and Gerald had been killed in action, aged 21. The Evesham Journal reported on 26th June 1915:

Mrs. Haines, Whinfield-road, Claines, near Worcester (late of Aston Somerville), has received from the War Office, the sad news that her fourth son, Private G. Haines, of the 2nd Worcesters, was killed in action on May 15. He joined Kitchener's Army at the outbreak of war, and was sent out to France in February. Pte. Haines was only twenty-one years of age, and was a favourite with all who knew him. Much sympathy is felt for the bereaved family.

Gerald has no known grave or memorial in France and no record of his death is held by the Commonwealth War Graves Commission. Gerald is commemorated on the brass plaque inside St Mary the Virgin Church, Aston Somerville. He is also commemorated alongside his brother Cecil on the Claines War Memorial in the churchyard at St John Baptist Church and on the memorial plaque inside the Claines Institute (see page 65).

Gerald completed a will after enlistment in which he left all his effects to his mother Annie Haines of 4 Granville Villas, Whinfield Road, Claines. His will, which was actioned by the War Office on 27th September 1915, confirms he was killed in action at Richebourg, near Festubert, on 15th May 1915[113].

The Memorial Plaque inside St Mary the Virgin Church, Aston Somerville.

---

112   Page 70, Worcestershire Regiment in The Great War by Captain H. FitzM Stacke MC.
113   Pte 13676, Henry John Nash 2nd Battalion Worcestershire Regiment was killed in action the following day (see page 125).

Claines War Memorial built by Haughton Builders with the Cross of
Sacrifice designed by Sir Reginald Blomfield. The Memorial was unveiled
by Lord Hampton at a Dedication Service held on 12th September 1920.

The Claines War Memorial bears the names of 28 men (including Privates Cecil F.
Haines and Gerald Haines) who died during the First World War and the inscription:
SEE YE TO IT THAT THESE SHALL NOT HAVE DIED IN VAIN.

George Hensley
Private M2/148096, 284th Company Army Service Corps

George Hensley was born in Broadway in 1891, the youngest son of John Hensley, a stonemason from Broadway, and Elizabeth Hensley (née Mumford) from Childswickham. George's parents had married in 1870 and they set up home on the High Street, Broadway, where they raised George and his seven brothers and two sisters. In the 1911 census George, and his older brothers Percy Joseph and Oswald, are recorded as being employed as gardeners in the village.

By 1915 George's parents had moved to Primrose Bank, High Street, and George was working as a chauffeur in Evesham for a doctor. George's brother Oswald married Marion Smith, known as Minnie, at St Saviour's Church, Broadway, on 8th September 1915. The Evesham Journal reported on the wedding the following Saturday:

On Wednesday afternoon a marriage was celebrated at St. Saviour's Church between Mr. Oswald Hensley, the seventh son of Mr. John Hensley, of Primrose Bank, Broadway, and Miss Marion Smith, second daughter of Mr. Robert Smith, of Cheltenham. The bride was given away by her father, and was attended as bridesmaid by her sister, Miss Ethel Smith. Mr. George Hensley, brother of the bridegroom acted as best man. The marriage ceremony was performed by the Vice Rector of St. Saviour's, the Rev. F. Bruno Townsend, C.P., and Miss E. Cotterell played bridal music on the organ as the party entered and left the church. The bride was attired in a dress of silver grey brocaded silk, wore veil and wreath, and carried a shower bouquet of choice exotics. The bridesmaid wore a champagne cashmere dress with silk trimmings, wore a white hat with pink carnations, and carried a shower bouquet of choice flowers. The presents received were useful and numerous. After the ceremony a large party was entertained at Primrose Bank.

Five of the ten Hensley siblings.
(Susan Woodhouse)

Five of the ten Hensley siblings.
(J. Jacques., Jnr/Susan Appleby)

George enlisted in Evesham in late 1915 and joined 284th Company, a Mechanical Transport Company of the Army Service Corps. He was posted to East Africa on 3rd February 1916 and whilst on leave, on 21st April 1917, he married Elsie May Morris at St Saviour's Church, Leamington Road. On 8th May 1917, George returned to East Africa but ill health forced his return home to England in November

1917. George was treated at Endell Street Military Hospital[114], Covent Garden, London, where he died of malaria on 14th May 1918.

Commemorative plaque on the wall of Dudley Court, London, the site of
Endell Street Military Hospital.

George's funeral took place at St Saviour's Church on 18th May 1918 and he is buried in the churchyard. George left the effects of his will totalling £65 9s 6d to his widow, Elsie May Hensley. The Evesham Journal of 15th June 1918 printed the following report of his funeral:

Pte. George Hensley, M.T., A.S.C., died in Endel-street Military Hospital on May 14 from malarial fever. The body was conveyed to Broadway on the 16th and the funeral took place on the 18th at St. Saviour's Catholic Church. A military funeral was given, the Dead March being played on the organ and the De Profundis sang by the choir. There were a large number present both in church and at the graveside. Flowers were sent by "His wife, Elsie, Mum and Dad"; "Georgina[115], Will and family"; "Andrew[116], Lizzie and Leonard"; "Austin[117] and Maud"; "Chris and Emmie"; "Nell and Louise"; Lill and Queenie"; Mrs. May; "Oswald and Minnie"; Mr. and Mrs. E. Kenyon Stow[118]; Madame de Navarro[119]; Mrs. Box; Mrs. Wm. Roberts; Miss Hawling; Kate Moore and May Watts. Pte. G. Hensley was the son of Mr. and Mrs. John Hensley of High-street, Broadway, and previous to joining the Army was in the employ of a doctor at Evesham as chauffeur. After a period of training in England he sailed for East Africa on February 3, 1916 returning to England March 6, 1917. He went to East Africa a second time and on May 8 1917, and on being invalided home reached England November 30, 1917. General sympathy is expressed with his wife, parents and family.

George's older brother Percy Joseph, who had been born in Broadway in 1885, married Hellinor Emma Maunders at St Peter's Church, Willersey, on 17th April 1911 and they had one daughter, Louisa

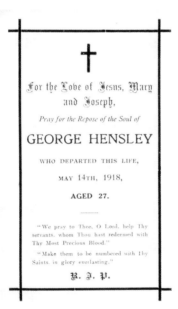

†

For the Love of Jesus, Mary and Joseph,

Pray for the Repose of the Soul of

GEORGE HENSLEY

WHO DEPARTED THIS LIFE,

MAY 14TH, 1918,

AGED 27.

"We pray to Thee, O Lord, help Thy servants, whom Thou hast redeemed with Thy Most Precious Blood."

"Make them to be numbered with Thy Saints, in glory everlasting."

R. I. P.

Funeral card for Pte George
Hensley, 14th May 1918.
(Susan Appleby)

---

114   The Endell Street Military Hospital was open from May 1915 to the end of 1919. The hospital was entirely staffed by women and run by militant suffragists, having been founded in 1914 by Dr Flora Murray and Dr Louisa Garrett, members of the Women's Social and Political Union.

115   George's sister Georgina Jelfs (née Hensley, 1871-1945) and her husband William Jelfs (1870-1923).

116   George's brother Andrew Hensley (1873-1961) his wife Sarah Elizabeth Hensley (née Sweetman,1875-1959) and son Leonard Joseph Hensley (1906-1945) of Leamington Road, Broadway. Andrew's grandson, Second Lieutenant Kenneth Andrew Hensley (1933-1955) died whilst on active service with the Royal Warwickshire Regiment, in Kuala Lumpur, Malaysia, and is commemorated on the Broadway War Memorial with a brass plaque.

117   George's brother Austin Hensley (1875-1949) and his wife Maud Elizabeth Hensley (née Yoxall, 1881-1925) of High Street, Broadway.

118   Edward Kenyon Stow and Norah Kenyon Stow (née Bentley) of Quad Mill, Broadway.

119   Mary Anderson de Navarro (1859-1940), American stage actress and wife of Antonio Fernando de Navarro (1861-1932) of Court Farm, Broadway.

Emma, born in 1912. Percy enlisted with the 11th (Service) Battalion Royal Warwickshire Regiment on 28th December 1914 in Stratford-upon-Avon. Percy (Private 11038) was posted to the Western Front on 31st July 1915. In mid-January 1916 Percy was hospitalised with pleurisy and on 4th February 1916 was transported on HMHS Copenhagen back to England where he was diagnosed as suffering from tuberculosis. On 3rd April 1916, Percy was discharged from the army under paragraph 392(xvi) of the King's Regulations 1912 as he was no longer fit for active service and he returned home to Willersey.

Percy died at home, aged 32, on 1st September 1917. He is buried in Willersey churchyard and commemorated on the Willersey War Memorial. The memorial commemorates 12 men of the village who died in the First World War including Albert Daffurn who was born in Broadway (see page 122).

The grave of Pte George Hensley (left), St Saviour's Churchyard, Broadway, and the grave of Pte Percy Hensley, St Peter's Churchyard, Willersey. (Susan Woodhouse)

Willersey War Memorial, Willersey.

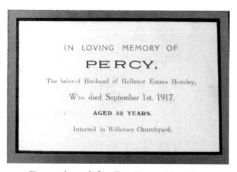

Funeral card for Pte Percy Hensley.
(Susan Woodhouse)

Reginald Bertram Hill
Private 9574, 1st Battalion Royal Warwickshire Regiment

Reginald Bertram Hill was born in Broadway in early 1894 and baptised in St Michael's Church on 22nd April 1894, the youngest son of William Richard Hill, a farm labourer from South Littleton, and William's second wife, Harriett Hill (née Jones), from Childswickham. His parents had married in 1891 and Reginald had two older siblings, Alfred Charles, born in Broadway in 1892, and a half-brother, William James, known as James who had been born in Buckland in 1879. Reginald's father had firstly married Esther Wright in Buckland in 1877 but she had died, aged 37, in 1888.

Pte Reginald B. Hill.
(Evesham Journal)

Reginald grew up in the cottages at Bury End, Broadway. Reginald's mother died in 1909 at the age of 51 leaving his father widowed for a second time. Reginald attended Broadway Council School and after leaving school was apprenticed as a baker and by 1911 was working at Louis J. Brown's bakery on the High Street. His father, William, worked as a market gardener and his brother, Alfred, as a farm labourer in the village. Reginald's half-brother, James, who had worked at the kennels for the North Cotswold Hunt, had moved by 1911 to Chepstow where he was working as a stableman for Colonel Reginald Bertie (retired Colonel of the Royal Welsh Fusiliers) and his wife, Amy.

On 4th December 1914, Reginald travelled to Stratford-upon-Avon to enlist with the Royal Warwickshire Regiment, the same day as Joseph Badger (see page 137), George Barnett (see page 8) and Frederick Goddard (brother of Arthur Goddard, see page 59). Reginald was posted with the 1st Battalion to the Western Front on 2nd May 1915 with the 10th Brigade of the 4th Division and from 1st June served in the trenches at Lancashire Farm during the Second Battle of Ypres.

On 26th June 1915, The Evesham Journal published a letter from Reginald and fellow serving Broadway men: George Barnett, Francis Edgar Bartlett, Harvey Carter, Harry Gilder, Frederick Goddard, Charles Walter Jarrett, Felix Lambley, Frank Phillips (see page 136), George Smith and Thomas Stanley (younger brother of Charles Robert Stanley, see page 102). Reginald's letter mentions a gas attack on Whit Monday, 24th May 1915, during the Second Battle of Ypres:

I am writing these few lines hoping that you will insert them in the 'Journal' just to let our friends know that we are all well. I am writing from the rest camp, which is the only place from which we have the chance of communicating with our friends. Please remember us to all the people at Broadway. We are all well and in the best of health and spirits thank God. We have had some rough times since we have been here. It is only six weeks since we came out but we know what it is to fight for our country, and live in hope of coming back safely to our dear old village of Broadway again. Some of the lads from home are wounded and missing, but we are glad to say none of us have been put under yet, and we hope by God's guidance that we shall pull through safely. G. Smith has a slight wound, but is with us again. We should have liked to have been at the Club, as we hear they had a nice time Whitsun week. We are glad to say that our regiment has done good work. Our motto is 'Heads up, Warwicks' but here it is a case of 'keep your heads down'. One has not the chance of showing his head over the top of the trench a second time. The German snipers do not miss such a mark, and are on duty day and night. I should like to get near one. We have lovely weather here except for thunderstorms now and then. We experienced one of our roughest times Whit Monday. We came from the trenches on the Sunday night for a rest, but about three o'clock the next morning we were aroused by our guns about ------- yards behind us. We were ordered to put our respirators on, fall in at once, and go up to the firing line. The beastly Germans sent over two doses of gas. This was the first lot we had experienced since we have been out, and I hope it will be the last. We were nearly choked to death with it; our eyes and noses ran with water, and we could not see for some time. I am glad to say we have had the wind in our favour nearly all the time since, and hope it will keep so. From the Broadway lads of the 1st Warwicks Regt., now doing a bit in France.

At 2.45am on 24th May 1915, a ferocious German artillery bombardment was accompanied by a simultaneous discharge of chlorine gas along almost the entire length of the British front line. Although the favourable wind had alerted the British to the likelihood of an attack, the proximity of the German trenches and the speed of the assault meant that many men failed to put their respirators on quickly enough and large numbers were overcome and many killed.

From 1st June 1915, the battalion served in the trenches at Lancashire Farm and during the first week of July 1915 was called on to support troops fighting to capture the International Trench at Boesinghe, along the Yser Canal. Casualties were high and on 4th July 1915 Reginald was killed in action at the age of 21. The Evesham Journal of 10th July 1915 reported:

We regret to learn that Pte. R.B. Hill, of 1st Warwicks, youngest son of Mr R.W. Hill, of the Bury End, Broadway, was killed in France on Sunday last. The sad news came in the following letter to the father from Pte. F. Phillips[120], who is in the same battalion – "Just a few lines with my deepest regret to tell you that your son, Pte. R.B. Hill was killed in action on Sunday July 4. He was hit with shrapnel and died almost immediately. It has put me about a lot as he has been my best pal since enlistment. I have got his badge, and will send it home to you for a keepsake. He will be very much missed in the company as he was liked by everyone." Pte. Hill was 21 years of age and single. He was a baker by trade, and previous to his enlistment worked for Mr. L. Brown, of Broadway. He joined the army in December, and went to the continent in May. He was a good hard working lad, esteemed by all who knew him. General regret is felt at his death, and sincere sympathy expressed with his father in his sore trial.

Reginald is buried in Bard Cottage Cemetery near Boesinghe, West-Vlaanderen, Belgium (grave I. D. 32) which at the time was known as 10th Infantry Cemetery. His epitaph reads: LOVINGLY REMEMBERED BY FATHER. Bard Cottage was a house set back a short way from the German line close to a bridge called Bard's Causeway. The cemetery was made nearby in a sheltered position under a high bank. All the headstones are of Hopton Wood Stone (not the usual Portland Stone) and there are now 1,639 Commonwealth casualties of the First World War buried or commemorated in this cemetery designed by Sir Reginald Blomfield[121]. Reginald is also commemorated on the Broadway Council School Memorial Board as 'Bertram Hill' (see page 128) and in the Roll of Honour 1914-1918 in St Michael's Church as 'Herbert Hill' (see page 3).

The grave of Pte Reginald B. Hill, Bard Cottage Cemetery, Belgium. (Aurel Sercu)

Five days after Reginald was killed, George Barnett, who served with Reginald, was killed in action (see page 8).

Reginald's brother, Alfred Charles (Private 12730), served during the war with the 9th (Service) Battalion Gloucestershire Regiment and in 1919 he married Tryphena Figgitt (née Cooke) the widow of Wilford Charles Figgitt (see page 42).

Bard Cottage Cemetery, Pte Reginald Hill's grave front row second from the right. (Aurel Sercu)

---

120   Pte Frank Alfred Phillips (see page 136).
121   Sir Reginald Blomfield also designed the Ypres (Menin Gate) Memorial (see page 9 and page 124).

Joseph Hilson
Private 12240, 1ˢᵗ Battalion Gloucestershire Regiment

Joseph Hilson (also spelt Hillson) was born in Bethnal Green, London, on 8ᵗʰ February 1892, the son of Joseph Hilson and Lucy Hilson (née Bridges) who had married on 5ᵗʰ November 1891 at St James the Great Church, Bethnal Green. Joseph was baptised on 7ᵗʰ October 1893 at St John's Church, Bethnal Green. At the time the family were living at 159 Quinn's Square, off Russia Lane, and Joseph's father was working as a potman in a nearby public house.

Pte Joseph Hilson.
(Evesham Journal)

Aged five, on 18ᵗʰ September 1897, Joseph and his older brother George Henry enrolled at Somerfield Street School[122], Tower Hamlets. Joseph's mother, Lucy, died a couple of years later at the age of 33 and by April 1901 Joseph had moved to 19 Knott Street, Stepney, with his widowed father, brother John Alfred and sister, Lucy. Joseph's brother, George, went to live with their paternal aunt and uncle, Frances Townsend (née Hilson) and Henry Townsend at 14 Wolverley Street, Bethnal Green.

On Tuesday 6ᵗʰ August 1901, Joseph was admitted to Mile End Old Town Children's Home, a scattered home[123] for poor law children attached to Mile End Workhouse run by the Guardians of the Poor of the Hamlet of Mile End Old Town, as his father had been sent to prison. His brother John and sister Lucy were admitted to the home a few weeks later on 25ᵗʰ September 1901 from the attached infirmary. John and Lucy were discharged from the home on 4ᵗʰ October into the care of their father who had been released from prison, and Joseph was released the following day. Whilst in the children's home, Joseph attended Ben Jonson School, Harford Street, on the edge of Mile End Park, east London from 27ᵗʰ August 1901 to 7ᵗʰ October 1901.

On 21ˢᵗ May 1903, Joseph was readmitted to Mile End Old Town School Children's Home. The register at the time records that Joseph had no known relative and that he was taken to the home by the police. This suggests that Joseph's father had by this time died or had been readmitted to prison. Joseph left the children's home in 1909 when he was apprenticed to Ernest Warren an ironmonger in Broadway. Joseph lived and worked for Ernest Warren and his family until he enlisted in September 1914.

Warrens, High Street, Broadway. (Peggy Hancock)

---

122   Somerfield Street School opened in 1881 and was re-named Stewart Headlam School in 1924.
123   Scattered or isolated homes placed small groups of children in ordinary houses scattered around the suburbs of the city, under the care of a foster-parent employed by the workhouse union

Joseph enlisted in Cheltenham and joined the 7th (Service) Battalion Gloucestershire Regiment of Kitchener's Army. The battalion trained at Tidworth and by January 1915 had moved to billets in Basingstoke. In February 1915 the battalion moved to Blackdown, Aldershot, before being mobilized at the beginning of June. On 19th June 1915, Joseph, part of 'B' Company embarked at Avonmouth bound for Gallipoli. The battalion landed at 'Y' Beach, Helles, Gallipoli at 10.30pm on 11th July 1915 and was engaged in various battles including: The Battle of Sari Bair, The Battle of Russell's Top and The Battle of Hill 60 (see map on page 108).

Joseph contracted dysentery whilst in Gallipoli and was transferred to a hospital in Malta before being transported back to England for further treatment and recuperation in Broadway. Joseph was able to rejoin his regiment in March 1916 and was posted to the 1st Battalion on the Western Front at the beginning of April. On 17th April 1916, his first day in the trenches at Double Crassier, south east of Maroc, Joseph was hit in the head by shrapnel and died within minutes. On 6th May 1916, the Evesham Journal reported:

News has reached Broadway that Pte. Joseph Hilson, of the Gloucestershire Regt., was killed in the trenches by shrapnel on April 17. Pte. Hilson, who was an orphan, came from Mile End Old Town Scattered Homes, and had been with Mr. E. Warren as an ironmonger's assistant for seven years. He enlisted in the Gloucesters early in September, 1914, and was sent in due course to the Gallipoli Peninsula, where he was attacked by dysentery, and was invalided to a hospital in Malta for several months. He was then transferred to a hospital in this country, and when convalescent had a furlough at Broadway. In March he went to the front again, and on his first day in the trenches he was struck by shrapnel on the head, and within a few minutes was dead. He was a smart and useful lad, a valued assistant, and was liked by all who had to do with him.

The grave of Pte Joseph Hilson,
Maroc British Cemetery.
(Margaret Dufay)

Joseph is buried in Maroc British Cemetery, Grenay, France (grave I. H. 49). The cemetery, designed by Sir Herbert Baker, was begun by French troops in 1915 and now contains 1,379 Commonwealth burials and commemorations. In 1920, Ernest Warren, Joseph's employer, contributed to the Broadway war memorial fund in Joseph's memory and requested that Joseph's name be inscribed on the war memorial.

Joseph's sister Lucy was admitted by the age of 14 as an inmate at Darenth Asylum in Dartford. Lucy was later transferred to the Leavesden Asylum[124] in Hertfordshire where she died, aged 21, in 1918.

Maroc British Cemetery, Grenay, Pas de Calais, France.
(Commonwealth War Graves Commission)

---

124   Darenth and Leavesden Asylums were set up by the Metropolitan Asylums Board. Children formed a large number of the Board's intake of infectious sick and mentally handicapped patients.

Francis Henry Ingles

Private TF/241275, 'C' Company, 7th (Service) Battalion The Queen's Own (Royal West Kent Regiment)

Francis H. Ingles.
(Peggy Hancock)

Francis Henry Ingles, was born in Broadway in 1891, the son of Emily Ingles. Francis, was brought up in Broadway by his maternal aunt and uncle, Eliza Ann Daffurn (née Ingles) and Charles Daffurn with his cousin Tom Daffurn (see page 31). Francis was a pupil at Broadway Council School and after leaving school worked as a kennelman and whipper-in at The Kennels, Broadway, for the North Cotswold Hunt.

Francis enlisted in Evesham after conscription was introduced in 1916 and he initially served as a Private, regimental number 22018, with the Somerset Light Infantry. Francis later transferred to the Royal West Kent Regiment and was allocated a new regimental number, TF/241275.

Francis served with 'C' Company of the 7th Battalion The Queen's Own (Royal West Kent Regiment) on the Western Front. In January 1918, the battalion moved to the 53rd Infantry Brigade of the 18th Division and during March 1918, was on the front line in the Battle of St Quentin during the German Spring Offensive. During the afternoon of 20th March 1918, the battalion was warned to prepare for attack and from the early hours of 21st March was subjected to a heavy bombardment by the Germans. By the time dawn broke the area was shrouded in a heavy mist which allowed the Germans to advance undetected and inflict considerable damage. 'C' Company suffered severe losses during the German advance and the battalion was overwhelmed. The battalion's war diary for that day records 20 officer casualties and 577 casualties amongst other ranks. Francis was one of the many men reported as missing in action on 21st March 1918.

A year after Francis was declared missing, the following announcement was published in the Evesham Journal on 26th April 1919:

In loving memory of Tom Daffurn, of Broadway, Worcestershire, who died at Malta, May 1st, 1917. Also of Frank Ingles, of the West Kents, who was reported as missing March 21st, 1918, the beloved sons of Charles and Elizabeth Daffurn. Their warfare o'er from earthly strife they're gone to hear their Lord's sweet gracious world. Well done.

It was later confirmed that Francis died on 28th March 1918 and he is commemorated on Pozieres Memorial, France (Panel 58 and 59) along with 88 other officers and men of the battalion who died on the same day. The memorial encloses Pozieres British Cemetery just outside the village of Pozières. Along the sides and the back are stone tablets fixed in the stone rubble walls bearing the names of the dead grouped under their regiments. Francis is also commemorated on the Broadway Council School Memorial Board (see page 128).

Pozieres Memorial, France. (Jeff Fox)

Francis's uncle, Walter Henry Ingles, farmed at Bury End where he had six acres of arable crops and five acres of orchard. Frank's cousin and Walter's son, Stephen John Ingles, known as Jack (see page 136), appealed against his conscription when his papers arrived when he reached the age of 18 in July 1916. Jack's father supported his exemption application stating at the Evesham Military Service Tribunal held in December 1916 that Jack was required to help with the cherry season the following year. The tribunal decided that Jack would be exempted until 1st April 1917 after which he enlisted with the Royal Field Artillery. Jack served with the RFA until his demobilization in 1919.

Francis H. Ingles, North Cotswold Hunt, Broadway.
(Peggy Hancock)

Pte Francis H. Ingles's inscription on Pozieres Memorial.
(Sarah Huxford)

Charles Jackson

Private 241170, 9th (Service) Battalion Worcestershire Regiment

Charles Jackson was born in 1887 and baptised at St Michael's Church later in the year on 11th December. Charles was the second son of eleven children of agricultural labourer, John Jackson from Broadway, and his wife Eliza Jackson from Willersey. Charles was brought up in the village in the family home at China Square. Charles was a pupil at Broadway Council School and after leaving school, firstly worked as an errand boy before finding work as a farm labourer. In 1913, Charles married Agnes Maria Taylor from Sedgeberrow near Evesham. Prior to their marriage Agnes had worked as a domestic servant for Mrs Eleanor Haines of Lauristine, Hales Road, Cheltenham.

China Square, Broadway, where Charles Jackson lived as a boy.
(J. Jacques, Junr., Broadway)

It is not known when Charles enlisted but he initially served as Private 3613 with the 2/8th Battalion Worcestershire Regiment. Charles later transferred to 9th (Service) Battalion Worcestershire Regiment and was given a new regimental number 241170.

From February 1916 the 9th Worcesters served in Mesopotamia. On 1st July 1918 the battalion, part of the 39th Brigade, received orders to leave the 13th (Western) Division in Mesopotamia and the Brigade proceeded to Baku on the western coast of the Caspian Sea in the Caucasus where on 24th August 1918 it joined the North Persia Force at Dunsterforce Headquarters (named after its commander Major General Lionel Dunsterville, CB). The aim of Dunsterforce was to organise and train local groups to counter Ottoman operations in the Caucasus and to prevent the port and oil fields from falling under Ottoman control. British forces, reinforced by Armenian and Russian volunteers occupied Baku, however, the following month they were forced to evacuate the city on 14th September when they came under threat of attack by a superior Ottoman force. After the Armistice Dunsterforce returned to Baku and remained there as an occupying force until September 1919.

Charles fell ill and died, aged 31, on 8th October 1918. He is buried in Belgaum Government Cemetery, in the state of Karnataka, near the west coast of India (plot C, grave 144). Charles would have been invalided to India from either Mesopotamia or Baku and he died in hospital in India (there was a British military hospital in Belgaum which had opened before the war). There are eight men from the Worcestershire Regiment buried in the cemetery with Charles. Charles is also commemorated on the Kirkee 1914-1918 Memorial (Face 5), on the plateau above Bombay, India. The Kirkee Memorial commemorates more than 1800 casualties who died during the war who are buried in civil and cantonment cemeteries in

India and Pakistan where there graves can no longer be properly maintained.

Charles completed a will in his army pay book leaving all his property and effects to his widow, Agnes who secondly married Thomas Bowles in 1920. In 1919, the parishioners of Sedgeberrow erected a war memorial cross, built of white Ashlar stone by W. & H. Gardiner[125] of Evesham, by the lychgate of St Mary's Church in the village. Charles is commemorated on the memorial alongside ten other men from Sedgeberrow who were killed in action or died of wounds or sickness during the war. Charles is also commemorated on the Broadway Council School Memorial Board (see page 128).

Unveiling and dedication of Sedgeberrow War Memorial, 1920. (Cyril Banks)

Sedgeberrow War Memorial, Worcestershire.

Kirkee 1914-1918 Memorial, India.
(Commonwealth War Graves Commission)

125 W. & H. Gardiner were asked to quote for the building of Alfred Parsons's design for the Broadway War Memorial (see page 4).

Walter Jordan

Private 202406, 1st Battalion Worcestershire Regiment

Born in late 1897, at Bowers Hill between Badsey and Willersey, Walter Jordan was the eldest son of Charles Jordan, a farmer's son from Hampton, and Bertha Jordan (née Stanley) from Willersey. His parents had married in Badsey on 11th September 1897 and by 1901 they had moved into the village of Willersey where Charles farmed. Walter had two younger brothers and two younger sisters. The family moved to Colletts Fields, Broadway, and Walter was enrolled at Broadway Council School. After leaving school, Walter worked as an errand boy for a grocer in the village and by 1914 the family had moved to 58 Council Cottages.

Walter enlisted in Evesham after the introduction of conscription in 1916 and joined the 1st Battalion Worcestershire Regiment. Walter served on the Western Front and at the end of July 1917 the battalion was involved in the first phase of the Battle of Ypres. On the 26th July 1917 the battalion had moved forward from their billets in Ypres to dugouts at Halfway House. During the night of 30th/31st July the battalion left the support trenches to prepare for an attack and by 3.50am the British infantry went 'over the top' and the great battle began. Little opposition was encountered as 'C' and 'D' companies of the battalion moved forward over rain-soaked ground towards the German front lines and on to the support trenches where they dug in. 'A' and 'B' companies followed and continued north eastwards through what remained of Chateau Wood to James Trench where they met fierce opposition. Their advance was halted by heavy shelling and machine gun fire but the brave actions of Lance-Corporal Charles Richards and Private Sydney Fudger (who were both later awarded the DCM) lead to the capture of a German machine gun which allowed the advance to continue to the intended target, a crest facing Westhoek Ridge where the remaining men of the battalion continued to come under heavy gun fire throughout the day. The first phase of the attack had been accomplished but the battalion had lost over 200 men during the attack. The heavy rain returned that evening and the battalion dug in as best they could until they were relieved by the 3rd Battalion towards the end of the following day.

Walter was killed in action, aged 19, during the action on 31st July 1917 but it is not known with which of the companies of the battalion he was with at the time. After the battle Walter was buried in Perth Cemetery (China Wall), Belgium (grave I. E. 12).

The cemetery west of Ypres in Belgium was begun by French troops in November 1914 (the French graves were removed after the Armistice) and was adopted by the 2nd Scottish Rifles in June 1917. It was called Perth Cemetery as the predecessors of the 2nd Scottish Rifles were raised in Perth, and China Wall after the communication trench known as the Great Wall of China. It is also known as Halfway House Cemetery and was used for front line burials until October 1917.

Walter is also commemorated on the Broadway Council School Memorial Board (see page 128).

The grave of Pte Walter Jordan,
Perth Cemetery (China Wall), Belgium.
(Sarah Huxford)

Charles Hubert Keyte

Private 27819, 3rd Battalion Worcestershire Regiment

Pte Charles H. Keyte.
(Evesham Journal)

Charles Hubert Keyte[126] was born in Broadway in 1891, the youngest son of Joseph Keyte and Emma Keyte (née Smith). Charles's parents had married in Broadway in 1876. His father was a painter and decorator and his mother, from Marcliff in Warwickshire, worked as a dressmaker. Charles was one of nine children, two of whom died during infancy.

Charles was brought up in Broadway and attended Broadway Council School. In the 1901 census Charles is recorded as living with his mother, Emma, in Rams Alley. By 1911 Charles had set up as a boot-repairing business at Fox House in the village where he had moved to with his mother.

In August 1913 Charles married Lillian Annie Slater in Milton under Wychwood, Oxfordshire, and they had two children, Philip born in 1914 and Charles Edward born in 1915. The family moved to The Shanty (later known as The Busy Bee) on the High Street from where Charles and Lillian continued to run the boot-repairers.

Charles voluntarily attested in 1915 under the Derby Scheme. Charles would have been paid a day's army pay and issued with a grey armband with a red crown to wear as a sign that he had volunteered. Charles was called upon for service in April 1916 with his group (no. 30) and was assigned to the 3rd Battalion Worcestershire Regiment. Charles was posted to the Western Front where the battalion formed part of the 74th Brigade of the 25th Division.

From July 1916, the battalion was involved in the battles of the Somme including the Battle of Bazentin Ridge 14th to 17th July and the Battle of Pozieres Ridge from 23rd July to 10th August 1916. The battalion then returned to billets at Bertrancourt before marching on to the training area at Puchevillers.

The grave of Pte Charles H. Keyte,
Authuile Military Cemetery, France.
(Sarah Huxford)

On 18th August the battalion returned to the front line trenches before the Leipzig Salient to the south of the village of Thiepval with the 1st Battalion Wiltshire Regiment. Here the battalion encountered shelling and sniper fire from the German trenches overlooking them, and on 22nd August 1916 two men of the battalion were killed and seven men were wounded. Charles was one of the men killed in action that day and he was buried by his regiment in Authuile Military Cemetery, Somme, France (grave I. 3). His epitaph reads: HE LEFT ALL AND FOLLOWED JESUS.

The Evesham Journal reported on 2nd September 1916:

On Saturday morning, in a letter from the chaplain of the regiment, the sad news was received that Private Charles Hubert Keyte, of the Worcester Regiment, had been killed in France on August 22. The place of his death was not known, but the letter stated that the nose cap of a shell struck him in the head, and that death was instantaneous. Pte. C.H. Keyte was in business as a bootmaker in High-street, Broadway, and was 24 (sic) years of age. He had for several years been a member of the Laverton Brass Band, in which he played the first cornet. He married Miss Annie Slatter, of Milton, in August 1913, and had two sons, aged two and one years. Pte. Keyte voluntarily attested under the Derby Scheme in 1915, and joined up with his group in April of the current year. He went to the front in July, and had been

---

126   Charles Hubert Keyte was first cousin to: Albert Henry Clarke (see page 18), brothers Bertie Vernon Keyte and Heber John Keyte (see page 133) and Wilson William Keyte (see page 138).

on several occasions in hot places before meeting with his death. At the time he was suffering from a bad throat, and might have had sick leave from duty, but gallantly decided to hold on as long as possible. Deep and general sympathy is expressed with his widow and family in their loss.

Charles is commemorated on the Broadway Council School Memorial Board (see page 128). Probate was granted to Charles's widow, Lillian, in Worcester on 9th October 1916, total effects were £98 4s 1d. Lillian continued to run the boot repairing business after Charles's death and placed the following announcement in the Evesham Journal on 30th December 1916:

Mrs. C.H. Keyte boot and shoe maker, wishes to express regret to her numerous customers for any delay in the execution of their orders. She is hoping soon to secure another workman, and will esteem the favour of continued patronage.

Charles's brother, William Joseph, who was born in Broadway on 11th August 1884, was a jobbing builder and decorator who was employed across many of the farms in the village. William appealed against his conscription at a Military Service Tribunal in Evesham at the beginning of March 1918. On 8th March 1918, The Evesham Journal published the grounds of William's appeal:

He said that if called up he would have to close his business. He complained that there were a dozen or two C3[127] men in Broadway who had not been called up, and who had no businesses of their own. He was a married man[128] with three children and had been rejected three times and examined five times. It was not until last April that he was passed in any category at all. He had lost one man. He was a one-man business.

William was granted conditional exemption from military service provided he continued to undertake work of national importance. William did not serve during the war and died in 1974.

Charles's elder brother William Joseph and Emily Keyte (centre), their two children James and Ivy Keyte and family, Broadway.

---

127   Under the Military Service Act of January 1916, recruits were graded from A1 to C3. The latter was the lowest grade, for men who were unsuitable for combat training, fit only for clerical and other sedentary jobs.
128   William Joseph Keyte married Emily Fathers in Evesham on 19th January 1912.

Alfred Layton

Private 22994, 9th (Service) Battalion Worcestershire Regiment

Pte Alfred Layton.
(Kim Workman)

Alfred Layton was born in London, on 18th June 1889, the youngest son of George Layton from Haslingfield, Cambridgeshire, and Ellen Layton (née Eden) from Harvington near Evesham. Alfred's parents married on 19th December 1874 at All Saints' Church, St John's Wood, London. At the time of their marriage, Alfred's father was employed as a cardboard maker but by 1887 he was employed as a wiremaker for the growing telecommunications industry.

Alfred had six siblings, four brothers and two sisters, and the family lived at 8 Tolmers Square, St Pancras, London. The year after Alfred was born, his sister May died, aged three, and his mother was admitted to Barnet Asylum. Alfred, the youngest member of the family, was sent to live with his maternal grandparents William James Eden, an agricultural labourer, and Hannah Eden (née Oliver) in Harvington whilst his father, brothers and sister stayed in London.

The following year his sister Annie died and his mother died later the same year on 17th September 1891. His father secondly married Susan Hicks who worked with him at the General Post Office and they moved with Alfred's brothers to Islington. George and Susan had three daughters but Susan died in 1905 and George and the children moved to 72 Waddington Street, Stratford, in the east end of London where George thirdly married his housekeeper Ada Jane Ann Streater (née Nicholls) in 1914.

Alfred was brought up in Harvington by his grandparents. Alfred attended Harvington School where his maternal aunt, Annie Pickering, worked as a teacher. Alfred's grandfather died in 1908 and in the 1911 census, Alfred is recorded as working as a labourer for a market gardener in Harvington, living with his widowed grandmother, Hannah Eden who later died, aged 79, on 26th January 1914.

On 7th June 1913, Alfred married Nora Carey, from Oddington, Gloucestershire, at St John the Baptist Church, Fladbury. Alfred and Nora set up home in Broadway where Nora worked as a domestic servant for Edwin Lewis Foss[129], the chemist, and his family on the High Street.

After his marriage, Alfred worked on the railways firstly for the Great Western Railway at Broadway railway station with his father-in-law, Thomas Carey, and later as a wharf-man for Wallis and Co. at Evesham station. Alfred and Nora had two children, Alfred William born in 1913 and Geoffrey Francis in 1915. In June 1915, Alfred enlisted in Broadway and he joined the 9th (Service) Battalion Worcestershire Regiment.

Alfred was posted to Mesopotamia in April 1916 where the battalion, part of the 39th Brigade of the 13th (Western) Division, had been transferred from Gallipoli as reinforcements for the Tigris Corps fighting the Ottoman forces. During April the battalion was

Nora Carey.
(Kim Workman)

---

129   Two of Edwin L. Foss's sons, Sidney Elliott and Alfred Edward, were awarded the Meritorious Service Medal during the war, see page 139.

involved in actions along the River Tigris and the unsuccessful relief of Kut-al-Amara. The battalion was back in the trenches at Bait Isa by 1st May where it encountered sporadic shell fire and sniper fire. By the end of May the heat was rapidly increasing, and on 23rd May the 39th Brigade marched back to a tented camp near Mason's Mounds for rest and training. On 8th June the 9th Worcesters marched four miles south into the desert at Twin Canals where they set up camp in the intense heat. Temperatures exceeding 110°F/43°C were common during the summer months and towards the end of June the division was relieved by the 3rd Indian Division (3rd (Lahore) Division).

After dark on 27th June 1916, the 9th Worcesters marched the six miles across uneven roads to the fortified post of Sodom where a light railway was being laid to improve supplies of equipment and food. Heat and sickness had taken its toll on the battalion which was in poor physical condition. It took until 10pm that evening before the leading platoons arrived at their destination with many following on several hours behind. Alfred, aged 26, who had been suffering from dysentery succumbed to exhaustion and lost his life during the march. On 22nd July 1916, the Evesham Journal reported:

Pte. Alfred Layton, of the 9th Worcester Regiment, previous to his enlistment lived at High-street, Broadway, and was wharf-man to Messrs. Wallis and Co. at Evesham station. He joined the army in June, 1915, and trained at Devonport. He sailed for Mesopotamia at the end of April, 1916, and safely landed, but after being at the front for a month died from the effects of heat at the age of 26 years. He leaves a wife and two children, with whom deep sympathy is felt.

Prior to his posting to Mesopotamia, on 2nd May 1916 Alfred completed a will in his pay book leaving all of his property and effects to his wife Nora on the event of his death.

Alfred is buried in Amara War Cemetery, Al Amara, on the banks of the River Tigris, Iraq (grave XII. D. 11). In 1933 all of the headstones were removed from the cemetery when it was discovered that salts in the soil were causing them to deteriorate. Instead a screen wall was erected with the names of those buried in the cemetery engraved upon it. The current situation in Iraq makes it impossible for the Commonwealth War Graves Commission to maintain the cemetery and Alfred's name appears in the Roll of Honour, which is displayed in the Commission's offices in Maidenhead (see page 39). Alfred is recorded in the Roll of Honour 1914-1918 in St Michael's Church as 'Albert Layton' (see page 3).

The Cross of Sacrifice in Amara War Cemetery, Al Amara, Iraq.
(Harry Fecitt)

Alfred, Geoffrey and Nora Layton.
(Kim Workman)

Alfred's widow Nora, secondly married Robert Cook in Broadway on 24th September 1919. Nora and Robert Cook's eldest son, Robert Leonard, served with the 5th Battalion Grenadier Guards and died on 23rd April 1943 in North Africa during the Second World War. Lance Corporal Robert Cook is buried in Medjez-El-Bab War Cemetery, Tunisia, and is one of the men of the Second World War commemorated on the Broadway War Memorial.

Alfred's older brother Harry Eden, who was born in 1885, served with the Essex Regiment during the war. His eldest brother, William George, who was born on 18th April 1880, worked as a telegraph boy after leaving school. At the age of 16, in June 1896 he joined the Royal Navy at Chatham, Kent, as a boy 2nd class on a training ship having signed up for a minimum of 12 years service. From the age of 18 he served overseas and completed 15 years service during which time he reached the rank of able seaman having served on HMS Boscowen, Minotaur, Pembroke, Victorious, Hawke and Egeria. After leaving the navy, William worked as a linesman and on 10th May 1915, William, aged 35, enlisted as a sapper (no. 1379) with the Royal Marines Divisional Engineers most likely with a Signals Company. On 31st December 1916, William transferred to the Royal Engineers (Sapper 207522) when the army took over responsibility for the unit.

Alfred's brother Samuel Sidney, who was born in 1888, enlisted, aged 18, with the Royal Fusiliers in Dalston on 7th December 1900. He served in Egypt, Bermuda and South Africa before being posted to the Western Front with the British Expeditionary Force on 13th August 1914. Samuel transferred to the Labour Corps during the war before he was discharged from the army on 14th August 1918.

Broadway Station opened on 1st August 1904. The above photo was taken in 1907.
William Robert Billey (see page 12), Alfred Layton (see page 81),
Frank Alfred Phillips (see page 136) and Wilfred George Tandy (see page 107)
worked for the Great Western Railway at Broadway.
(J. Jacques, Junr., Broadway/John Alsop)

Sidney John Painter
M2/033139 Private, 5th Divisional Supply Column, Army Service Corps

Sidney John Painter was the eldest son of George Isaac Painter, a grocer from Bourton-on-the-Water, and Sarah Painter (née Hutt) from Standlake, near Witney. Sidney was born in 1892 in Castle Eaton, a small Wiltshire village between Cirencester and Swindon. His parents had married in 1888 and settled in the village of Lower Swell where George worked as a grocer.

When Sidney was a young boy, the family moved to Broadway where his father found work as a baker and Sidney was enrolled at Broadway Council School. By 1911 the family had moved to Fairfield, Station Road. Sidney and his younger brother Bertie William were apprenticed as motor engineers and his elder sister, Gwendoline Alice Sarah[130] as an assistant school mistress in the village.

Sidney's training as a mechanic and later employment as a driver no doubt influenced his decision to enlist in Birmingham on 11th January 1915 with a Mechanical Transport Company of the Army Service Corps. By the end of January Sidney had been posted to France and embarked from Avonmouth on 28th January 1915. On arriving in France he joined the 5th Divisional Supply Column[131], No. 48 Mechanical Transport Company. Sidney was taken ill on the way to France and was admitted to hospital in Rouen on 17th March suffering from influenza. Sidney's health never recovered and he was transferred to No. 4 General Hospital, Versailles, where he died of meningitis, aged 23, on 9th May 1915. The Evesham Journal published the following report of his death on 5th June 1915:

We regret to learn that Pte. Sidney Painter, of the Army Service Corps, died in the 4th General Hospital, Versailles, on May 9 from cerebro-spinal fever, Pte. S. Painter was the son of Mr G.J. and Mrs Painter, of Fairfield, Broadway, and was twenty-three years of age, and a skilled automobile engineer and driver. He joined the Army Service Corps at Birmingham and was at once transferred to Grove Park[132], Lewisham. A motor convoy being then ready for the front, Pte. Painter volunteered to go with the same and assisted in conducting to Avonmouth. The convoy was two nights on the road and on the journey Pte. Painter picked up a bad cold. A rough forty-eight hours' passage to France followed and further trying journey with motor wagons to the base, where he was attached to the Fifth Divisional Supply Column and assisted in motor repairs, working out of doors and sleeping under the detached cover of a motor van. In addition to mechanical work Pte. Painter took his share in guard duties and one night per week formed part of the guard mounted over the workshops. Though the work was hard and under rough conditions, Pte. Painter wrote home that he liked the work and was very happy.

On April 9 he wrote from the General Hospital that though he suffered with severe pains in the head and back he was feeling better and hoped it would not be long before he was about again and able to come home for a few weeks to get strong again.

On April 12 an orderly of the R.A.M.C. wrote that Pte. Painter was progressing well as could be expected. On April 17 Pte. Painter wrote himself that his eyes had been bad but he had got up one day. That, however, rather upset him and he had been in bed since; he hoped to be up again in a few days and then to get on all right.

Next a communication came from the General Hospital at Versailles that Pte. Painter was suffering from scarlet fever and that his condition was serious. On May 2 a further communication from a R.A.M.C. orderly stated that Pte. Painter was progressing favourably he hoped to sit up in a week and to be in England before the end of the month. He had the best of treatment and wanted for nothing. This hopeful letter was in only a week's time followed by the sad news that on May 9 Pte. Painter passed away in the same hospital from cerebro-spinal fever. Mr. and Mrs. Painter have received from Lord Kitchener the assurance of the true sympathy of the King and Queen in their trouble and general sympathy is felt with them throughout Broadway in their bereavement.

---

130   Alice Painter worked as a school teacher in Broadway from 13th April 1905 when she started as a trainee at Broadway National Infants' School until her retirement and was affectionately known in the village as 'Teacher Alice'. Alice never married and died in 1981.

131   Divisional Supply Column Companies were responsible for maintaining the supply of goods, equipment and ammunition.

132   Grove Park Workhouse, Marvel Lane, was requisitioned by the Army Service Corps in 1914 and used as a training and mobilization centre.

Sidney's funeral took place in Versailles and he is buried in Cimetière des Gonards, Rue de la Porte de Buc, Versailles, Yvelines, France (grave 3. 15). His epitaph reads: SAFE IN THE ARMS OF JESUS. The vicar of St Michael's Church wrote in Broadway's Parish Magazine of June 1915:

Everyone has felt deeply the loss of Sidney Painter, who died at Versailles from fever, and much sympathy is with the family in their sorrow. He was a good lad, and devoted to his parents and home.

Sidney is commemorated on the Broadway School Memorial (see page 128).

Cimetière des Gonards, Versailles and the grave of Pte Sidney J. Painter.
(Keith Pearey and The British School of Paris)

Sidney's brother Bertie, who was born on 11th December 1893, emigrated to Canada in 1912. Bertie moved from Canada to the United States where he initially settled in New York and found work as a chauffeur. On 5th June 1917, Bertie completed a Draft Registration Card[133] in Morristown, New Jersey, but it is not known whether or not he saw active service. On 11th March 1918, Bertie married Marie Brigant in New York and they had two children. Bertie died in New Jersey in 1971.

Sidney's younger sister Doris (see page 136), who was born on 13th November 1897 near Tewkesbury, married Alfred Hinton of Glebe Farm, Saintbury, in Broadway in 1923. Alfred's older brother, Gerald Charles (see page 131), enlisted with the Warwickshire Territorial Force, aged 17, in Weston-sub-Edge on 10th March 1911. On 8th April 1915 Gerald entrained for Avonmouth with the 1/1st Warwickshire Yeomanry, part of the 1st South Midland Mounted Brigade within the 2nd Mounted Division. The Yeomanry embarked for Egypt on 11th April[134] on SS Saturnia and SS Wayfarer. The Wayfarer was damaged by an explosion off the coast of the Scilly Isles and eventually arrived in Alexandria, Egypt, on 24th April. The Yeomanry proceeded to Gallipoli in August where they arrived at Suvla Bay on 18th August 1915. Three days later, Gerald was wounded in the arm by shrapnel during the advance on the Ottoman positions at Chocolate Hill (see map of Gallipoli on page 108). Gerald was disembodied[135] from the army on 8th April 1916 having served for five years with the Territorial Force. Gerald re-enlisted in Warwick on 19th July 1916 with the 3/1st Warwickshire Yeomanry. He was transferred to the Royal Warwickshire Regiment and posted to the Western Front in January 1917. Gerald (Private 307582) was killed in action in France on 18th April 1918 whilst serving with the 2/7th Battalion and he is commemorated on the Loos Memorial (Panel 22 to 25).

133   On 6th April 1917, the United States declared war on Germany and officially entered the First World War. Six weeks later on 18th May 1917, the Selective Service Act was passed, which authorised the President to increase the U.S. military and every male living in the U.S. between the ages of 18 and 45 was required to register for the draft.

134   William John Parker who also served with the 1/1st Warwickshire Regiment fell ill during the train journey to Avonmouth and died a few days later, see page 90.

135   Disembodiment was the term used when a member of the Territorial Forces was released from full-time active service.

Ernest Harold Parker

Private 17070, 14th (Service) Battalion (1st Birmingham) Royal Warwickshire Regiment

Ernest Harold Parker was born in 1885 in Brettell Lane, Stourbridge, the son of Herbert Henry Parker and Amelia Parker (née Fiddian), an upholsteress, from Old Swinford, Stourbridge. His parents had married in Old Swinford in 1872. Whilst Ernest was growing up his family lived at Heath Lane, Upper Swinford, and 24 Lower Hill Street, Stourbridge. Ernest's father worked as a glass blower and etcher in the Stourbridge glass industry. Although his eldest brother George Herbert Parker also became a glass engraver, Ernest did not follow in his father's footsteps and by 1901 Ernest had moved to Nottingham and was working as a footman for Mrs Harriet Matilda Smith[136] at Bramcote Hall.

Brettell Lane, Stourbridge c1900. (Amblecote History Society)

Ernest's mother died on 16th February 1914 and shortly afterwards his father moved to 30 Council Cottages, Broadway, to live with his daughter, Ernest's older sister, Edith Amelia Hensley. Edith had married Hubert Edward Hensley[137], a Broadway postman, in Broadway in 1910 and they had lived in one of the cottages overlooking the village green before moving to the new council cottages.

It has not been possible to determine exactly when Ernest enlisted but at the time he was living and working in Birmingham and he joined the 14th Battalion Royal Warwickshire Regiment one of the Birmingham Pals Regiments[138]. Ernest was posted to the Western Front in 1916 where he joined his battalion, part of the 13th Brigade of the 5th Division. From July 1916, the battalion was involved in the Battle of the Somme at High Wood, Guillemont and Morval. On 29th September, following the end of the Battle of Morval, the battalion left the Somme and entrained for Abbeville before moving to the vicinity of Béthune where they spent a relatively quiet and bitterly cold winter in and out of the line at La Bassée around Festubert and Givenchy. During March 1917, the battalion left the La Bassée front and moved

---

136 Mrs Harriet Smith (née Pym, 1839-1914) was the widow of Frederic Chatfield Smith (1823-1905), head of Smith's Bank, Nottingham, and a Conservative Party politician.

137 Hubert Hensley (1879-1925) was cousin to George Hensley (see page 68).

138 The Birmingham Pals were the three battalions of the Royal Warwickshire Regiment raised from men volunteering in the city of Birmingham in September 1914. They became respectively the 14th, 15th and 16th (Service) Battalions of the Royal Warwickshire Regiment. A further battalion, 17th, was formed in June 1915 as a reserve battalion and was reformed in September 1916.

to the Bruay district ahead of the Battle of Arras (9th April to 16th May 1917). On 3rd May the 14th Royal Warwicks took over the front line trenches in the Arras Road near Oppy where they were subjected to constant shelling, as well as machine gun and sniper fire.

According to the Commonwealth War Graves Commission, Ernest died on 7th May 1917[139] and he is commemorated on the Arras Memorial (Bay 3). The Arras Memorial is in the Faubourg-d'Amiens Cemetery and commemorates almost 35,000 servicemen from the United Kingdom, South Africa and New Zealand who died in the Arras sector between the spring of 1916 and 7th August 1918, the eve of the Advance to Victory, and have no known grave.

Ernest's death is recorded as 28th July 1916 in the UK, Soldiers Died in the Great War, 1914-1919 database, however, 7th May 1917 is the most probable date of Ernest's death as his battalion was not in line at the end of July 1916. The UK, Soldiers Died in the Great War, 1914-1919 database is a historical document originally compiled in 1921 by clerks in the War Office and includes over 703,000 names. It is known to contain many errors but as the original records from which it was compiled have been destroyed, it is not possible to attempt to correct errors with any authority. Ernest is also commemorated in his home town on the Stourbridge War Memorial in Mary Stevens Park.

Stourbridge War Memorial, designed by Ernest Pickford and unveiled by the 9th Earl of Coventry
on 16th February 1923. 377 names from the First World War are listed on the bronze plaques.
135 names were added after the Second World War.
(Charlie Hulme)

Ernest's younger brother Theodore Parker (1889-1957) also served on the Western Front from 19th January 1915 as a mechanic with a Mechanical Transport Company of the Army Service Corps (M2/033499). Ernest's older brother, Francis William (1880-1940), enlisted in Plymouth on 11th January 1917 and served as a gunner with the Royal Garrison Artillery until he was discharged in early 1919.

---

139   The Commonwealth War Graves Commission records Ernest as being 26 years of age but he would have been 32 years old in May 1917.

The Arras Memorial at Faubourg d'Amiens Cemetery, France.
(Commonwealth War Graves Commission)

Arras Flying Services Memorial at the Arras Memorial, which
commemorates nearly 1,000 airmen of the Royal Naval Air
Service, Royal Flying Corps and Royal Air Force who were
killed on the Western Front and have no known grave.
(James A.T. Williamson)

William John Parker
Private 2444, 1/1ˢᵗ Warwickshire Yeomanry

William John Parker, known as Willie, born in Broadway in 1895 and baptised at St Michael's Church on 1ˢᵗ December 1895. Willie was the eldest son of seven children born to Arthur Parker, a postman from Broadway, and Ann Alice Parker (née Aston) from Snowshill. Willie grew up in the village and attended Broadway Council School. After leaving school Willie worked as a butcher's assistant and in the 1911 census the family is recorded as living along the Leamington Road. His parents later moved to 2 Council Cottages.

Willie enlisted, aged 19, on 1ˢᵗ September 1914 and joined the 1/1ˢᵗ Warwickshire Yeomanry part of the 2ⁿᵈ Mounted Division based at Newbury. In November 1914, the battalion moved to Norfolk to defend the coastline and having received orders to proceed to Gallipoli, entrained for Avonmouth on 8ᵗʰ April 1915. Willie fell ill during the train journey and never embarked for Egypt on 11ᵗʰ April with his regiment on either the troopship SS Saturnia or the horse transporter SS Wayfarer which was damaged by an explosion during its journey to Alexandria.

Willie was admitted to Ham Green Hospital in Bristol and died aged 20, a week later on 17ᵗʰ April 1915 and he is buried in Bristol (Arnos Vale) Cemetery. Willie's grave is not marked by a headstone and his name is inscribed on a bronze plaque in the memorial cloisters (Screen Wall 4. 653). Willie is also commemorated on the Broadway Council School Memorial Board (see page 128). Following his funeral the Evesham Journal reported on 8ᵗʰ May 1915:

We record with regret the death of Pte. W. Parker, which occurred at the Ham Green Hospital, Bristol, after a short illness, at the age of 19 years. Pte. Parker was the eldest son of Mr. and Mrs. Arthur Parker, of Leamington-road, Broadway. He enlisted in the Warwickshire Yeomanry on September 1 and proved a good, keen soldier, volunteering for the first company for active service. He was taken ill in the train when on the way to embark for abroad, and despite all that could be done died a week later from fever. His funeral took place at Arnos Vale Cemetery, Bristol. The coffin was conveyed to the cemetery in a hearse, and there carried by six members of the Red Cross detachment. The funeral was carried out with full military honours, a detachment of the Black Watch furnishing the firing party and sounding the "Last Post". The father and mother and most of his near relatives attended. The service which was a most impressive one, was conducted by an Army Chaplain. Wreaths were sent by: Father, mother and family. Mrs Wells, Mrs Gibson, Mrs Kemp, Mrs M. Richardson, Mr. J. Payne, the Misses A. and D. Painter[140], the Misses Margery and Maud Folkes and Miss H. Morris, Mrs Badger and Miss Parker. The Captain of Pte. Parker's company motored over to Broadway specially to offer his condolences to the parents and tell them what a good lad he was, how well he did his work and that he was a soldier to the backbone. General sympathy was expressed with the family in their bereavement.

Willie's younger brother Arthur, who worked as a telegraph messenger in the village prior to his enlistment, served with the Gloucestershire Regiment on the Western Front from 8ᵗʰ December 1915. Arthur was awarded the Military Medal for bravery in the field during the war (see page 138).

Bristol (Arnos Vale) Memorial built of Bath Stone by funds raised by the Red Cross.

---

140   Alice and Doris Painter, sisters of Sidney John Painter, see page 85.

John Perry

Serjeant SE/17110, Royal Army Veterinary Corps attached 1st Guards Brigade

John Perry was born in Overton, Hampshire, in 1883, the youngest son of Thomas Perry from Arrow near Alcester, and Angelina Perry (née Turner) from Broadway. John's parents had married in Birmingham in 1872 and he had five sisters and three older brothers. His mother had grown up in Broadway and on leaving school had worked at home as a gloveress. John's father was a huntsman and had met Angelina whilst working with Angelina's brother, Richard, at the kennels of the North Cotswold Hunt in Broadway.

Whilst John was growing up, the family moved several times from hunt to hunt and in the 1891 census the family is recorded as living in Kintbury, Berkshire, where John's father worked as a huntsman for either The Vine or the Craven Hunt. John followed in his father's footsteps and became a hunt groom. By 1901 the family had moved to Stedham near Chichester where John and his father were working together as grooms. John's father had retired by 1911 and his parents moved back to Broadway where they lived at 2 Leamington Road. His father died in 1913 and he is buried in St Eadburgha's churchyard alongside John's youngest sister, Angelina, who died in 1911. After his father's death, John's mother moved to live at 32 Council Cottages.

The Perry family: Thomas and Angelina Perry and their children. (Jacqueline Walker)

John went on to work for the Fife Foxhounds, the David Davies Hunt in Montgomeryshire, Wales, the New Forest Staghounds and as a whipper-in for the North Staffordshire Hunt. In 1914, John married Annie Martindale in Cumbria and they had a daughter born in 1915.

John enlisted voluntarily with the Royal Army Veterinary Corps in 1916 and he served as a Serjeant with the 46th Mobile Veterinary Section, a first aid unit which provided medical care for sick and wounded horses, attached to the 1st Guards Division. John was posted to the Western Front where he remained with his division until after the Armistice on 11th November 1918.

Following the Armistice, the general advance by British Forces into Germany did not begin until December when the 1st Cavalry Division crossed the frontier between Belgium and Germany. The division crossed the Rhine into Germany on 12th December 1918 and was involved in the occupation of the bridgehead east of the Rhine at Cologne. Part 1 of Field Marshal Sir Douglas Haig's despatch on 21st March 1919 mentions the exemplary conduct of the troops during the difficult period following the Armistice:

For those who went forward, the real hardships of the long marches, poor billets, and indifferent food constituted a strange contrast to ideas which had been formed of victory.

John died on 15th February 1919, aged 35, in hospital in Cologne after contracting pneumonia probably as a complication of influenza, at a time when many of the men in his division were returning home. He was posthumously mentioned in Haig's final despatches (London Gazette 16th March 1919) for his good work during the occupation of the Cologne bridgehead and was awarded the Emblem, a small bronze oak leaf emblem to be worn with the ribbon of the Victory Medal denoting that he had been mentioned in despatches.

John's funeral took place on 17th February with full military honours and he is buried in Cologne Southern Cemetery, Germany (grave II. D. 8). His epitaph reads: UNTIL THE DAY BREAK AND THE SHADOWS FLEE AWAY. His mother Angelina died in 1928 and she is buried in the family plot in St Eadburgha's churchyard alongside John's father, Tom, and sister Angelina. Between their headstones is a stone cross engraved with John's name, age, rank[141] and regiment.

Cologne Southern Cemetery, Germany. (Commonwealth War Graves Commission)

The grave of Serjeant John Perry, Royal Army
Veterinary Corps, Cologne Southern Cemetery,
Germany. (Naturstein, Find A Grave)

---

141   The spelling 'sarjeant' is still used in a few regiments of the British Army. Both 'sergeant' and 'serjeant' were used in the First World War.

Southern Cologne Cemetery, Germany. Serjeant John Perry's grave centre, front row.
(Naturstein, Find A Grave)

The grave of Angelina Perry (1888-1923) left of photo, Tom Perry (1845-1913)
and his wife Angelina Perry (1850-1923) right of photo, with a memorial cross in
memory of Serjeant John Perry (middle), St Eadburgha's Churchyard, Broadway.

Frank Rastall

Private 241819, 1/8th Battalion Worcestershire Regiment

Born in Broadway in 1890, Frank Rastall was the youngest son of eight children of Elisha Rastall and Harriet Rastall (née Smith). Frank was baptised at St Michael's Church on 16th June 1890. His parents, both natives of Broadway, had married at St Michael's on 20th April 1864. Frank's father was employed as a gardener and agricultural labourer in the village and worked for many years for Edward and Ellen Stanley who farmed 100 acres at Bibsworth Farm. Frank attended Broadway Council School and after leaving school he initially worked as agricultural labourer but by 1911 Frank was employed as a groom. Frank's father died in early 1911 and his mother died four years later in 1915.

Frank enlisted in October 1914, as Private 5161, with the 1/8th Battalion Worcestershire Regiment, a battalion of the Territorial Force. At the time of his enlistment Frank gave his home address as Willersey. Frank served with fellow Broadway men, Leonard Green (see page 62) and Edgar Turner. The battalion spent the winter of 1914 in billets at Maldon, Essex, and was posted to on the Western Front at the end of March 1915 where it joined the 144th Brigade of the 48th (South Midland) Division on 15th May 1915. After the relatively quiet winter of 1915/1916 the battalion was involved in the many battles of the Somme during the latter half of 1916.

Following the renumbering of the territorial battalions in March 1917, Frank was assigned a new regimental number, 241819. During July the battalion was involved in the Battle of Passchendaele. After Passchendaele, the battalion moved to Italy at the end of 1917. The battalion arrived on 24th November but they did not go into line until April 1918 when they took up a position on the Asiago Plateau, north of Vicenza, in north east Italy. Here the battalion was involved in trench raiding often wading through deep snow to penetrate the Austro-Hungarian lines. In June the battalion was engaged in fierce fighting during the Battle of Piave River, the last major Austro-Hungarian attack on the Italian Front. The British advance met little opposition and the front line was recaptured with the taking of many prisoners.

The battalion returned to France in September 1918 and on 17th September 1918 joined a newly reformed 75th Brigade of the 25th Division part of the Fourth Army commanded by Sir Henry Rawlinson with the aim of breaking through the German's Hindenburg Line. The battalion was involved in the victorious advance across Picardy including the Battle of Beaurevoir Line in early October 1918, followed by the Battle of Cambrai, the Battle of the Selle and the Battle of the Sambre. If was during one of these battles in the Final Advance in Picardy that Frank was wounded and died, aged 28, on 19th October 1918. Frank is buried in Serain Communal Cemetery Extension (grave B. 20), Aisne, France, and he is also commemorated on the Broadway Council School Memorial Board (see page 128).

Serain Communal Cemetery Extension where Private Frank Rastall is buried. His grave is in the back row of the photograph 9th grave from the left.
(Commonwealth War Graves Commission)

Frank's brother, Harry (1881-1953), was called up for service following the extension of conscription in May 1916 to include married men, and he enlisted in Worcester on 8th September 1916. Harry was posted to the 14th (Labour) Battalion Devonshire Regiment and was sent to the Western Front at the beginning of October 1916. On 28th April 1917 Harry was transferred to 155th Company, Labour Corps, and was issued with a new regimental number 92702. Harry returned to Chiseldon Camp, Wiltshire, for demobilization in February 1919 and he returned home to his wife, Eleanor Annie Rastall (née Nash), and family at 5 Council Cottages, Broadway.

Joe Edgar Russell
Private 9570, 9th (Service) Battalion Royal Warwickshire Regiment

Pte Joe E. Russell. (Jacky Cook)

The eldest son of Joseph Russell and Frances Harriet Russell (née Matthews), Joe Edgar Russell was born in Broadway in 1886. His father had been born in Stanway and his mother in Broadway and they had married in 1884. Joe had two younger brothers and two younger sisters. In the 1901 census the family are recorded as living at Forley, Kintbury, Berkshire. Whilst living in Forley, Joe and his father worked as gamekeepers most likely on the nearby Hungerford Park Estate. By 1911 the family had moved back to Broadway and they were living at Wellsville, Leamington Road.

Joe initally found work in Broadway as a footman but later worked for the builders Espley & Company. His brother, Algernon John, known as Jack, worked as a yardman at The Lygon Arms Hotel. Joe and Jack both enlisted in Stratford-upon-Avon in December 1914 with the Royal Warwickshire Regiment. Joe was posted to the 9th (Service) Battalion, one of Kitchener's Army battalions, and Jack to the 3rd Battalion. Joe trained with his battalion on the Isle of Wight and Salisbury Plain and served with Wilfred Tandy (see page 107). Jack also trained on Salisbury Plain but was transferred to the Duke of Cornwall's Light Infantry and was posted to the Western Front the end of April 1915.

Men from Broadway who enlisted with the
9th (Service) Battalion Royal Warwickshire Regiment on the Isle of Wight.
(Jacky Cook)

Shortly before being posted to Gallipoli in June 1915, Joe married Josephine Rose Coxhill, known as Rose, in Broadway. Rose was the daughter of George and Helen Coxhill of Colletts Fields. After leaving school Rose entered into service and at the time of her marriage to Joe, was working as a cook for Antonio de Navarro and his wife Mary Anderson de Navarro at Court Farm in the village.

After his wedding Joe rejoined his battalion on Salisbury Plain a few days before the battalion, part of the 39th Brigade of the 13th Division, left Avonmouth on 17th June 1915 bound for Mudros, on the island of Lemnos. The battalion arrived on 9th July and four days later they landed at 'V' Beach, Cape Helles, Gallipoli (see map on page 108). The battalion was in and out of the trenches until the end of the July when they returned to Lemnos. After a short rest the battalion crossed the Aegean Sea once again and landed on the peninsula at Anzac Cove on 4th August and headed towards Koja Chemen Tepe (Hill 971). Three days later, fellow Broadway man, Wilfred Tandy (see page 107), was killed when the battalion came under fire whilst stopped at a nullah for water. On 9th August, during the assault on Koja Chemen Tepe in full view of the enemy, the battalion suffered heavy losses. All of the battalion's officers were killed and only 248 men including Joe survived. The battalion later received reinforcements and remained in Gallipoli until the end of the year but during that time Joe contracted dysentery and he was invalided to Alexandria, Egypt.

Joe recovered enough to return to his battalion which had left Gallipoli and was at Port Said in Egypt. The battalion, part of the 13th (Western) Division, was en-route to Mesopotamia as reinforcements of the Tigris Corps. The battalion left Port Said and reached Kuwait Bay in the Persian Gulf on 29th February 1916 where a week later they disembarked at Basra. On 15th March 1916, the battalion began its journey up the Tigris River to Sheikh Saad, behind the British Front, where they arrived on 21st March.

On 3rd April 1916, the battalion moved forward to the front line and at 4.45am during the morning of 5th April the attack on the Ottoman lines started in an attempt to relieve the Ottoman siege of Sir Charles Townshend's 10,000 troops garrisoned at Kut-al-Amara. The battalion, along with the 9th Battalion Worcestershire Regiment, successfully took Falahiyah about 16 miles from Kut but by 9th April had been unable to capture Sanniyat. After a brief rest the battalion started its attack on the fort at Biet Essa and during the three days of 17th to 19th April, it is recorded that there was more hand-to-hand fighting than during any other battle in Mesopotamia . It was during this battle that Joe was killed in action on 19th April 1916, one of 21 officers and men of the 9th Royal Warwicks who lost their lives. Four officers (one of whom later died) and 68 men were wounded. The attempt to relieve Kut failed and on 29th April General Townshend was forced to surrender. Over 13,000 British and Indian troops were taken into captivity, one of the worst defeats in the history of the British Army. Joe is commemorated on the Basra Memorial, Iraq (Panel 9, see page 39). Joe's widow, Rose, never remarried and died in Broadway on 9th January 1963.

Joe's brother, Reginald Oscar, who was born in Broadway on 7th August 1881, was the first of the brothers to enlist. On 19th August 1914, whilst working as a gardener for Charles John Philip Cave, Ditcham Park[142], Petersfield, Hampshire. Reginald enlisted with the 6th Battalion Hampshire Regiment later transferring to the Royal Army Medical Corps (Private 435510). After training on Salisbury Plain, Reginald set sail from Southampton on 16th August 1916 arriving in Rouen, France, the following day. On 13th September Reginald was posted to the 1/1st South Midland Field Ambulance on the front line. During his time in France, Reginald contracted a fever (recorded as pyrexia of unknown origin in his army service records) and he was transported back to England to No. 11 Station Hospital, Bethnal Green Military Hospital, Cambridge Heath, London. Reginald was admitted on 5th February 1917 and spent 51 days in hospital being treated for rheumatic fever which was attributed to the damp and exposure during the winter of 1916/17. Following his recovery, Reginald was transferred to the South Midland Company, Royal Army Medical Corps of the Territorial Force, and after further training at Blackpool was posted with the 10th Company Royal Army Medical Corps to Salonika. He left Southampton on 16th August 1917 arriving in Salonika on 7th September 1917 where he was attached to No. 42 Hospital. In September 1918 Reginald was posted to the Dardanelles on general duties but his health deteriorated and he returned to England in February 1919. Reginald was disembodied on 14th June 1919 under paragraph 392(xvi) of the King's Regulations 1912 as he was no longer medically fit for service, and he returned home to Broadway.

Jack (Private 20136 Algernon John Russell) was injured on 20th May 1915, whilst serving with the Duke of Cornwall's Light Infantry, just three weeks after he had arrived on the Western Front. Jack was transported back to England where he convalesced at the Manchester Hospital before returning to Broadway. Jack later transferred to the Devonshire Regiment (Private 267356) and served with the 1/6th Battalion in Mesopotamia. The battalion remained in Mesopotamia until the Armistice of Mudros on 31st October 1918 which ended hostilities with the Ottoman Empire.

---

142   Ditcham Park was designed by Sir Reginald Blomfield in the mid 1880s for the meteorologist Laurence Trent Cave.

Reginald O. Russell. (Jacky Cook)

Pte Algernon J. Russell
with his mother Frances Harriet Russell (inset).
(Jacky Cook)

Pte Algernon J. Russell (centre) in Mesopotamia.
(Jacky Cook)

George Sandel
Lance Corporal 3674, 1/8th Battalion Worcestershire Regiment

George Sandel, who is commemorated on the war memorial as 'G. Sandals', was born in Broadway in 1885[143], the son of James Sandel, an agricultural labourer and Sarah Ann Sandel (née Green), known as Annie. George's parents had married in Broadway in 1869 and they lived at Bury End. George had three brothers and five sisters. George was a pupil at Broadway Council School and after leaving school worked as a farm labourer.

At the age of 18, George joined the army. He enlisted with the Worcestershire Regiment at Worcester on 2nd October 1902. His army pension record states that he was 5' 6¾" tall, of fresh complexion with brown hair and blue eyes. On 8th October 1902 George was posted to the 3rd Battalion as Private 7206. After training with the 3rd Battalion, George was transferred, on 7th February 1903, to the 2nd Battalion and posted to South Africa where the battalion undertook garrison duties in Bloemfontein.

Due to sickness, George returned to England on the SS Dunora on 12th February 1904 and was admitted as a patient at Royal Victoria Hospital[144], Netley, near Southampton, before being discharged from the army on 8th March 1904 on an army pension. George returned to Broadway where he took up work as a market gardener.

In 1910 George married Mabel Lilian Luker in Stow-on-the-Wold. Mabel had been born in 1889 in Shangton, Leicestershire. Mabel's mother had died whilst Mabel was young and she had moved to live with her maternal aunt and family at Park Street, Stow-on-the-Wold. After their marriage, George and Mabel moved to live on Leamington Road and on 4th April 1915, their daughter, Lilian Mabel, was born.

On 2nd October 1914, George re-enlisted with the 1/8th Battalion Worcestershire Regiment as a Lance Corporal joining the battalion at Maldon, Essex. However, within a year, at the age of

Royal Victoria Hospital, Netley, Hampshire.
(Julie Green)

31, on 20th October 1915, whilst stationed at Halton Park Camp, Aylesbury, George was discharged on the grounds of being medically unfit for further service under Paragraph 392(xvi) of the King's Regulations 1912 and was awarded an army pension.

George returned to 35 Council Cottages to live with his wife and daughter but died, aged 32, on 8th December 1917 at Bury End. His death certificate states that he died of phthisis (tuberculosis) and that at the time of his death he was working as a motor driver. A funeral service was held at St Eadburgha's for George on 12th December 1917 but it has not been possible to locate his grave. Following his death his widow, Mabel, was awarded an army pension on 17th June 1918 for herself and daughter. Mabel died in 1967.

Although George is commemorated on the war memorial, George is not listed by the Commonwealth War Graves Commission or in the Worcestershire Regiment Roll of Honour as being a casualty of war. George is commemorated on the Broadway Council School Memorial Board as 'George Sandals' (see page 128).

---

143 George's surname is recorded in the 1885 Register of Births as 'Sandalls'.
144 The foundation stone of the Royal Victoria Hospital was laid by Queen Victoria on 19th May 1856. The hospital was built to cope with the injured returning from the Crimea War and was demolished in 1966.

Wilfred George Scrivens
Private 21387, 4th Battalion Worcestershire Regiment

Wilfred George Scrivens, known as George, was the son of Thomas Scrivens, an agricultural labourer from Buckland, and Harriett (née Hartwell) from Willersey. Thomas and Harriett had married in 1875 and set up home in Willersey. Wilfred had seven brothers and sisters and by 1891 the family had moved to Bell Yard, Broadway. George went to school in Broadway and after leaving school worked as a builder's labourer for Steward & Co. in Broadway. By 1911 George had moved away from the village to Watford where he was working as a bricklayer, boarding with Mr. J. Goldsney (a labourer at a gas works) at 5 Bridge Place.

Following the outbreak of war, George enlisted in 1915 and initially trained with the 5th Battalion Worcestershire Regiment before transferring to the 4th Battalion. At the beginning of July 1915, the battalion was posted to Gallipoli to join the 88th Brigade of the 29th Division described by Sir Ian Hamilton as the 'incomparable 29th Division'. George was one of the many reinforcements that were sent to Gallipoli after the battles of Krithia in the south of the peninsula (see map on page 108). The battalion travelled by ship via Malta and Alexandria arriving at Mudros, Lemnos, on 16th July 1915 where they transferred ship for the final stage of the journey to Cape Helles. Shortly after his arrival in Gallipoli, Wilfred wrote the following letters home which were printed in the Evesham Journal on 25th September 1915:

22nd July 1915: We have landed at the base after a splendid voyage, but very hot. This is a rum place, it is shoe-top deep in sand, and with the wind blowing you can't see half the time. We have to sleep in the open with one blanket, so you can tell it is no picnic. I wish you could see the warships here; it is a fine sight; you can hear their guns going at the Turks as I write. This is a somewhat different country to England; all you can see is bare sand. You would laugh if you could see us. We have cut our trousers off at the knees, and with helmets on look like Boy Scouts. Excuse the dirty paper; between sweat and sand I can't keep it clean.

3rd August 1915: This is a rum place and a rum life. If you get any money there is nothing to buy. The worst job is getting something to drink. We are given two cups of tea a day and that is not much. I should like to get hold of a pint of beer or cider and a good plate of cabbage and sprouts out of the garden. There's nothing of that here, but all tinned stuff, and that salty, but it is no good grumbling. I should like some of them that sit in the pubs at home and talk about how it should be done to be out here.

Three days after George's letter of 3rd August, at 4am on 6th August, the battalion left Gully Beach, Cape Helles, to attack and seize the tip of a well-defended salient based on the hamlet of Krithia between Krithia Nullah and the Gully Ravine. The battalion, which had been reinforced by fresh troops to 800 men, moved to the assembly trenches in preparation of an attack on the Ottoman trenches following heavy bombardment of artillery accompanied by naval gunfire from the bay. However the Ottoman forces replied with heavy gun-fire causing great damage to the British trenches and many casualties. At 3.50pm, when the whistle sounded, the battalion left the trenches and some made it through heavy machine gun fire across to the Ottoman trenches only to enter into fierce hand to hand fighting. Casualties were high and the remaining men withdrew. Over 60 men were taken prisoner and the battalion had lost 16 officers and 752 men. Despite the heavy losses the battle was deemed a success as it had drawn the Ottoman forces to Krithia enabling an attack to the north to be successful.

George was confirmed as having died, aged 27, on 6th August 1915. His body was never recovered after the battle and he is commemorated on Helles Memorial, Helles, Turkey, on a panel dedicated to the Worcestershire Regiment (Panel 104 to 113). The memorial stands on the tip of the Gallipoli peninsula near Sedd al Bahr, and serves the dual function of Commonwealth battle memorial for the whole Gallipoli campaign and place of commemoration for many of those Commonwealth servicemen who died there and have no known grave. The memorial bears the names of over 21,000 men and takes the form of an obelisk over 30 metres high that can be seen by ships passing through the Dardanelles.

Helles Memorial, Cape Helles, Turkey.
(Commonwealth War Graves Commission)

George's younger brother, James Thomas (1893-1966), joined the army at the age of 18, on 29th November 1911, and served with the 1st Battalion Gloucestershire Regiment. Following the outbreak of war, the battalion was mobilized on 4th August from Bordon, near Aldershot, where it was stationed and sailed for France on the SS Gloucester Castle, from Southampton at 12.10pm on the 12th August. The battalion landed in Le Havre on 13th August, one of the first to arrive in France, where it joined the 1st Division. The battalion proceeded to the Western Front and the front line at Landrecies near Mons on 23rd August 1914 where the battalion saw its first action of the war three days later. It is not known how long James served on the Western Front with the Gloucestershire Regiment as at some stage he was transferred to the 17th Battalion Essex Regiment. James received a gunshot wound to his right foot during the war and was discharged with the Silver War Badge on 4th June 1919 whereupon he returned home to Broadway.

Alec Silvester Stanley
Private 42530, 2ⁿᵈ Battalion Worcestershire Regiment

Alec Silvester Stanley, born in Offenham in 1896, was the son of William Stanley, a bricklayer from Snowshill, and Alice Adela Stanley (née Knight). Alec's parents had married in 1894. His mother had been born in Laverton but grew up in Broadway where she worked from home as a gloveress, employed as an outworker for the Fownes Glove Factory at Worcester. Alec had two siblings but both died in infancy.

Alec attended Broadway Council School and in the 1901 census the family are recorded as living along Back Way. The family later moved to Colletts Fields and by 1911 Alec was employed, aged 15, as a domestic servant working as a hall boy in one of the houses in the village.

Alec enlisted in Chipping Campden and joined the Gloucestershire Regiment as Private 24385. Shortly after his enlistment, on 8ᵗʰ March 1916, Alec completed a short-form will in his army pay book in which he left his property and effects to his mother Mrs. A. Stanley of 27 Council Cottages, Broadway. It is likely that Alec embarked for a theatre of war shortly after that date.

At some stage before April 1918, Alec transferred from the Gloucestershire Regiment to the 2ⁿᵈ Battalion Worcestershire Regiment. The change of regiments suggests that Alec had been wounded whilst serving with the Gloucestershire Regiment and that after recovering from his wounds re-enlisted with the Worcestershire Regiment as Private 42530.

Alec was posted to the Western Front and fought alongside Bertram Clarke (see page 21) in the Battle of Lys during the German Spring Offensive which began on 7ᵗʰ April 1918. Both Alec and Bert were initially reported as missing in action between 11ᵗʰ and 18ᵗʰ April. Alec's mother appealed for information about her son in the Evesham Journal on 3ʳᵈ August 1918 and his parents had still not heard the following year as they placed the following announcement in the Evesham Journal on 19ᵗʰ April 1919:

STANLEY – Reported missing between 11ᵗʰ and 17ᵗʰ April, 1918. Pte. Alec Stanley, 2ⁿᵈ Worcesters, of Broadway. The hardest and bitterest blow of all is not knowing where he is. – From loving mother and dad.

Alec's body was never found and he is commemorated on Ploegsteert Memorial to the Missing, Belgium, on the same panel (Panel 5) as Bertram Clarke. Alec's date of death is given as the 17ᵗʰ April 1918, one day later than Bertram's. Alec is also commemorated on the Broadway Council School Memorial Board (see page 128).

Ploegsteert Memorial, Belgium.
(Norman)

Pte Alec S. Stanley's inscription on the
Ploegsteert Memorial, Belgium.
(Sarah Huxford)

Charles Robert Stanley

Gunner, 59030 'B' Battery 86th Brigade Royal Field Artillery

Charles Robert Stanley[145] was the eldest son of Thomas Stanley, a carpenter, and Mary Ann Stanley (née Daffurn). His parents had married in Broadway in 1884. Charles was born in Broadway in 1886 and was baptised at St Michael's Church on 4th July 1886. Charles and had two younger brothers and four younger sisters.

The family lived on the High Street and Charles attended Broadway Council School. By the age of 14, Charles had left school and was working as a telegraph messenger. Charles's mother died a few months later and by 1911 Charles was working for the local builders Steward & Co. living with his widowed father who was also employed in the building trade.

Charles enlisted with the Royal Field Artillery in Worcester in January 1915 and was posted to the 86th Brigade part of the 19th (Western) Division. The division was inspected by HM King George V on 23rd June 1915 at Tidworth before it left for the Western Front. The brigade arrived in France on 18th July 1915 and assembled near St Omer before moving to the front. The brigade was involved in the Action of Pietre in 1915 and in 1916 the many battles of the Somme. Charles was killed in action, aged 30, on 14th September 1916, and he was buried by men of his battery in the Royal Berks Military Cemetery Extension, Ploegsteert, Belgium (grave I. H .8). The cemetery had been started in June 1916 and within the cemetery stands the Ploegsteert Memorial (see page 22 and page 101). On 23rd September 1916, the Evesham Journal reported:

Gunner Charles Robert Stanley, of the R.F.A., gave his life for his country on the 14th inst. His father Thomas Stanley, carpenter, of High-street, Broadway, has received a letter from Captain L.J. Paterson, commanding the battery, in which he states: "It is with great regret that I inform you of the death of your son, Gunner Stanley, who was killed in action on the afternoon of the 14th inst. Death was instantaneous. A burying party from the battery attended the burial, which was conducted by the Divisional Chaplain. A cross is being made by his comrades to mark the spot. My officers unite in sending you and his relatives our deep sympathy." Gunner Stanley, was the eldest son of Mr. Thomas Stanley and was 30 years old, and unmarried. Previous to enlisting he was a builder's labourer in the employ of Messrs. Steward and Co. He joined the army in January, 1915, and went to France in June, 1915. From that time onwards he was at the front and in most of the heavy fighting, but escaped untouched till he received the fatal shot.

Royal Berks Military Cemetery Extension in 1919 now known as
Berks Cemetery Extension, Ploegsteert, Belgium.

---

145   Charles Robert Stanley was first cousin to Tom Daffurn (see page 31) and Francis Henry Ingles (see page 75).

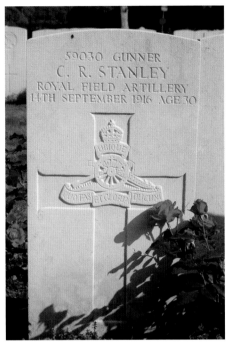

The grave of Gunner Charles R. Stanley,
Berks Cemetery Extension, Belgium.
(Sarah Huxford)

Berks Cemetery Extension, Belgium.
(Commonwealth War Graves Commission)

Charles is also commemorated on the Broadway Council School Memorial Board (see page 128). His brother Walter, who had been born in Broadway in 1890, worked as a farm labourer in the village. In 1908 Walter joined the army and was a reservist when he was called up on 14th August 1914. Walter served with the 1st Battalion Worcestershire Regiment (Private 8673) on the Western Front arriving in France on 5th November 1914 where he served for the duration of the war.

Charles's brother Thomas William, who had been born in Broadway in 1897, enlisted on 4th December 1914, aged 18, with the Royal Warwickshire Regiment (Private 9560). Thomas enlisted with George Barnett and several other men from the village (see page 8) and was posted to the Western Front with his battalion on 1st June 1915. He was wounded in June 1916 but returned to France a couple of months later. Thomas was honourably discharged from the army before the end of the war with the Silver War Badge.

Edith Elizabeth Stanley, Charles's sister, married George Thomas Newman, a general labourer from Murcot, near Broadway on 19th March 1913. George Newman was called up for service following the introduction of conscription in 1916 and he enlisted with the Devonshire Regiment in Bristol on 3rd November 1916. He served in France from 27th February 1917 with the No. 3 Infantry Labour Company which on 28th April 1917 became 168th Company. George was posted back to England in the autumn of 1918 and was transferred to the 424th Agricultural Company, Labour Corps, on 17th October 1918. He was posted to Southern Command Labour Centre, Fovant, on 10th June 1919 before being posted to Germany on 8th July 1919. George remained in Germany until 24th February 1920. He was posted back to England for demobilization and returned home to Broadway the following month.

Stanley Alfred Talbot

Second Lieutenant 11th (Service) Battalion The Prince of Wales's (North Staffordshire Regiment) attached 9th (Service) Battalion The Loyal North Lancashire Regiment

Stanley, Walter and Charles Talbot.
(Jane M. Barker)

Stanley Alfred Talbot was born at 133 Hartfield Road, Wimbledon, on 13th January 1884, the youngest of three sons of the Reverend Walter Charles Talbot, a Congregational Minister, and his wife Alice Maria Talbot (née Ansell). Stanley's parents had married on 24th July 1878 at Falkenham Chapel, Woodbridge, Suffolk.

In 1880, Stanley's father Walter was appointed Pastor of Wimbledon Congregational Church, Worple Road, Wimbledon. Walter's next ministry from 1888 to 1902 was at Buckland Chapel, Portsmouth, Hampshire, and the family moved to 105 Queen's Road, Portsmouth.

Following his older brothers, Walter Ansell (born 1881) and Charles Leslie (born 1882), Stanley started in the Michaelmas Term of 1895 at Caterham Congregational School, Surrey, a boarding school for sons of Congregational Ministers. After Stanley left school he was articled to an auctioneer in Portsmouth and by the 1911 census Stanley was working as an auctioneer's clerk in Surrey, whilst living with his brothers and their families at 33 Purley Oaks Road, Sanderstead.

In 1914 Stanley's parents moved from Horsham to Smallbrook, Broadway, when his father took up what was to be his last ministry at the Congregational Church in the village.

Stanley enlisted on 2nd February 1915 and joined the 18th (Service) Battalion (1st Public Schools) Royal Fusiliers also known as the City of London Regiment. Stanley served as Lance Corporal 6419 with the battalion on the Western Front from 14th November 1915 until March 1916 when he returned to England. The battalion disbanded on 24th April 1916 and many of the men were commissioned as officers. On 4th August 1916, Stanley received his commission as a Second Lieutenant with the North Staffordshire Regiment and he returned to France on 16th September where he was attached to the 9th (Service) Battalion The Loyal North Lancashire Regiment.

During the final phase of the Battles of the Somme, during operations to clear the northern end of Thiepval Ridge, Stanley was killed in action on 19th October 1916. Major William Humphrey Meyrick Wienholt, Stanley's commanding officer wrote to his parents:

We quickly learned his sterling worth. He had already done some splendid work, and it was with feelings of genuine regret that I heard he had been killed.

The battalion's Chaplain wrote:

He had only been with us a short time, but was universally liked and he will be very much missed in the battalion, both himself and as an officer.

Second Lieutenant L. A. Kemp also wrote to Stanley's parents:

He was easily the coolest man in the whole battalion. I and others went to talk to him to get back nerve, and we got it. Your son was the bravest man in a thousand.

Charles is buried in Tincourt New British Cemetery (plot VI. E.12), Tincourt-Boucly, Somme, France. His epitaph reads: FOR EVER WITH THE LORD. Charles is also commemorated on the 1914-1919 Memorial Plaque at Caterham School. Following his death probate was granted in 1917 to his father Walter, effects £267 14s 1d.

Tincourt New British Cemetery, Somme, France. (Peter Woodger)

The grave of Second Lieutenant Stanley A.
Talbot, Tincourt British Cemetery,
Somme, France.
(Peter Woodger)

Memorial Plaque Caterham School,
Surrey: IN HONOUR AND REMEMBRANCE
OF OLD BOYS OF THE SCHOOL WHO GAVE
THEIR LIVES FOR PEACE AND FREEDOM.
(Caterham School)

Stanley's brother Charles was exempted from war service on medical grounds. His eldest brother Walter enlisted as a Private with the Middlesex Regiment and was posted to the Western Front on 3rd July 1917. Walter later received a commission with the 16th (Service) Battalion (Church Lads Brigade) King's Royal Rifle Corps, known as The Churchman's Battalion, and as a Temporary Second Lieutenant was awarded the Military Cross for great gallantry in rallying his men on April 13th and 14th 1918 during the Battle of Neuve Église. Supplement to the London Gazette, 24th September 1918:

T. 2nd Lt. Walter Ansell Talbot, K.R.R.C. For conspicuous gallantry and devotion to duty. When the right flank of his company had been turned, he formed a strong point on the exposed flank and delayed the attack on the front held by his battalion. Next day when his company was almost surrounded, he ordered them to remain in position and fight to the last. The enemy were repulsed, leaving 100 killed and wounded. He showed fine leadership and determination.

Walter was subsequently promoted to the rank of Lieutenant and transferred to the 5th Battalion before he was demobilized at the end of the war.

Following Stanley's death, his father's health declined and Walter retired from the ministry at the age of 69. Walter and his wife Alice moved away from Broadway to Sunshine Cottage, Hinchwick Wellingborough, Northamptonshire, to be near their two remaining sons. Walter died, aged 92, on 28th August 1942.

Lieutenant Walter Ansell Talbot, MC.
(Jane M. Barker)

Reverend Walter Charles Talbot Minister of
Broadway Congregational Church 1914-1916.
(Jane M. Barker)

Second Lieutenant Stanley A. Talbot.
(Berrows Worcester Journal)

Wilfred George Tandy
10754 Private, 9th (Service) Battalion Royal Warwickshire Regiment

Wilfred George Tandy was the third son of Richard Tandy and Emma Jane Tandy. Wilfred was born in 1885 in Broadway and he had two older brothers and five sisters. Wilfred's father had been born in Hampton on 8th March 1846 but had grown up in Broadway, working as an agricultural labourer for Edward and Mary Stanley at Bibsworth Farm. Wilfred's mother was from Childswickham and after his parents married they settled in Broadway where Wilfred and his brothers and sisters grew up and went to Broadway Council School. His father found work in the village as a gardener and the family are recorded as living along Pinhorn's Alley off the High Street. In 1897, Wilfred's eldest sister married Thomas William Vincent, the older brother of Ernest Edward Vincent (see page 113).

Pte Wilfred G. Tandy.
(Evesham Journal)

Wilfred was a member of Broadway Football Club, and prior to his enlistment Wilfred worked for the Great Western Railway[146] as a packer in the Engineering Department at Broadway station. Wilfred's elder brother Ernest Dennis enlisted with the Royal Warwickshire Regiment on 26th October 1914. Early the following year Wilfred also enlisted with the Royal Warwickshire Regiment. Wilfred was posted to the 9th (Service) Battalion and he served with Joe Russell (see page 95). The battalion was one of four that formed part of the 39th Brigade of the 13th (Western) Division and from February 1915 trained at Blackdown on Salisbury Plain. The 9th (Service) Battalion Worcestershire Regiment were in the same brigade and Wilfred (and Joe Russell) would have been on Salisbury Plain at the same time as Albert Clarke (see page 18) who was with the 9th (Service) Battalion Worcestershire Regiment.

In June 1915 the division was called upon to provide reinforcements in Gallipoli and they entrained for Avonmouth. On the 17th, the battalion embarked at Avonmouth and reached Mudros, on the island of Lemnos, on 9th July. The battalion remained on board their troopship until further orders were received and on 13th July 1915 they proceeded to the Gallipoli peninsular where they landed at 'V' Beach at Cape Helles at the southern end of the peninsula (see map on page 108). The battalion went into the trenches of Gully Ravine the night of 14th July and remained there or in reserve until the early hours of 29th July. Although there were several rumours that the Ottoman forces would attack, there was little heavy fighting and there were only a few casualties. The battalion was withdrawn at the end of the month and marched to Gully Beach and along the coast back to 'V' Beach where they boarded the minesweeper 'Ermine' for the four hour sailing back to Lemnos.

On 4th August 1915, the battalion returned to the peninsula and landed at Anzac Cove[147] to the north of Cape Helles on the Aegean Coast. The battalion marched northwards through the night of 6th/7th August from Plugge's Plateau near Anzac Cove towards Koja Chemen Tepe (Hill 971), the highest point on the Sari Bair Ridge. Conditions in Gallipoli were extremely hot and dry and water was scarce. On 7th August 1915, four months after his arrival in Gallipoli, Wilfred, aged 30, was killed by enemy fire whilst the battalion had stopped to refill their water bottles at a stream in a valley, known locally as a nullah.

Wilfred's death was reported in the Evesham Journal on Christmas Day, Saturday 25th December 1915:

Mrs. Tandy, of High-street, Broadway, had previously only been notified that her son, Pte. Wilfred Tandy, of the 9th Royal Warwicks, had been killed in action at the Dardanelles on August 7. In response to a request for some further information,

---

146   Wilfred had worked for the Great Western Railway for 8 years before his enlistment in 1915.

147   Anzac Cove was the site of the Australian and New Zealand Army Corps (ANZAC) landings on the Gallipoli peninsula on 25th April 1915 and the beach became the main base for the ANZACs for the eight months of the Gallipoli campaign.

Mrs. Tandy has received a letter from Sergt. G.H. Lamb, dated Gallipoli, October 3, in which the following particular are given:- "Pte. Tandy was killed by a bursting shell (shrapnel), sustaining several wounds, one in the head and one in the back. He died almost at once, and from my own observations could not have felt much pain. It happened whilst we halted behind a nullah to fill our water bottle, as we had till then nothing to drink for thirty hours. Then suddenly the enemy commenced to shell us, and I am sorry to say we had several casualties. Your son was buried next morning by our burying party. We were very sorry to lose a good comrade, for that is how we look upon him. He had not been a member of the 9th Battalion for very long, but he was well liked by all. I trust that this scanty information may bring you a little of that consolation which you and your family must much need."

Although Wilfred's was reported as having been buried by his battalion he has no known grave and he is commemorated on the Helles Memorial, Cape Helles, Turkey (Panel 35 to 37, see page 100). Two days later the battalion lost all of its officers and hundreds of men during the assault on Koja Chemen Tepe. Joe Russell survived but was later invalided to Egypt with dysentery (see page 95). Wilfred is also commemorated on the Broadway Council School Memorial Board (see page 128).

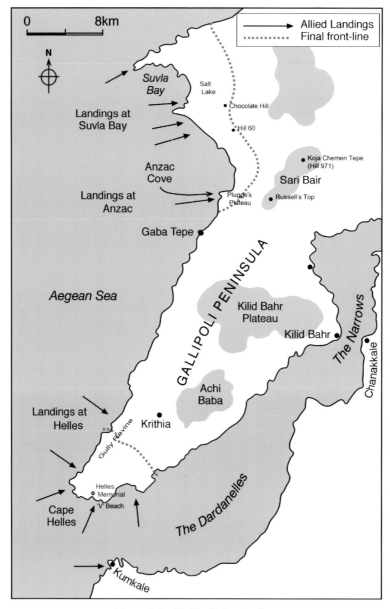

Map of the Gallipoli Peninsular.

Walter John Tebby
Private 29004, 14th (Service) Battalion (Swansea) Welsh Regiment

Walter John Tebby was the second son of Thomas Tebby and Mary Jane Tebby (née Horn). His father was from Arncott, Oxfordshire, and his mother from Luffield Abbey a small village near Stowe, Buckinghamshire. Walter's father was a jobbing farm labourer and travelled from farm to farm for work. His parents married in 1888 in Syresham near Brackley, Northamptonshire, and Walter was born in Syresham in 1896. Walter had an older brother, William Henry born in 1889, and a sister Marion Jane[148] born on 9th October 1890.

Pte Walter J. Tebby.
(Evesham Journal)

Walter's mother died in Syresham in 1906 and the following year Walter's father married Lydia Rosa Stephens in Herefordshire. Walter's half-brother, Charles Thomas was born in Syresham in 1909. By 1911 the family had moved to Broadway Wood, a thatched cottage on West End, Broadway. Walter, aged 14, had left school and was working as a farm labourer and his father as a cowman for one of the local farms. The family later moved into the centre of the village to The Orchard, a thatched cottage behind The Lygon Arms Hotel.

Walter went on to work for Henry J. Patten at The Kite's Nest Dairy and he was working as a milkman in Swansea when war broke out in August 1914. Walter enlisted shortly after war was declared and he joined the 14th (Service) Battalion Welsh Regiment, known as the Swansea Pals. The battalion was formed in Swansea in October 1914 by the Mayor, Swansea Football Club and Swansea Cricket Club.

After training near Swansea the battalion joined the 129th Brigade, 43rd Division, at Rhyl. On 28th April 1915, the battalion became part of the 114th Brigade of the 38th (Welsh) Division known as Lloyd George's Division[149] and from August the battalion trained at Winchester, Hampshire, before it was mobilized to the Western Front in December 1915.

The first major engagement the battalion took part in was the Battle of Albert, the first phase of the Battle of the Somme 1916, from the 1st to 13th July 1916. The battalion moved forward from its billets at Septenville on 2nd July. Three days later the 38th Division relieved the 7th Division at the front opposite Mametz Wood and the battle to clear German positions from Mametz Wood started at 8.30am on the 7th July. The 14th (Swansea) Battalion entered the battle on the 10th July with 676 men and by nightfall 75 men and one officer had died and there were 376 injured, more than half the battalion had been lost in one day. Walter was wounded in the head at Mametz Wood and he was transferred to the Royal Victoria Hospital (also known as Netley Hospital, see page 98) near Southampton. Walter died, aged 20, of his wounds in hospital a few days later on 23rd July 1916.

Walter's funeral took place at St Eadburgha's Church on 26th July 1916 after which he was buried in the churchyard (grave N1. 3. 19). His grave is marked by a private headstone[150]. The following Saturday the Evesham Journal printed the following article on Walter's death and funeral:

It is with regret that we record the death of Private Walter John Tebby, of the Welsh Regiment, which occurred at Netley Hospital on the 23rd inst. Pte. Tebby was the younger son of Mr. Tebby, of The Orchard, Broadway, and for some time worked for Mr. Patten of Kite's Nest Dairy. About the middle of 1914 he went to assist with a milk round in Swansea and soon after the outbreak of war there joined the Welsh Regt. After a full home training he went to France at the end of

---

148   Walter's sister, Marion Jane Tebby, who worked as a servant for the Flower family at Middle Hill, see page 45, married Ebenezer Ernest Emms, see page 40.

149   The 13th Battalion Royal Welsh Fusiliers also formed part of the 38th (Welsh) Division, see page 46.

150   Private memorials also mark the grave of two other First World War casualties in the churchyard, Captain W.R. Ponsonby, DSO and Private 25302 T. Gould, see page 126.

1915, and did eight months at the front, till he sustained a serious rifle shoot wound to the head. Pte. Tebby was brought back to England to Netley Hospital, where everything possible was done, but notwithstanding all he passed away on Sunday last. The funeral took place at St. Eadburgh Church, Broadway, on Wednesday afternoon. The coffin was covered with the Union Jack, and was carried by four friends in uniform – Sergt. A. Box[151], Ptes. A. Knight, R. Russell[152], and T. Stanley[153]. There followed as mourners Mr. and Mrs. Tebby (father and mother), Mrs. E. Emms (sister), Mr. E. Emms, Tro. William Tebby (Shropshire Yeomanry, brother), Pte. Stephens (Shropshire Light Infantry, uncle), Mrs. Sayer. There were also present Mr. Rees Price, Mrs. Russell, Mrs. Kemp. The service was conducted by the Rev. E. Dove. Sincere sympathy is expressed to the family in their loss.

After Walter died his father, Thomas, moved to Fowlers Wells Farm, Chobham, Surrey. Thomas was contacted by the Broadway War Memorial Committee and he contributed to the war memorial fund and requested that his son's name be inscribed on the war memorial.

In 1987, a memorial to the 38th (Welsh) Division was erected by the South Wales Branch of the Western Front Association at Mametz. The memorial commemorates the 4,000 men of the division killed or wounded at Mametz Wood on the Somme in 1916.

Pte Walter J. Tebby's grave, St Eadburgha's Churchyard, Broadway.

Mametz Wood Memorial to the 38th (Welsh) Division overlooking the fields at the southern end of Mametz Wood by sculptor and blacksmith David Petersen. (Norman)

---

151   Sergeant 202847 Albert Henry Box, Worcestershire Regiment.
152   Private Reginald Oscar Russell, 6th Battalion Hampshire Regiment, brother of Joe Edgar Russell, see page 95.
153   Private Thomas William Stanley, Royal Warwickshire Regiment, brother of Charles Robert Stanley, see page 102.

Jack Tustin

Lance Corporal 36116, 14th (Service) Battalion (1st Birmingham) Royal Warwickshire Regiment

Lance Corporal Jack Tustin.
(Evesham Journal)

Jack Tustin was the eldest son of Algernon Tustin, a kennelman with the North Cotswold Hunt in Broadway, and Emma Tustin (née Clarke[154]). Jack was born in Broadway in 1899 had two younger brothers, Albert Ernest and Charles Thomas and two younger sisters, Laura Maud and Edith Beatrice. Jack's father was from Bourton-on-the-Hill and had moved to Broadway when he married Emma Clarke in 1895.

Jack was baptised at St Michael's Church, on 18th September 1899. He grew up in the village and was a pupil at Broadway Council School. Jack enlisted in Worcester after 31st December 1915 but it is not known exactly when. Unless he enlisted on or after his 18th birthday in 1917 he would have been too young to legally enlist and may have told the recruiting officer he was 18 or older as recruits under the age of 19 were not allowed to be posted overseas.

Jack enlisted with the 14th (Service) Battalion (1st Birmingham) Royal Warwickshire Regiment, one of the Birmingham Pals regiments, and served with the battalion, part of the 13th Brigade of the 5th Division, on the Western Front.

From the end of August 1918, after two weeks' rest, the battalion was involved in a series of battles and attacks in the Pas de Calais, the Battles of the Hindenburg Line, also known as the Hundred Days Offensive that forced the German Army into retreat and the end of the war. On 8th September, at Leuze Wood, the General commanding the division, Major General Sir John Ponsonby, KCB, CMG, DSO addressed the 13th Brigade making special mention of the bravery of the regiment:

The 2nd King's Own Scottish Borderers and the 14th Royal Warwickshire Regiment advanced gloriously and with the utmost gallantry. Their advance was witnessed by officers of the General Staff. I am sorry that the Brigade failed to carry through their objective, through no fault of yours. The advance was pressed on with the utmost determination and perseverance.

You have had bad luck in the last three shows, the two previous being in High Wood and Wood Lane area, but I know that whatever the 13th Brigade are asked to do in the future they can be relied upon to carry through as they have done in the past. Thank you very much for all you have done. By advancing as you did under hellish artillery and machine-gun fire you did something better than if you had succeeded. I can trust the 13th Brigade to do anything on earth.

Jack was wounded in action in September and died at one of the three casualty clearing stations in Grevillers, near Bapaume, aged 19, on 30th September 1918. Three days earlier during the first day of the Battle of Canal du Nord[155], the battalion was involved in the attack on African Trench just outside the village of Gouzeaucourt and it is likely that Jack was wounded during the ensuing battle. The Evesham Journal reported on 14th December 1918:

Lance-Corpl. J. Tustin, Royal Warwick Regt., son of Mr. and Mrs. G. Tustin, of Broadway, has died of wounds received in action. A letter from the Sister-in-charge of the clearing station said he was shot in the thigh and body, but was bright and cheerful till the last.

Jack is buried in Grevillers British Cemetery (grave XII. D. 19). His epitaph reads: CHRIST HAS GATHERED IN HIS OWN. The cemetery was designed by Edwin Lutyens and there are 2,106 Commonwealth servicemen of the First World War buried or commemorated in Grevillers British Cemetery. Jack is also commemorated on the Broadway Council School Memorial Board (see page 128).

---

154 Emma Clarke was the sister of Charles Clarke, step-father of Bertram Clarke, see page 21.
155 The Guards Division were also involved in the Battle of Canal du Nord and on the first day of the battle Guardsman Ernest Edward Vincent was killed in action, see page 113.

Grevillers British Cemetery, Pas de Calais, France.
(Commonwealth War Graves Commission)

The grave of Lance Corporal Jack Tustin,
Grevillers British Cemetery, France.
(Sarah Huxford)

A Field Dressing Station, Canal du Nord, 1918.
(WW1 Daily)

Ernest Edward Vincent
Guardsman 27767, 1ˢᵗ Battalion Grenadier Guards

Ernest Edward Vincent was born in Broadway in 1880 and baptised at St Michael's Church on 30ᵗʰ April 1881. Ernest was the youngest son of five children of William George Vincent and Mary Ann Vincent (née Burrows) from Buckland. At the time of Ernest's birth, the family was living at Phillipps Cottages[156], Leamington Road, Broadway, and his father was working as an agricultural labourer. The family later moved to live at Pike Row Cottages, Leamington Road.

Guardsman Ernest E. Vincent.
(Evesham Journal)

Ernest had three older brothers[157] and a younger sister, Elizabeth Mary Jane. After leaving school Ernest left Broadway and moved to Bristol, Somerset, where he met and married Ethel Kate Banwell in 1904.

Ethel was the daughter of Mark Banwell, a house painter, and Lavinia Banwell (née Day). Ernest and Ethel moved to Weston-super-Mare where their three sons, were born. Their eldest, Percival William Mark was born on 18ᵗʰ May 1905, followed by Harold Sidney Clifford in 1907 and Leslie Wilfred Ernest on 23ʳᵈ April 1909. After Harold was born the family moved to Christchurch, Hampshire, where Ernest was employed as a cast iron pipe jointer on the railways. The family lived at 20 Millhams Street, Christchurch, next door to Ethel's parents. In 1911, Ernest's youngest son Harold died, aged four.

The grave of Guardsman Ernest E. Vincent, Grenadier Guards, Sanders Keep Military Cemetery, France. (Marijke Taffein)

It is not known when Ernest enlisted but he enlisted in Bristol and joined the 1ˢᵗ Battalion Grenadier Guards as a Private[158] and served with the 3ʳᵈ Guards Brigade of the Guards Division on the Western Front.

The Grenadier Guards played an important role in the Allied push to victory in the final advances of the war which started on 18ᵗʰ August 1918. At the end of September 1918, the 1ˢᵗ Battalion was engaged in the Battle of Canal du Nord, one of the battles of the Hindenburg Line, which led to the eventual breakthrough of the line on 29ᵗʰ September 1918 and a German retreat. Ernest died, aged 37, on 27ᵗʰ September 1918 on the first day of the Battle of the Canal du Nord.

Ernest is buried in Sanders Keep Military Cemetery, Graincourt-Les-Havrincourt, south-west of Cambrai in France (grave III. A. 6). His headstone is engraved with the epitaph: ONE OF THE BEST. Sanders Keep was a German fortification stormed by Scots Guards on 27ᵗʰ September 1918. After the battle both British and German dead were buried by the Guards Division Burial Officer.

156　The Vincent family were neighbours of William and Mary Barnett, parents of George Barnett, see page 8.

157　Vincent's brother Thomas William Vincent (1873-1942) married Amy Cecilia Tandy (1879-1942) sister of Wilfred George Tandy, see page 107.

158　In 1919 HM King George V commanded that the rank of Guardsman replace that of Private in recognition of the regiment's efforts during the war.

Sanders Keep Military Cemetery, Graincourt-les-Havrincourt, France.
(Commonwealth War Graves Commission)

Sanders Keep Military Cemetery, Graincourt-les-Havrincourt, France.
Ernest Vincent's grave is in the centre of the above photograph.
(Commonwealth War Graves Commission)

Edmund Joseph Wale

Lance Corporal 30871, 8th (Service) Battalion Royal Berkshire Regiment

Edmund Joseph Wale was born in 1885 in Carrickfergus, Ireland, the middle son of Joseph Samuel Wale from Suffolk, and Mary Ann Wale (née Fox) from Margate, Kent. Edmund had two brothers, Alfred James also born in Ireland in 1880, and Frederick William born in Leysdown, Kent, in 1890.

At the time of Frederick's birth Edmund's father was working as a Commissioned Boatman for HM Coastguard in Ramsgate and the family were living at 9 Coastguard Cottages. Following Joseph's promotion to Coastguard Officer, the family moved to the Coastguard Cottages at Dunwich.

Edmund J. Wale.
(The Wale Family)

Edmund had left school by 1901 and was employed as a gardener in Dunwich. He later moved to London where he was employed by the landscape painter and gardener Alfred Parsons, RA[159] at 54 Bedford Gardens, Kensington. Alfred Parsons was a regular traveller to the United States and on 3rd January 1908, Edmund travelled with him as his companion on SS Mauretania to New York from Liverpool. Whilst in London, Edmund married Millicent Mary Smedley in 1910. Millicent, the daughter of an ironworker, was born in 1883 in Peterborough, Northamptonshire. Her sister, Clara Jane Smedley, was employed by Alfred Parsons in London as his parlour maid.

Alfred Parsons was a member of the colony of artists[160] who lived and worked in London and Broadway in the late 1890s many of whom were expatriate Americans. Within a year of their marriage, Edmund and Millicent had moved to Broadway and were living in Russell House Cottage next to the Broadway home of Francis Davis Millet[161] and not far from Alfred Parsons's Broadway home, Luggershill, on Springfield Lane. Edmund had been employed by Frank Millet and his wife Elizabeth Millet, known as Lily, as one of their gardeners in the extensive gardens and orchards at Russell House.

Edmund was supposed to accompany Frank Millet on RMS Titanic to New York on 10th April 1912 but did not travel due to the birth of his son, Brian, who had been born on 15th February 1912. Frank Millet died in the sinking of the Titanic on 15th April 1912 and Edmund remained in the employ of Frank's widow, Lily, until his conscription in August 1916.

Edmund received his conscription papers in early 1916 and Lily Millet appealed against his conscription. The Evesham Journal reported on the meeting of the Evesham Military Service Tribunal held at the end of May 1916:

Mrs. F. D. Millet, of Russell House, Broadway, asked for total exemption of Edmund Joseph Wale (31), head gardener in her employ at Russell House cottages. Wale is a married man with one child. Mrs. Millet said two of her lads had already gone. She had sent hampers of fruit to the soldiers and sailors and the hospitals, so that Wale was very usefully employed. Wale also looked after her cattle and poultry, and had been with her seven or eight years. In reply to a remark by the Chairman, Mrs. Millet said that she was too loyal a citizen to wish to have a man especially to tend to her garden. – The Chairman: I know you are. Her gardens and orcharding were about 14 acres, including a cherry orchard. – Exemption granted until July 1.

---

159   Alfred Parsons was a Broadway Parish Councillor and Chairman of the Broadway War Memorial Committee (see page 4).

160   The Broadway Colony of artists was a group of predominately American artists, writers, actors and musicians who made Broadway their home in the late 1800s and included Francis Davis Millet, Edmund Gosse, Mary Anderson de Navarro, John Singer Sargent and Edwin Austin Abbey.

161   At the time of the 1911 census, Frank and Lily Millet had just returned from Panama and had rented Russell House to Sir Ralph St George Claude Gore, 10th Baronet Gore, of Magherabegg, County Donegal and his wife Lady Elsie Vaughan Gore.

Just before Edmund's exemption was due to expire, Lily Millet again appealed on his behalf at the Evesham Military Service Tribunal at the end of June 1916. The Evesham Journal on 24th June 1916 reported:

Mrs. F. D. Millet, of Russell House, Broadway, appealed for her gardener, Edmund J. Wale. He is a married man with one child, and Wale said that he managed the whole of the garden for Mrs. Millet. They had 3 milking cows and 3 heifers, 15 store pigs and 2 breeding sows, 300 heads of poultry, and a pony. They sent all the fruit to market. By Lieut. Glanfield: It was an appeal by Mrs. Millet. He himself was quite willing to serve his country – Mrs Millet was in court but was taken ill just before the case was called on, and had to leave the Court.

Edmund was granted further exemption until 31st July 1916 and afterwards he enlisted in Evesham with the 8th (Service) Battalion Royal Berkshire Regiment. Edmund joined the battalion as they were withdrawing from the front line on the Somme. The battalion spent the winter of 1916 in and out of the trenches around Albert, the main town behind the British front line. Christmas 1916 was spent in the front line trenches at Flers but by New Year's Eve, the battalion was back in billets in Albert. The battalion returned to the front line in the spring and in June 1917 moved north to the Belgian border to guard the Yser Canal. The battalion later withdrew to Le Clipon near Dunkirk (known as Hush Hush Land), where the battalion received training on amphibious warfare as they were designated to take part in a British landing on the Belgian coast as a follow up to the Third Battle of Ypres. This plan was abandoned and during October the battalion marched from Le Clipon to Passchendaele where the battalion joined the Second Battle of Passchendaele near Poelcapelle. Christmas 1917 was spent in billets at Reninghof near Houthhulst Forest where the men enjoyed Christmas dinner and presents from Queen Alexandra's Field Force Fund.

In the great reorganisation of the army, on 3rd February 1918, Edmund's battalion was sent to join the 18th Division in the St Quentin area on the Somme. The Battalion suffered heavy casualties as it came under heavy fire and gas shelling in the German Spring Offensive on 21st March and a number of the men were taken prisoner. The remains of the battalion withdrew gradually to Nampcel where a composite battalion was formed with the remnants of the 7th Battalion of the Royal West Kent Regiment and 53rd Trench Mortar Battery.

During the morning of 4th April 1918, during the Defence of Amiens, the battalion marched from billets in Gentelles to the Bois de Hangard in preparation for an expected German attack. The attack took place at 4.30pm that afternoon following heavy bombardment. The battalion forced the Germans to call off the attack but suffered many casualties, 6 officers and 45 other ranks were wounded or killed. Edmund was one of the men killed in action on that day. His body was never recovered and he is commemorated on Panel 56 and 57 of Pozieres Memorial (see page 75).

Edmund is recorded in the Roll of Honour 1914-1918 in St Michael's Church as 'Edward Wale'. He is also commemorated on the Cheltenham War Memorial, The Promenade, Cheltenham. His name is on the west panel of the memorial and was added after the unveiling of the memorial in 1921. Edmund's widow, Millicent had moved to Cheltenham during the war and she died there in 1925 at the age of 42.

Ramsgate Coastguard Cottages where Edmund Wale lived as a boy.
(Marguerite Wiewel)

Russell House, Broadway, c1910, home of Francis Davis Millet (1848-1912)
and Elizabeth Greely Merrill 'Lily' Millet (1855-1932)
where Edmund Wale worked as head gardener.

First World War embroidered silk postcard.
(Mary Smith)

Appendix I: Abbreviations

The following abbreviations have been used:

ASC	Army Service Corps
BA	Bachelor of Arts
Batt	Battalion
Capt	Captain
CB	Companion of the Most Honourable Order of the Bath
CBE	Commander of the Most Excellent Order of the British Empire
CMG	Companion of the Order of St Michael and St George
Cpl	Corporal
CVO	Commander of the Royal Victorian Order
DSO	Distinguished Service Order
HMHS	His Majesty's Hospital Ship
HMS	His Majesty's Ship
HMT	Hired Military Transport/His Majesty's Troopship
HRH	His/Her Royal Highness
JP	Justice of the Peace
KCB	Knight Commander of the Most Honourable Order of the Bath
JP	Justice of the Peace
Lieut/Lt	Lieutenant
L/Corporal	Lance Corporal
MA	Master of Arts
MC	Military Cross
MM	Military Medal
MRCVS	Member of the Royal College of Veterinary Surgeons
MSM	Meritorious Service Medal
MVO	Member of the Royal Victorian Order
NCO	Non-commissioned Officer
OBE	Order of the British Empire
Pte	Private
RA	Royal Artillery
RAMC	Royal Army Medical Corps
Regt	Regiment
RFA	Royal Field Artillery
RGA	Royal Garrison Artillery
RFC	Royal Flying Corps
RMS	Royal Mail Ship/Steamer
Sergt/Sgt	Sergeant
SS	Steam Ship
SWB	Silver War Badge
VC	Victoria Cross

Appendix II: Date of Death, Campaign Medals, Memorial/Cemetery and Country of Death

The following table lists the men commemorated on the war memorial in order of their date of death. It details the location of the cemetery or memorial where they are buried or commemorated, and the details of any campaign medals awarded.

The Victory Medal 1914-1919 (VM), a bronze medal, was issued to all those who entered a theatre of war. The British War Medal 1914-1920 (BWM), a silver medal, was issued to all those who went overseas. The 1914 Star (1914) also known as the Mons Star was issued to those who served with their unit in France and Belgium between 5th August 1914 and midnight of 22nd/23rd November 1914. The 1914-15 Star (1914/15) was issued to all those (with a few exceptions) who had served in a theatre of war before 31st December 1915 and had not qualified for the 1914 Star.

Name	Date of Death	Campaign Medals Awarded	Memorial or Cemetery	Country of Death
Parker, William J	17/04/1915	VM, BWM, 1914/15	Bristol (Arnos Vale) Cemetery	England
Painter, Sidney J	09/05/1915	VM, BWM, 1914/15	Les Gonards Cemetery, Versailles	France
Haines, Gerald	15/05/1915	VM, BWM, 1914/15	Unknown	France
Hill, Reginald B	04/07/1915	VM, BWM, 1914/15	Bard Cottage Cemetery	Belgium
Barnett, George	09/07/1915	VM, BWM, 1914/15	Ypres (Menin Gate) Memorial	Belgium
Scrivens, Wilfred G	06/08/1915	VM, BWM, 1914/15	Helles Memorial	Turkey
Tandy, Wilfred G	07/08/1915	VM, BWM, 1914/15	Helles Memorial	Turkey
Figgitt, Wilford C	25/09/1915	VM, BWM, 1914/15	Loos Memorial	France
Collins, Archibald W	26/09/1915	VM, BWM, 1914/15	Noeux-les-Mines Communal Cemetery	France
Hilson, Joseph	17/04/1916	VM, BWM, 1914/15	Maroc British Cemetery	France
Russell, Joe E	19/04/1916	VM, BWM, 1914/15	Basra Memorial	Iraq
Folkes, Francis A	23/04/1916	VM, BWM, 1914/15	Jerusalem Memorial	Israel
Layton, Alfred	27/06/1916	VM, BWM	Amara War Cemetery, Al Amara	Iraq
Flower, Oswald S	12/07/1916	VM, BWM, 1914/15	Morlancourt British Cemetery No. 1	France
Tebby, Walter J	23/07/1916	VM, BWM, 1914/15	St Eadburgha's, Broadway	England
Keyte, Charles H	22/08/1916	VM, BWM	Authuile Cemetery	France
Haines, Cecil F	09/09/1916	VM, BWM	Thiepval Memorial	France
Stanley, Charles R	14/09/1916	VM, BWM, 1914/15	Berks Cemetery Extension	Belgium
Talbot, Stanley A	19/10/1916	VM, BWM, 1914/15	Tincourt New British Cemetery	France
Edwards, Henry H	25/03/1917	VM, BWM,	Basra Memorial	Iraq
Clarke, Albert H	25/04/1917	VM, BWM, 1914/15	Doiran Memorial	Greece
Daffurn, Tom	01/05/1917	VM, BWM, 1914/15	Addolorata Cemetery	Malta
Parker, Ernest H	07/05/1917	VM, BWM	Arras Memorial	France

Name	Date of Death	Medals Awarded	Cemetery or Memorial	Country of Death
Billey, William R	21/05/1917	VM, BWM	Croisilles British Cemetery	France
Game, Hubert J	08/06/1917	VM, BWM, 1914	All Saints', Narborough	England
Jordan, Walter	31/07/1917	VM, BWM	Perth Cemetery (China Wall)	Belgium
Green, Leonard F	27/08/1917	VM, BWM, 1914/15	Tyne Cot Memorial	Belgium
Earp, John W	17/11/1917	VM, BWM, 1914/15	Tyne Cot Cemetery	Belgium
Sandel, George	08/12/1917	Unknown	Unknown	England
Box, Arthur	14/01/1918	VM, BWM	Dar Es Salaam War Cemetery	Tanzania
Bishop, William	22/03/1918	VM, BWM	Beaumetz Cross Roads Cemetery	France
Ingles, Francis H	28/03/1918	VM, BWM	Pozieres Memorial	France
Wale, Edmund J	04/04/1918	VM, BWM	Pozieres Memorial	France
Goddard, Arthur H	14/04/1918	VM, BWM	Ploegsteert Memorial	Belgium
Clarke, Bertram	16/04/1918	VM, BWM	Ploegsteert Memorial	Belgium
Stanley, Alec S	17/04/1918	VM, BWM	Ploegsteert Memorial	Belgium
Hensley, George	14/05/1918	VM, BWM	St Saviour's, Broadway	England
Vincent, Ernest E	27/09/1918	VM, BWM	Sanders Keep Military Cemetery	France
Tustin, Jack	30/09/1918	VM, BWM	Grevillers British Cemetery	France
Jackson, Charles	08/10/1918	VM, BWM	Belgaum Government Cemetery	India
Rastall, Frank	19/10/1918	VM, BWM	Serain Communal Cemetery Extension	France
Cull, John S	25/10/1918	VM, BWM	Tehran Memorial	Iran
Folkes, Alfred	29/10/1918	VM, BWM, 1914/15	St Eadburgha's, Broadway	England
Emms, Ebenezer E	06/11/1918	VM, BWM	St Eadburgha's, Broadway	England
Perry, John	15/02/1919	VM, BWM	Cologne Southern Cemetery	Germany
Bayliss, Josiah James	02/03/1919	Unknown	St Eadburgha's, Broadway	England
Crump, William G.	16/03/1919	VM, BWM, 1914	Ford Park Cemetery, Plymouth	England
Gardner, William	Unknown	Unknown	Unknown	Unknown

Appendix III: Casualties not included on the Broadway War Memorial by the Broadway War Memorial Committee

The following men were considered by the Broadway War Memorial Sub-Committee for inclusion on the war memorial but were not included as they were categorised as 'non-residents' by the sub-committee:

Lieutenant The Honourable Charles Lindsay Claude Bowes-Lyon
3rd Battalion attached 1st Battalion Black Watch (Royal Highlanders)

Charles Lindsay Claude Bowes-Lyon, born near Luton on 15th September 1885, was the eldest son of The Honourable Francis and Lady Anne Catherine Sybil Bowes-Lyon (née Lindsay), of Ridley Hall, Bardon Mill, Northumberland, and a cousin of Her Majesty Queen Elizabeth The Queen Mother. Charles joined the Forfarshire and Kincardine Militia Artillery in 1906 and in 1910 was gazetted to the 3rd Battalion (Special Reserve) Black Watch.

Attached to the 1st Battalion, he joined the Expeditionary Forces in France in early September 1914 and was twice slightly wounded. On 23rd October 1914, after three days incessant fighting at Pilken, near Ypres, Charles was killed in action, aged 29, during an attack to recover the lost trenches. Charles is buried in New Irish Farm Cemetery, Ypres (grave XXX. X. 11), and is commemorated on the war memorial in Lyndhurst in the New Forest and on the memorial plaque inside St Cuthbert's Church, Beltingham. Charles was considered for inclusion on the Broadway War Memorial as his aunt Lady Maud Agnes Bowes-Lyon lived at Orchard House (now The Orchard Farm).

Captain The Honourable Fergus Bowes-Lyon
8th Battalion Black Watch (Royal Highlanders)

Fergus Bowes-Lyon was considered for inclusion on the Broadway War Memorial as he was a nephew of Lady Maud Bowes-Lyon. Fergus was born at Glamis Castle on 18th April 1889, the fourth son of Claude George Bowes-Lyon, 14th Earl of Stathmore and Kinghorne and Nina Cecilia Bowes-Lyon, Countess of Strathmore and Kinghorne (née Cavendish Bentinck). Fergus was an older brother of Her Majesty Queen Elizabeth The Queen Mother. On 17th September 1914 Fergus married Lady Christian Norah Dawson-Damer and they had one daughter born the following summer.

Fergus arrived in France on 10th May 1915 and was killed in action on 27th September 1915, the third day of the Battle of the Hohenzollern Redoubt during the Battle of Loos. Fergus was buried in a quarry at Vermelles and although the quarry was later adopted as a military cemetery, Quarry Cemetery, the details of his grave were lost and he was recorded as being amongst the missing on the Loos Memorial.

In 2011 Fergus's grandson traced his grave and provided the Commonwealth War Graves Commission with sufficient evidence that Fergus had been buried in Quarry Cemetery, Vermelles. A special memorial headstone was commissioned in 2012 and erected in the cemetery (grave A. 15) with the wording: BURIED NEAR THIS SPOT as there is no certainty as to the exact location of his original burial spot. Fergus's name was subsequently removed from the Loos Memorial. He is also commemorated on the Glamis War Memorial, the Lyndhurst War Memorial, and the war memorial in St John's Church, Forfar.

Captain The Honourable Fergus Bowes-Lyon.

Charles Collins

At the time of writing it has not been possible to identify this casualty. Charles is also commemorated on the Broadway Council School Memorial Board (see page 128).

Edgar Cook, MM
Second Corporal 86297, 254th Tunnelling Company, Royal Engineers

Edgar Cook was the youngest son of five children of William Henry Cook, a farm labourer from Fairford, and Emma Clara Cook (née Masslin). Edgar was born in Cheltenham in 1888 and by the time of the 1901 census, Edgar and his family were recorded as living on Claines Lane, Claines. By early 1911 the family had moved to Cleeve Prior near Evesham.

Edgar enlisted in Birmingham with the King's Royal Rifle Corps (Corporal 8057). During the war Edgar was awarded the Military Medal and was transferred to the 254th Tunnelling Company, Royal Engineers. Edgar was wounded in action and died on 29th October 1917. Edgar is buried in Lijssenthoek Military Cemetery (grave XXI. DD. 6). The Commonwealth War Graves Commission records Edgar as having been as a native of Broadway.

Albert Daffurn
Private 118, Princess Patricia's Canadian Light Infantry (Eastern Ontario Regiment)

Pte Albert Daffurn.
(Evesham Journal)

Albert Daffurn, a farm labourer, was born in Broadway on 22nd September 1869, the third son of Charles Daffurn, a stonemason and quarryman from Broadway, and Mary Daffurn. Albert was baptised at St Michael's Church on 14th November 1869. After leaving school Albert joined the army and served for eight years with the 3rd Battalion Rifle Brigade during which time he was posted to India. After completing his service Albert returned to Broadway but six months later, following the outbreak of the Boer War, he was re-called and he served in South Africa. Albert returned to Broadway following his discharge from the army and in 1906 he married Elizabeth Smith, known as Bessie. Bessie, from Willersey, was the daughter of Thomas Smith, the village grocer. After their marriage Albert and Bessie settled in Willersey where their four children were born.

On 5th April 1912, Albert sailed on SS Corsican bound for Ingersoll, Ontario, to seek work as a farm labourer. The number of immigrants to Canada from England reached its peak in 1912/13 as many English farm labourers were attracted to opportunities arising on dry-land farms on the plains in Canada. Indeed many of Albert's fellow passengers on the Corsican are recorded as seeking work as farm labourers. The ship's manifest has 'British Bonus Allowed' stamped next to Albert's name confirming that he intended to settle in Canada. The bonus was a commission paid by the Canadian Government's Immigration Branch to steamship booking agents in the United Kingdom for each suitable immigrant who purchased a ticket to sail to Canada. Albert settled in Canada and found work on the railways and as a builder's labourer.

After Britain declared war against Germany on 4th August 1914, Canada, a loyal member of the British Empire, also declared war. A week later, on 10th August 1914, Captain Andrew Hamilton Gault, a veteran of the Boer War, founded the Princess Patricia's Canadian Light Infantry in Ottawa, Ontario. The regiment was named after HRH Princess Patricia of Connaught, daughter of the Duke of Connaught and granddaughter of Queen Victoria. Fourteen days after recruiting started, Albert enlisted in Ottawa.

The regiment was to be made up of mature men who had seen active service and his previous military experience is recorded on Albert's enlistment papers.

The regiment's first formal parade took place on 23rd August at which HRH Princess Patricia presented the Camp Colour that she had designed and made by hand. Albert and his regiment left Ottawa on 28th August and embarked at Montreal in SS Megantic. The sailing, however, was cancelled due to enemy action in the Atlantic and the regiment disembarked at Lévis, Québec, where the regiment set up camp. After a month's training, on 27th September, the regiment once more set sail for England on the SS Royal George arriving at Bustard Camp, Salisbury Plain, on 18th October. In early November the regiment moved to Winchester where they joined the 80th Brigade of the 27th Division. On 4th November HM King George inspected the regiment along with Lords Kitchener and Roberts and is reported as saying "This is the finest battalion I have ever inspected."

Albert landed in France with his regiment on 21st December 1914. The regiment was the first and only Canadian Infantry Regiment in a theatre of war that year. Shortly after Christmas, Albert was wounded in the leg at La Bassée and returned to Willersey to recuperate. By May 1915, Albert had returned to his regiment and the Western Front.

From 20th April 1915, the regiment was in the trenches at Polygon Wood between St Julien and Hill 60. Although not directly involved in the battles that raged at St Julien and Hill 60, the regiment was badly depleted and, facing a vastly superior force, was forced on 3rd May 1915 to retreat three miles to an exposed position in front of Bellewaerde Lake and Bellewaerde Wood. The regiment suffered badly during the following day when they were shelled continuously. Nearly 200 men were lost that day most of whom were in the exposed front trench (some of the men in support in Bellewaerde Wood were also killed) and as a result the line was taken over by the King's Shropshire Light Infantry but the regiment, with a fresh draft of troops, returned to the trench only a couple of days later.

From 4am on 8th May the regiment came under the most intense bombardment it had experienced with heavy fire from howitzers, field guns and sniper fire, as the Germans made several attempts to advance, eventually reaching the front line trenches. Despite suffering heavy losses during the attack, the regiment managed to hold their position until they were relieved at 11.30pm by the 3rd Battalion King's Royal Rifle Corps who helped bury the men that had died in the support and communications trenches but it was not possible to reach the front line. Casualties were high: two officers and 93 men were killed, two officers and 79 men were reported as missing and six officers (including Major Andrew H. Gault who had just returned to the regiment having been injured at St Elio on 1st March) and 203 men were wounded. Albert was one of the 93 Princess Pats killed in action on that day.

Corporal 39, Edward Edwards[162], was one of only 49 men of the Princess Patricia's Light Infantry who survived that terrible day which he later called the 'Last Stand of the Princess Pats'. He was taken prisoner during the evening of 8th May and recounted in the book 'The Escape of a Princess Pat' by George Pearson:

The general result was beyond any poor words of mine. All spoken language is totally inadequate to describe the shocks and horrors of an intense bombardment. It is not that man himself lacks the imaginative gift of words but that he has not the word tools with which to work. They do not exist. Each attempt to describe becomes near effrontery and demands its own separate apology.

In addition, kind Nature draws a veil for him over so much of all the worst of it that many details are spared his later recollection. He remembers only the indescribable confusion and the bursting claps of near-by flame, as foul in color and as ill of smell as an addled egg. He knows only that the acid of the high-explosive gas eats into the tissue of his brain and lungs, destroying with other things, most memories of shelling.

After Albert's death, his widow Bessie received the following letter from Major General Sam

---

162   During the war, Sergeant Edward Edwards from Rosedale, Toronto, was wounded twice, declared missing and officially declared dead, escaped twice from German prison camps before escaping to Holland and returning to England in September 1916.

Hughes[163], the Canadian Minister for Militia and Defence which was published in the Evesham Journal on 21st August 1915:

Will you kindly accept my sincere sympathy and condolence in the decease of that worthy and heroic soldier, Pte. Albert Daffurn. While one cannot too deeply mourn the loss of such a brave comrade, there is a consolation in knowing that he did his duty fearlessly and well and gave his life for the cause of liberty and the upbuilding of the Empire. Again extending to you my heartfelt sympathy. Faithfully, Sam Hughes.

Albert is commemorated on Panel 10 of the Ypres (Menin Gate) Memorial and, although not commemorated on the Broadway War Memorial, he is included on the Roll of Honour 1914-1918 in St Michael's Church (see page 3) and on the Willersey War Memorial (see page 70).

Ypres (Menin Gate) Memorial, designed by Sir Reginald Blomfield nears the names of more than 54,000 officers and men whose graves are not known.
(Commonwealth War Graves Commission)

Lewis Diston
Private 21284, 10th (Labour) Battalion Royal Berkshire Regiment
transferred to 30th Labour Group HQ Labour Corps

Lewis Diston, born in Snowshill in 1897, was the son of William Diston and Amelia Diston (née Rouse). Lewis married Gladys Ethel Gardiner from Cutsdean near Stow-on-the-Wold in 1916 and they lived at Bell Yard, Broadway. Lewis enlisted with the Royal Berkshire Regiment and served with the 10th (Labour) Battalion before he was transferred to the Labour Corps. He died, aged 21, on 1st June 1918 and is buried in Nine Elms British Cemetery, Poperinge, Belgium (grave XI. D. 17).

Lewis is commemorated on Snowshill War Memorial in St Barnabas churchyard in the centre of the village. The memorial, erected in 1923, was designed by Frederick Griggs and carved by Alec Miller in stone donated by Sir Philip Sidney Stott from his quarry at Stanton.

---

163   Sir Sam Hughes was Canada's Minister of Militia and Defence from October 1911 to November 1916.

Dennis William Diston
Lance Corporal 17261, 10th (Service) Battalion Gloucestershire Regiment

Lance Corporal Dennis Diston.
(Evesham Journal)

Dennis William Diston was born in Stanton in 1887. Dennis was the son of Charles Diston, an agricultural labourer from Snowshill, and Julia Ann Diston from Laverton. In 1891, a year after his youngest sister Mabel was born, Dennis's mother died.

After leaving school, Dennis worked as a farm labourer and jobbing gardener. On 6th July 1912 he married Mabel Elizabeth Grove, the daughter of Frederick and Martha Grove, at St Michael's Church. At the time of their marriage Mabel was working as a kitchen maid for Mr R.G. Hardy at Holland House, Lansdown Road, Cheltenham. After their marriage the couple moved to 41 Council Cottages, Broadway, and they had two children, George born in 1913 and Dorothy born in 1915.

Dennis enlisted with Kitchener's Army. He joined the 10th (Service) Battalion Gloucestershire Regiment and was posted to the Western Front on 9th August 1915. The following year Dennis was initially posted as wounded and missing in action. It was later confirmed that he was killed in action, aged 29, on 22nd July 1916 and he is buried in Pozieres British Cemetery, France (grave IV. 2. 30). Dennis is commemorated on Snowshill War Memorial, Prestbury War Memorial and on the memorial inside St Mary's Church, Prestbury.

Henry John Nash
Private 13676, 2nd Battalion Worcestershire Regiment

Henry John Nash, known as Harry, was born about 1891 in Limerick, Ireland, the son of Henry John Nash, a general labourer from Worcester and Mary Ann Nash from Jersey. In 1891 at the time of the census that was taken at the beginning of April, the family is recorded as living at 5 Little Charles Street, Worcester.

Harry enlisted with the 2nd Battalion Worcestershire Regiment in 1914 and arrived in France on 18th February 1915 where he joined the battalion at billets in Les Choquants. Harry served on the Western Front and was killed in action during the Battle of Festubert on 16th May 1915, the day after Gerald Haines, who was in the same battalion, was killed (see page 66). Harry is commemorated on Le Touret Memorial, Pas de Calais, France (Panel 17 and 18).

At the time of writing, no records have been found linking Harry to Broadway except for his inclusion in a list of Broadway casualties published in the Evesham Journal at the end of 1915.

Le Touret Memorial, France.
(Commonwealth War Graves Commission)

Appendix IV: Casualties buried in St Eadburgha's Churchyard not on the Broadway War Memorial

The following two men are buried in private graves in the churchyard at St Eadburgha's. They are both recognised by the Commonwealth War Graves Commission as First World War casualties and their graves as war graves but neither of them is commemorated on the Broadway War Memorial.

Thomas Gould
Private 25302, 3rd (Reserve) Battalion Oxfordshire and Buckinghamshire Light Infantry

Thomas Gould was born about 1880 near Aston, Warwickshire. Prior to his enlistment Thomas worked as a coachman and he married Helen Graham in Witton, near Aston, in 1917. Thomas enlisted in Birmingham and initially served with the Royal Warwickshire Regiment (Private 14284).

During the war Thomas was transferred to the 3rd (Reserve) Battalion Oxfordshire and Buckinghamshire Light Infantry. The battalion did not serve overseas during the First World War and from October 1917 until November 1918, played an important coastal defence and garrison role at Dover, the centre of defence of the English Channel during the war. The battalion trained officers and men for service overseas, and often the sick and wounded who had returned home were posted to the battalion after leaving hospital for convalescence and re-training before being sent back to the front.

Thomas was admitted to Farncombe Voluntary Aid Detachment Hospital in Broadway (see page 49) during the war where he died of pleurisy and pericarditis, aged 38, on 30th March 1918. His funeral was held at St Eadburgha's on 3rd April 1918 and he is buried in a private grave in the churchyard (grave N2. 4. 7). His epitaph reads: JESUS LIVES HENCEFORTH IS DEATH BUT THE GATE OF LIFE IMMORTAL "LOVE CONQUERS ALL".

The grave of Pte Thomas Gould, St Eadburgha's Churchyard, Broadway.

Captain William Randall Ponsonby, DSO
3rd (Prince of Wales's) Dragoon Guards

William Randall (also spelt Rundall) Ponsonby was born on 8th August 1876 on the Isle of Wight, the second son of Colonel Justinian Gordon Ponsonby and Elizabeth Sophia Ponsonby from Clifton, Bristol. William's father served in the army and in the 1881 census William is recorded as living with his mother, two brothers (George Montagu born in India in 1875 and Reginald Gordon born in Farnham in 1878) and two sisters (Cara Lilian born in Farnham in 1879 and Olive Mary born in Farnham in 1881) at 5 Queen's Villa, Queen's Road, Farnham.

In early 1890, William's mother died in Sedbergh, Cumbria, and William along with his brother George, was sent to Sedbergh School as a boarder. The school records William as having been a boarder in Lupton House from 1890 to 1891. During his time at Sedbergh School William's home address was firstly recorded as Templemore, County Tipperary, and then Cork, Ireland, where his father was stationed. In 1895, William's father remarried Augusta Blanche Cook in London and his half-brother Bertie Hastings was born in London in 1898.

After leaving school, William travelled to Australia where he settled and served in the Royal Navy and as a Police Officer in Pilliga, New South Wales, Australia. William enlisted in South Africa with D Troop Thorneycroft's Horse and served with the troop from 12th November 1899 to 8th April 1901 attaining the rank of Lieutenant. William was wounded at Colenso on 15th December 1899. He was created a Companion of the Distinguished Order in 1901 in recognition of his service during operations in South Africa and was presented the insignia by the King on 29th October 1901. After serving with Thorneycroft's Mounted Infantry, he transferred to the South African Constabulary.

In February 1900 the Newcastle Morning Herald and Miners Advocate reported:

A Victoria Cross is pretty sure to be awarded Lt Ponsonby, of D Troop Thorneycroft's Light Horse. Mr. Ponsonby is well known in the Pilliga NSW district, having served in the Police Force there. The conspicuous deed of gallantry which is going to earn him this distinction is described in the Natal 'Witness' of December 22, which giving an account of the battle of Colenso, says: - Thorneycroft's provided a hero in the person of Lt Ponsonby, of D troop, who when his section was recalled, on account of the heavy fire remained behind with a wounded man, whose wounds he dressed. Then he tried to carry the man to safety. Whilst so engaged his helmet was pierced with a bullet, but he stuck with his task and moved forward with his burden. The injured man's life was, however, short, as while being carried a bullet lodged in his stomach, causing almost instant death. The dying man's movements when writhing on the ground drew fresh fire and Ponsonby sought shelter for a short time. He then pushed on, receiving a flesh wound on the left arm, while his coat was perforated. Noticing his condition a Boer advanced to 80 metres to make sure of his victim, but Ponsonby drew his revolver, and shot him dead. When he returned to camp he received a well merited ovation from his friends. Later on our hero went back to the fighting line, and again succoured a wounded comrade, this time saving him.

In 1902, William married Lillian Patteson Nickalls, daughter of Sir Patteson Nickalls and Lady Florence Nickalls (née Womersley) in London, and they moved to The Grange Cottage, Church Street, Broadway.

During the First World War William was gazetted to the 3rd (Prince of Wales's) Dragoon Guards and he served as a Captain with the Guards until ill health forced him to retire. William returned home to Broadway and he died, aged 42, on 18th January 1919 of tuberculosis. His funeral service was held at St Eadburgha's Church on 21st January 1919. He is buried in the south side of the churchyard along the east boundary. Probate was awarded to his widow Lilian on 7th November 1930, total effects £5. His epitaph is taken from the last verse of Rudyard Kipling's *The Galley-Slave*:

The grave of Captain William R. Ponsonby, St Eadburgha's Churchyard, Broadway.

It may be that Fate will give me life and leave to row once more -
Set some strong man free for fighting as I take awhile his oar.
But today I leave the galley. Shall I curse her service then?
God be thanked - whate'er comes after, I have lived and toiled with Men.

William's brother George Montagu, who served as a Lieutenant in the 2nd Battalion West African Frontier Force, died on the 13th December 1901. His younger half-brother, Bertie, served in the First World War as a Midshipman with the Royal Navy. Bertie died, aged 16, on HMS Bulwark on 26th November 1914. During the morning of 26th November, while the ship was anchored in the estuary of the River Medway near Sheerness, she was destroyed by a large internal explosion killing 738 of the 750 crew members. Bertie is commemorated on The Portsmouth Naval Memorial, on Southsea Common, Hampshire (Panel 1).

Appendix V: Broadway Council School Memorial Board

The Broadway Council School Memorial Board, at Broadway First School, commemorates 27 pupils of Broadway Council School who lost their lives in the First World War.

Broadway Council School Memorial Board.

The following pupils are commemorated on the memorial board which is inscribed with the words: AT THE GOING DOWN OF THE SUN AND IN THE MORNING WE WILL REMEMBER THEM.

George Barnett (see page 8)	John Grimmett (see page 129)	Sidney Painter (see page 85)
Robert Billy (see page 12)	Cecil Haines (see page 64)	William Parker (see page 90)
Arthur Box (see page 16)	Reginald Handy	Frank Rastall (see page 94)
Bertram Clark (see page 21)	Thomas Handy (see page 129)	George Sandals (see page 98)
Archibald Collins (see page 23)	Bertram Hill (see page 71)	George Scrivens (see page 99)
Charles Collins (see page 122)	Frank Ingles (see page 75)	Alec Stanley (see page 101)
Thomas Daffurn (see page 31)	Charles Jackson (see page 77)	Charles Stanley (see page 102)
Ebenezer Emms (see page 40)	William Jones	Wilfred Tandy (see page 107)
Wilfred Figgett (see page 42)	Walter Jordan (see page 79)	James Tomes
Frank Folkes (see page 50)	Charles Hubert Keyte (see page 80)	Jack Tustin (see page 111)
Leonard Green (see page 62)		

At the time of writing it has not been possible to identify Charles Collins, Reginald Handy, William Jones and James Tomes. It is likely, however, that Reginald Handy is Richard Keyte Handy, the brother of George Thomas Handy (see page 129).

John William Grimmitt
Gunner 246724, 'C' Battery, 275th Brigade Royal Field Artillery

John William Grimmitt (also spelt Grimmett), known as Jack, was born in Buckland in 1898, Jack was the eldest son of Albert George Grimmitt, a carpenter, and Rhoda Ann Grimmitt (née Holmes). Jack grew up in Buckland and Broadway and was educated at Broadway Council School. After leaving school worked as a farm labourer.

Jack enlisted with the Royal Field Artillery and served on the Western Front with 'C' Company of the 275th Brigade. Jack was killed in action, aged 19, on 18th April 1918, at Fouquières near Béthune and he is buried in Fouquieres Churchyard Extension, Pas de Calais, France (grave II. F. 5). His epitaph reads: IN EVER LOVING MEMORY OF OUR DEAR BOY FOR EVER WITH THE LORD.

Jack is also commemorated on the stone tablet inside St Michael's Church, Buckland (see page 17) alongside William Arthur Box.

The grave of Pte John W. Grimmitt, Fouquieres Churchyard Extension. (Margaret Dufay)

Fouquieres Cemetery Extension, designed by Sir Edwin Lutyens, contains 387 Commonwealth burials of the First World War. (Commonwealth War Graves Commission)

George Thomas Handy
Private 29206, 9th (Service) Battalion Gloucestershire Regiment

George Thomas Handy, known as Thomas, was the eldest son of Thomas Handy, a baker, and Mary Handy (née Keyte). Thomas was born in Broadway in 1880 and baptised at St Michael's Church on 26th December 1880. Thomas was first cousin to Albert Clarke (see page 18) and grew up in Broadway.

Thomas was a pupil at Broadway Council School and after leaving school was apprenticed to the Broadway baker William Smith. In 1901 Thomas married Clara Porter, from Kingham, Oxfordshire, and they moved to Moreton-in-Marsh where Thomas opened his own bakery. Thomas was also groundsman

Pte George T. Handy.
(Berrows Worcester Journal)

at Moreton-in-Marsh Cricket Club and greenkeeper for both the Golf and Bowling Clubs for many years.

Thomas and Clara had two sons, Thomas William born in 1902 and Albert George born in 1905. At the time of his enlistment Thomas and his family were living at Croxdale Terrace, Evenlode Road, Moreton-in-Marsh.

Thomas enlisted with the 9th (Service) Battalion Gloucestershire Regiment and was posted to Salonika. He was killed instantaneously by a shell during the night of 24th/25th April 1917 (the same day as his cousin Albert Clarke) and he is buried in Karasouli Military Cemetery, Polykastro (formerly Karasouli), Greece (grave A89). Thomas is also commemorated on the Moreton-in-Marsh War Memorial as 'Thomas G. Handy'.

After his death his widow, Clara, received the following letter from Second Lieutenant A.E. Farmer:

He was killed instantaneously by a shell on the night of April 24 during a heavy bombardment. He always showed great courage and devotion to duty, and is a great loss to me and my company. He has been laid to rest with a number of others who fell that night, in a cemetery near the firing line. Please accept the company commander's and my sincerest sympathies in your bereavement.

Jim Franklin who served with Thomas also wrote:

I beg to add my deepest sympathy. I am very sorry, for the two of us worked together as mates, being the only two together in the line from Moreton. We have had a terrible time of it I assure you. We laid him to rest last night by the side of many more who have given their lives for their country. This is a small consolation for one's loss, but one must comfort oneself with the knowledge that those who die here die a noble death. All the chaps in the same platoon are very sorry, as well liked him very much. He was a good soldier.

Thomas's younger brother, Richard Keyte Handy, was born in Broadway in 1883. After leaving Broadway Council School, Richard found work as an agricultural labourer in the village. He married Sarah Ann Hartwell in 1905 and they moved to Evesham where Richard worked as a builder's labourer. Richard and Sarah had two sons, Arthur David Thomas born in 1908 and Albert Richard George born in 1909. Richard enlisted with the 9th (Service) Battalion Worcestershire Regiment (Private 19218) and was posted to Gallipoli at the beginning of October 1915. Richard died in Gallipoli on 4th November 1915 and he is commemorated on the Helles Memorial, Turkey (see page 100) and the Evesham War Memorial.

Karasouli Military Cemetery, Polykastro, Greece.
(Commonwealth War Graves Commission)

Appendix VI: Other Broadway Casualties

The table below lists casualties who were found to have been born or lived in Broadway, that are not commemorated on either the Broadway War Memorial or the Broadway Council School Memorial Board (see page 128), or buried in St Eadburgha's churchyard.

Included in the table is Private 5767, William Harold Gabb 3rd Battalion Coldstream Guards. William was the first man born in Broadway to die in the First World War. He died of wounds received in action in Rentel, Belgium, on 7th November 1914. William, born in 1880, was the son of William Thomas Gabb and Jane Gabb (née Cole). After leaving school William was employed at John Morris's bakery in the village and he later joined the railway police and was stationed at Cheltenham and in the Forest of Dean before joining the Coldstream Guards. William served for three years with the Guards before transferring to the reserve and emigrating to Canada in 1912 with his wife, Ellen Eliza Gabb (née King-Ottley) whom he had married in London in 1908. As a reservist, William was recalled on mobilization and served with the 3rd Battalion Coldstream Guards on the Western Front. In October, a few weeks before he died, William's wife and two children returned to England to live with his widowed mother on Northwick Road, Evesham in October 1914. William's is commemorated on the Ypres (Menin Gate) Memorial, Belgium, and the Evesham War Memorial.

Name	Year of birth	Rank and Number	Battalion and Regiment	Date of Death	Cemetery or Memorial
Annesley, James Howard Adolphus	1868	Lieutenant Colonel CMG, DSO	6th Dragoon Guards (Carabiniers)	22 Apr 1919	Brookwood Cemetery, Surrey
Batchelor, George Walter Raymond	1893	Private 9569	15th Entrenching Battalion, late 11th Battalion Royal Warwickshire Regiment	22 Mar 1918	Pozieres Memorial, France
Cunnington, Charles Chamberlain	1885	Corporal 7931	2nd Battalion Dorsetshire Regiment	1 May 1916	Amara War Cemetery, Iraq
Dale, Ernest Stocks	1891	Corporal 17842	1/7th Battalion Worcestershire Regiment	15 Jun 1918	Magnaboschi British Cemetery, Italy, and Aston Somerville War Memorial
Dale, John S.	1886	Company Sergeant Major 13784	8th Battalion Gloucestershire Regiment	4 May 1918	Klein-Vierstraat British Cemetery, Belgium
Gabb, William Harold	1880	Private 5767	3rd Battalion Coldstream Guards	7 Nov 1914	Ypres (Menin Gate) Memorial, Evesham War Memorial

Name	Year of birth	Rank and Number	Battalion and Regiment	Date of Death	Cemetery or Memorial
Ganderton, Thomas Henry	1894	Private 17267	3rd Battalion Worcestershire Regiment	10 Jul 1916	Thiepval Memorial, France, Holberrow Green War Memorial, St Peter's Church and Inkberrow Council School
Handy, Richard Keyte	1883	Private 19218	9th Battalion Worcestershire Regiment	4 Nov 1915	Helles Memorial, Turkey, Evesham War Memorial
Hartwell, Arthur James	1893	Private 240100	8th Battalion East Surrey Regiment	10 Apr 1918	Abbeville Communal Cemetery Extension, France
Hinton, Gerald Charles	1895	Private 307582	2/7th Royal Warwickshire Regiment formerly 3645 Warwickshire Yeomanry	18 Apr 1918	Loos Memorial, France
Huxley, Albert	1895	Lance Corporal 241169	2/8th Worcestershire Regiment	21 Nov 1917	Sunken Road Cemetery, Fampoux, France
Matthews, William Henry	1887	Private 28859	3rd Garrison Battalion Oxfordshire and Buckinghamshire Light Infantry	8 Jul 1917	England
Perkins, George Thomas	1896	Private 14453	2nd Battalion Royal Warwickshire Regiment	4 May 1917	Arras Memorial, France
Sadler, Ernest Charles	1899	Guardsman	2nd Battalion Coldstream Guards	13 Apr 1918	France (1914-1918) Memorial, France
Smith, William Thomas	1885	Private 290802	4th Battalion Bedfordshire Regiment	21 Aug 1918	Achiet-le-Grand Communal Cemetery Extension, France
Spiers, Walter Edward	1884	Private 19365	4th Battalion Worcestershire Regiment	31 Aug 1915	Helles Memorial, Turkey, St Peter's Church, Inkberrow
Turner, Lambert	1886	Private 41726	2/4th Battalion Princess Charlotte of Wales's (Royal Berkshire Regiment) formerly 145506 Labour Corps	26 Oct 1918	Villers-Pol Communal Cemetery Extension, France
Walker, Henry Austin	1895	Private 20806	1st Battalion Coldstream Guards	27 Mar 1918	Arras Memorial, France

Appendix VII: Broadway Men who Enlisted in 1914

The table below lists the names of men born or living in Broadway, who were found during the research for this book to have enlisted in 1914. Where known their rank, regimental number and date of their enlistment is given.

Name	Rank	Regiment	Date of Enlistment
Andrews, George Gazey	Private	1/8th Battalion Worcestershire Regiment	17 Nov
Badger, Joseph Lawrence	Private	1st Battalion Royal Warwickshire Regiment	4 Dec
Bandey, Thomas Charles	Private	Active Service Company, National Reserves	
Barnett, George	Private	1st Battalion Royal Warwickshire Regiment	4 Dec
Bayliss, Walter Henry	Private	Army Service Corps	9 Dec
Berry, Arthur Edwin	Private	Worcestershire Regiment (Territorials)	Sep
Box, Albert Henry	Private	Worcestershire Regiment (Territorials)	Sep
Bridges, Albert Arthur	Private	Worcestershire Regiment	
Brookes, Thomas Henry	Private	9th Battalion, Essex Regiment	
Burrows, Edgar	Private	Active Service Company, National Reserves	
Canham, George Charles	Private	6th Battalion Essex Regiment	11 Sep
Clarke, Albert Henry	Private	Worcestershire Regiment	Sep
Clarke, Frank	Private	Unknown	
Clarke, Herbert James	Rifleman	King's Royal Rifle Corps	31 Aug
Clarke, John	Private	Worcestershire Regiment	
Colley, Albert	Private	8th Battalion Gloucestershire Regiment	
Collins, Albert	Driver	Army Service Corps	14 Dec
Cook, Frank	Private	Worcestershire Regiment	
Corbett, Charles	Private	Army Service Corps	27 Aug
Cotterell, Frank	Private	Warwickshire Yeomanry	Sep
Coxhill, Gerald	Private	11th Hussars	Sep
Crump, Francis Laurent D.	Private	Worcestershire Regiment	8 Sep
Crump, William George	Yeoman of Signals	Royal Navy (HMS Marlborough)	
Dale, John S.	Company Sergeant Major	8th Battalion Gloucestershire Regiment	Sep
Denton, Malcolm John	Private	6th Battalion Worcestershire Regiment	5 Sep
Dowdeswell, John	Private	Worcestershire Regiment	16 Nov
Edwards, Henry Harold	Private	Worcestershire Regiment	
Elliott, E.	Private	Worcestershire Regiment	
Figgitt, Wilford Charles	Private	Royal Warwickshire Regiment	Nov
Folkes, Francis Alfred	Private	Worcestershire Regiment	Sep
Franklin, Gilbert	Private	Gloucestershire Regiment	
Gabb, William Harold	Private	3rd Battalion Coldstream Guards	Aug
Game, Henry Clement	Lieutenant	Royal Field Artillery	

Name	Rank		Date of Enlistment
Game, Hubert John	Lieutenant	Royal Artillery	
Glover, William	Private	Unknown	
Goddard, Frederick	Private	1st Battalion Royal Warwickshire Regiment	4 Dec
Green, Leonard Frank	Private	Worcestershire Regiment (Territorials)	Sep
Griffin, Albert John	Nagsman	Remount Company, Army Service Corps	26 Sep
Haines, Conway	Private	Welsh Pals	20 Sep
Haines, Gerald	Private	2nd Battalion Worcestershire Regiment	
Halford, Sidney	Private	Worcestershire Yeomanry	14 Oct
Hall, William	Private	Royal Flying Corps	
Handy, Frederick H.	Unknown	Hampshire Regiment (Territorials)	
Hardwick, Albert H.	Trooper	Worcestershire Yeomanry	1 Sep
Hill, Alfred Charles	Private	Worcestershire Regiment (Territorials)	
Hill, Reginald Bertram	Private	1st Battalion Royal Warwickshire Regiment	4 Dec
Hilson, Joseph	Private	Gloucestershire Regiment	
Ingles, Charles Edward	Private	Worcestershire Regiment	
Ingram, Arthur James	Driver	Army Service Corps	4 Dec
James, Joseph Charles	Private	2/8th Battalion Worcestershire Regiment	
Jarrett, Charles Walter	Private	Royal Warwickshire Regiment	
Jarrett, John William C.	Private	Worcestershire Regiment	
Jelfs, E.	Private	Worcestershire Regiment	
Johnson, W.E.	Trooper	Worcestershire Yeomanry	
Jones, P.	Ship's Corporal	Royal Navy	
Kennewell, John	Private	Foot Guards	
Keyte, Algernon John	Private	Royal Warwickshire Regiment	4 Dec
Keyte, Charles Herbert	Private	Worcestershire Regiment	4 Dec
Keyte, Heber John	Private	Worcestershire Regiment	17 Nov
Keyte, Horace Cuthbert	Private	Worcestershire Regiment	7 Aug
Keyte, Hubert Vernon	Private	Worcestershire Regiment	7 Aug
Keyte, Walter George	Private	Worcestershire Regiment	28 Aug
King, Aloysius	Trooper	Warwickshire Yeomanry	Sep
Knight, William Lloyd	Private	Warwickshire Yeomanry	Sep
Lambley, Felix Wilfred	Private	Royal Warwickshire Regiment	9 Dec
Ligham, Dr. W.		Royal Army Medical Corps	
Malin, Walter	Trooper	Worcestershire Yeomanry	3 Sep
Merriman, John	Private	Active Service Company, National Reserves	
Mingo, Hugh	Petty Officer	Royal Navy	
Morris, Crescens Lindsay	Private	Active Service Company, National Reserves	
Nash, Henry John	Private	2nd Battalion Worcestershire Regiment	
Newbury, George	Private	Active Service Company, National Reserves	
Oram, John	Private	Worcestershire Regiment (Territorials)	Sep
Parker, William John	Private	Warwickshire Yeomanry	1 Sep

Name	Rank	Regiment	Date of Enlistment
Phillips, Frank Alfred	Private	Royal Warwickshire Regiment	4 Dec
Plain, Edward	Trooper	Worcestershire Yeomanry	
Ponsonby, William R.	Captain	3rd (Prince of Wales's) Dragoon Guards	
Pugh, R.	Able Seaman	Royal Navy	
Rastall, Frank	Private	Worcestershire Regiment (Territorials)	Oct
Rastall, William	Corporal	Active Service Company, National Reserves	
Roberts, John	Private	Duke of Cornwall's Light Infantry	
Russell, Reginald Oscar	Private	Hampshire Regiment	19 Aug
Russell, Sydney Gordon	Private	Worcestershire Regiment	
Sandals, George	Private	Active Service Company, National Reserves	
Sandel, George	L/Corporal	Worcestershire Regiment (Territorials)	
Sanford, Henry Ayshford	Captain	Active Service Company, National Reserves	
Scrivens, James Thomas	Private	Gloucestershire Regiment	4 Aug
Seabright, Henry	Private	Worcestershire Regiment	3 Sep
Seabright, Hubert	Private	Worcestershire Regiment	7 Sep
Shillam, Walter	Trooper	Worcestershire Yeomanry	
Simms, Harold	Private	Kitchener's Army (Regiment unknown)	
Smith, Charles	Private	Duke of Cornwall's Light Infantry	3 Sep
Smith, George Walter	Private	Hampshire Regiment	19 Sep
Smith, Henry Jesse	Private	Grenadier Guards	12 Oct
Smith, Herbert	Private	Rifle Brigade	Aug
Stanley, Edward	Private	Worcestershire Regiment	16 Nov
Stanley, James	Private	Worcestershire Regiment	25 Sep
Stanley, R.	Sergeant	Worcestershire Regiment	
Stanley, Walter	Private	Worcestershire Regiment	14 Aug
Such, Francis	Private	Worcestershire Regiment	
Tandy, Ernest Dennis	Private	Royal Warwickshire Regiment	26 Oct
Tanner, A.H.	Private	Kitchener's Army (Regiment unknown)	
Tebby, Walter John	Private	14th (Service) Battalion Welsh Regiment	
Tooley, Victor Alan	Private	Army Service Corps	
Turner, Edgar	Private	Worcestershire Regiment (Territorials)	Sep
Tustin, William H.	Private	Worcestershire Regiment (Territorials)	
Vellender, William	Private	Worcestershire Regiment	9 Sep
Walker, John	Private	Royal Warwickshire Regiment	14 Dec
Watts, Francis John	Seaman	Royal Navy (HMS Bellerophon)	
West, William	Private	Army Service Corps	30 Dec
Williams, A.B.	Lieutenant	Active Service Company, National Reserves	
Williams, N.A.T.	Corporal	Army Service Corps	
Wooton	Private	Worcestershire Regiment	
Worton, R.	Lieutenant	The Scottish Rifles	
Yates, J.	Private	Worcestershire Regiment	
Yorke, Alfred Christopher	Private	Worcestershire Regiment (Territorials)	

Appendix VIII: Broadway's Boy Soldier, Frank Alfred Phillips
Private 9572, 1st Battalion Royal Warwickshire Regiment

Frank Alfred Phillips was born in Broadway on 1st September 1897, the youngest son of Robert Phillips, a coachman from Oddington, and Mary Phillips (née Waddoup) from Ettington near Stratford-upon-Avon. Frank's father worked for Viscount and Viscount Lifford of Austin House, Broadway, and the family lived at Stable Cottage. As a boy Frank was a member of Broadway Football Club and Broadway Cricket Club, and he was a member of St Michael's Church Choir. After leaving school Frank was employed as a gardener in the gardens at Austin House.

Pte Frank Phillips.
(Evesham Journal)

Frank enlisted with the Royal Warwickshire Regiment with George Barnett (see page 8) and Frederick Goddard (older brother of Arthur Goddard, see page 59) and a number of other Broadway men in Stratford-upon-Avon on 4th December 1914. Frank was only 17 years of age at the time and it was at his own request that his parents refrained from insisting on his return home as he was under military age.

Frank trained for five months on the Isle of Wight before he volunteered for a draft and was posted to the Western Front with George Barnett and the 1st Battalion Royal Warwickshire Regiment on 2nd May 1915. Frank was involved in the Battle of Ypres before moving to Arras in July 1915 where he remained until May 1916. Frank returned to Broadway on leave in May before returning to the front in June where his battalion was involved in the Battle of the Somme.

On 19th May 1917 it was reported in the Evesham Journal that Frank had been killed in action at the beginning of the month. It was later reported that Frank had been killed on 3rd May 1917 in an attack on the Chemical Works at Roux during the Battle of Arras but his body had not been buried by his own battalion but by another and that his family could obtain further details from the Burial Board, London.

St Michael's Church Choir 1909.
Back row: Sidney Halford, F. Packer, Albert Henry Box, Reginald Bertram Hill (see page 71), Leonard Frank Green and Sid Knight.
Middle row: Charles Ingles, Frank Phillips, Allan George Richardson, Stephen John (Jack) Ingles, Ernest Nichols.
Front row: Doris Painter (sister of Sidney John Painter, see page 85), Doris Green (sister of Leonard Green), D. Brown and M. Keen.
(Evesham Journal)

A memorial service was held for Frank in Broadway but a month later his parents received a postcard from him from Camp of Prisoners of War, Cassel (Kassel), in central Germany, dated 15th May 1917. It read:

I have just arrived here, so please send all letters to the above address. With best love, Frank.

Frank was released from prison in Germany at the end of the war and he returned home to Broadway. In 1924, Frank married Doris Green (pictured left), the sister of Leonard Green (see page 62) and they had two children.

Frank worked for a number of years for the Great Western Railway as a signalman in Broadway. Frank died, aged 96, in 1993. His wife Doris died in 1930 shortly after their daughter was born.

Appendix IX: Broadway Men awarded the Military Medal

Over 115,000 Military Medals were awarded in the First World War. The medal, introduced by Royal Warrant on 25th March 1916, was the other ranks' equivalent of the Military Cross (which was awarded to commissioned officers) and was awarded 'for bravery in the field'. The Military Medal was discontinued in 1993. The following men from Broadway were awarded the Military Medal:

Joseph Lawrence Badger, MM
Private 9559, 3rd Battalion Royal Warwickshire Regiment
transferred Corporal 30883, 14th Service Battalion Machine Gun Corps,

Joseph Lawrence Badger was born in Broadway on 15th August 1896, the eldest son of Adam Badger, a travelling salesman and labourer from Daventry, Northamptonshire, and Sarah Jane Badger (née Ellis) from Broadway. Joseph had a younger sister, Mary, who was born in 1905.

After leaving school Joseph was worked an errand boy in the village. He enlisted with the Royal Warwickshire Regiment in Stratford-upon-Avon on 4th December 1914 with George Barnett (see page 8) and Frederick Goddard (older brother of Arthur Goddard, see page 59). His enlistment records state that Joseph was 5' 9" tall and weighed 9st 10lbs.

Joseph was posted to the 3rd Battalion Royal Warwickshire Regiment on 12th December 1914 and to the Western Front on 2nd May 1915 with the first British Expeditionary Force. Just over two weeks later on 19th May 1915 Joseph received a gunshot wound to the head at Ypres and was admitted to hospital at Étaples before being transported home on 29th May 1915 to Fort Pitt Chatham Hospital and then to Rusthall Military Hospital, Tunbridge Wells.

Joseph returned to duty with the 3rd Battalion by the middle of July 1915 and was posted to Gallipoli with the 9th (Service) Battalion at the beginning of September. Within a few weeks, on 13th October 1915, Joseph received a bullet wound to the left thigh at Suvla and he was transported back to England on 21st October 1915.

On 18th February 1916, Joseph returned to the 3rd Battalion and on 8th May 1916 transferred to the Machine Gun Corps. After training at Belton Park, near Grantham, Joseph was posted back to the Western Front on 25th June 1916. He arrived at the depot at Camiers, in the Pas de Calais, the following day and joined the 119th Company at the front on 5th July 1916. Joseph was promoted to the rank of Lance Corporal on 23rd July 1916 but was demoted on 27th January 1917 for neglecting his duty in the field the previous day. In April 1917, whilst on the Western Front, Joseph was hospitalised with pyrexia of unknown origin or trench fever.

Joseph was granted 11 days' leave at the end of August 1917 after which he returned to the front. He was reported as being missing in action on 24th November 1917 at Boudon Wood during the Battle of Cambrai. He was found the following day with gunshot wounds to the left knee and elbow and was transported back to England a couple of days later. He was admitted to Kitchener Hospital, Brighton, for 13 days before he was transferred to Seaside Hospital, Seaford, on 17th December 1917 where he was a patient for two weeks before he was transferred back to Kitchener Hospital for further treatment.

Joseph returned to the 4th Reserve Battalion Machine Gun Corps at Alnwick in early 1918. In the middle of June 1918, he was admitted to hospital in Alnwick with influenza and after he recovered he was posted back to France on 6th July with the 14th Service Battalion. Whilst in France, Joseph was promoted to the rank of Acting Corporal on 29th September 1918 and to Corporal on 9th November 1918.

Joseph returned to England on 12th February 1919 and he was demobilized the following month on 15th March 1919 and Joseph returned to Broadway to live with his father at 33 Council Cottages. After his demobilization Joseph was awarded the Military Medal (London Gazette 17th June 1919) and he married Elizabeth Dunn the same year. Joseph died, aged 86, in 1983.

Edgar Cook, MM
Second Corporal 86297, 254th Tunnelling Company, Royal Engineers

Edgar Cook (see page 122) died on 29th October 1917. He is buried in Lijssenthoek Military Cemetery (grave XXI. DD. 6) and is recorded by the Commonwealth War Graves Commission as being a native of Broadway.

Wilson William Keyte, MM
Private 30818, 11th (Service) Battalion Worcestershire Regiment

Wilson Keyte was born in Broadway in 1885, the son of Ann Keyte, a domestic servant and gloveress. Wilson was brought up in China Square in the village and after leaving school worked as a grocer's assistant. He married Ada Ethel Such in Chipping Norton in 1904 and they had three children. In the 1911 census, the family are recorded as living on Leamington Road, Broadway.

Wilson enlisted with the Worcestershire Regiment and was posted to Salonika with the 11th (Service) Battalion. Wilson was awarded the Military Medal in 1917 for stretcher-bearing duties during the Battle of Doiran. Two of Wilson's cousins, George Thomas Handy (see page 129), and Albert Henry Clarke (see page 18) were involved in the same battle. Albert was killed in action on 24th April 1917 and George was killed instantaneously by a shell during the night of 24th/25th April 1917.

The 11th Battalion saw action in Salonika from November 1915 until September 1918. The battalion was then posted to Bulgaria and Turkey and at the end of September 1919 was amalgamated with the 9th Battalion. After the end of the war, Wilson was awarded the Greek Military Cross, conferred by His Majesty The King of The Hellenes, the highest decoration awarded by the Greek Government, for meritorious service in action. Wilson Keyte died, aged 64, in 1949.

Arthur Parker, MM
Private 24387, 8th (Service) Battalion Gloucestershire Regiment

Arthur Parker, was born in Broadway in 1897, the son of Arthur Parker, a postman from Broadway, and Ann Alice Parker (née Aston) from Snowshill. Arthur was the younger brother of William Parker (see page 90). Arthur worked as telegraph messenger in the village prior to his enlistment with the Gloucestershire Regiment on 28th August 1915. Arthur was posted to the Western Front in December 1915 with the 10th (Service) Battalion.

When the 10th (Service) Battalion was disbanded in February 1919, Arthur transferred to the 8th (Service) Battalion. He was awarded the Military Medal for bravery in the field during 1919 (London Gazette 13th June 1919). Arthur died, aged 69, in 1966.

Appendix X: Broadway Men who were Serving in 1918

The table below which lists the men of Broadway who were serving in 1918 has been based on the 1918 Absent Voters List for the Parish of Broadway. An Act of Parliament, passed on 6th February 1918, allowed servicemen over the age of 21 to be eligible to vote in their home constituency and the Absent Voters List, published on 15th October 1918, was compiled from details supplied by the men themselves before the closing date for applications of 18th August 1918.

Included below are brothers Sidney Elliott and Alfred Edward Foss sons of Edwin Lewis Foss, the village Chemist, and Eliza Foss (née Elliott). Sidney was born in Broadway in 1887 and Alfred in 1889. Sidney, who trained as a chemist, enlisted with the Royal Army Medical Corps and served as a Quartermaster Sergeant (regimental number 437365) on the Western Front. Sidney was awarded the Meritorious Service Medal[164] in 1919. Alfred, worked as a farm labourer after leaving school. He enlisted with the Army Service Corps (regimental number 1241) and was attached to the 2/2nd South Midland Field Ambulance (regimental number T4/248876). Alfred was awarded the Silver War Badge during the war and the Meritorious Service Medal in 1919.

The table also includes George Geoffrey Game who served as a Lieutenant with Royal Field Artillery and was awarded the Military Cross in 1919 (see page 55). Also included is Private 14969, John William Charles Jarrett 2nd Battalion Worcestershire Regiment. John was born in 1893 and enlisted in 1914. He was wounded three times during the war and in 1918 was awarded the Croix de Guerre avec Étoile. The Evesham Journal reported on 30th November 1918:

Pte. J. Jarrett of the 2nd Batt. Worcestershire Regiment, eldest son of Mr and Mrs Charles Jarrett of Bury End, Broadway, has received the following official communication from the headquarters of the 100th Infantry Brigade:- "You have been awarded the undermentioned French decoration for devotion to duty during the operations at Neuve Eglise in April last 'Croix de Guerre avec Estoile (sic)'. Your name appeared in the London Gazette on 10th October 1918. The Divisional Commander and Brigadier-General desire me to express their congratulations on the honour you have brought to your division and brigade.

On the back of the official communication the Brigadier-General wrote the following personal letter: "Private Jarrett, I write to say how thankful I was to hear that the earlier report of your death was incorrect and how delighted I am to think that you have been awarded the French decoration, I only wish that I was going to have the pleasure of pinning it on your coat, but I enclose it with best wishes instead."

Name	Rank and Number	Battalion and Regiment or Corps
Adams, Thomas	236186	ASC
Andrews, George Gazey	Private 247503	446th Agricultural Company, Labour Corps
Annesley, CMG DSO, James Howard Adolphus	Lieutenant Colonel	6th Dragoon Guards (Carabiniers)
Aston, Charles William	Signalman BZ/3274	Royal Navy (HMS Wigan)
Badenoch, David Sutherland	Captain	RAMC
Badger, Joseph Lawrence	Private 30833	Machine Gun Corps
Bartlett, Francis Edgar	Private 9561	9th Battalion Royal Warwickshire Regiment
Bartlett, James Frederick	Unknown	9th Battalion Royal Warwickshire Regiment
Bayliss, Josiah James	Private 25249	Labour Corps
Biles, Frank Arthur	Private 202905	3rd Battalion Royal Sussex Regiment

---

164   The Meritorious Service Medal was awarded to non-commissioned officers for distinguished service of for gallantry.

Name	Rank and Number	Battalion and Regiment or Corps
Biles, Percy George	Corporal 15528	9th Battalion Gloucestershire Regiment
Biles, William Henry	Private S-43932	Gordon Highlanders
Bishop, William	Private 203259	10th (Service) Battalion Worcestershire Regiment
Bonham, John Wroughton	Major	Remounts Service, ASC
Box, Albert Henry	Sergeant 202847	3rd Battalion Worcestershire Regiment
Box, Frank	Air Mechanic 3rd Class 82919	RFC
Bridges, Albert	M2/164233	Mechanical Transport Company, ASC
Brookes, Harry	Private M2/033641	Mechanical Transport Company, ASC
Brookes, Thomas Henry	Lance Corporal 85855	Unknown
Brown, William Barclay	Second Lieutenant	66th Indian Labour Company
Burrows, Edgar	34498	Royal Defence Corps
Cameron, Norman Ogilvie Monah	Lieutenant	1st Battalion Queen's Own Cameron Highlanders
Canham, Charles George	Acting Corporal 206285	2nd Battalion Northumberland Fusiliers
Carter, Francis Henry	Private 269685	RFC
Carter, Harvey Bertram	Private 9635	3rd Battalion Royal Warwickshire Regiment
Chandler, Frank	392154	424th Agricultural Company, ASC
Chandler, Noah	Private 24376	12th (Service) Battalion (Bristol) Gloucestershire Regiment
Clark, John Seymour	Guardsman 17203	2nd Battalion Grenadier Guards
Clarke, Bertram	Private 30483	15th Platoon, 'D' Company, 2nd Battalion Worcestershire Regiment
Clarke, Ernest Arthur	103881	Labour Corps
Clarke, Frank Thomas	187021	Devonshire Regiment
Clarke, Herbert James	Corporal R595	12th Battalion King's Royal Rifle Corps
Clarke, John	Gunner 2485	Motor Machine Gun Service, RA
Close, William Charles	Private 36586	'C' Company, 2/5th Battalion Somerset Light Infantry
Collier, Vincent Henry	Private S/420084	Mechanical Transport Company, ASC
Collins, Albert	Driver T4/035709	ASC
Collins, Alfred George	9748	'C' Company, 10th Battalion Royal Warwickshire Regiment
Collins, Horace Leigh	Private 201474	'C' Company, 1/4th Battalion Welsh Regiment
Collins, Oscar James	Private 361040	Labour Corps attached Royal Engineers
Cope, Frederick John	Sergeant 116844	RGA
Crump, William George	Yeoman of Signals 220097	Royal Navy (HMS Revenge)
Cull, John Sydney	Private 47588	15th Machine Gun Squadron, 6th (Poona) Cavalry Brigade
Days, Wilfred	Private 29138	'B' Company, 7th Battalion Oxfordshire and Buckinghamshire Light Infantry
Denton, Malcolm John	Private 21305	1st Battalion Oxfordshire and Buckinghamshire Light Infantry
Diston, Lewis	Private 94935	30th Labour Group, (HQ Labour Corps) ASC

Name	Rank and Number	Battalion and Regiment or Corps
Ellis, Austin	Private 27655	14th Battalion Worcestershire Regiment
Emms, Ebenezer Evelyn	Private 146497	424th Agricultural Company, Labour Corps
Emms, Nelson Reginald	Gunner 23341	RGA
Exon, Albert George	Private 29869	6th Battalion Worcestershire Regiment
Figgett, Arthur Stanley	Ordinary Seaman J65590	Royal Navy (HMS Tyne)
Figgett, Harry	Private 33908	7th Battalion Gloucestershire Regiment
Figgitt, Walter	Private 5379	6th Battalion Australian Imperial Force
Fletcher, Alfred	Sapper 275487	Royal Engineers
Folkes, Charles	Private 35005	King's Shropshire Light Infantry
Folkes, Jim	Private R4/146084	No 2 Advanced Remount Depot, ASC
Folkes, Reginald Duncan	Private 14959	4th Battalion Worcestershire Regiment
Foss, Alfred Edward	Sergeant 1241, T4/248876	61st Divisional Supply Column, ASC
Foss, Sidney Elliott	Quartermaster Sergeant	Royal Army Medical Corps attached 2/2nd (South Midland) Field Ambulance
Franklin, Gilbert Charles	Private 48830	81st Machine Gun Company
Fridlington, William Charles	Private 343201	ASC
Game, George Geoffrey	Lieutenant	RFA
Gardner, Joseph	Private 24386	8th Platoon, 'B' Company, 9th Battalion Gloucestershire Regiment
Gardner, William	Private M2/153742	ASC attached 2nd Siege Artillery Battery (Australia)
Gardner, William Henry	Private M/402734	Mechanical Transport Company, 3rd Cavalry Division, ASC
Glover, Arthur	Gunner 199609	406th Battery, 166 Brigade, RFA
Grantham, Frank	Private 136647	50th Company, Labour Corps
Green, Frank James	Private 31142	6th Platoon, 'B' Company, 3rd Battalion Worcestershire Regiment
Hacklett, Stephen Ralph	483757	Agricultural Company, Labour Corps
Haines, Frank Richard	Able Seaman SS7622	27 Mess Royal Navy (HMS Queen)
Halford, Sidney	Private H/325463	1/1st Worcestershire Yeomanry
Halford, Walter	Private 11238	6th (Service) Battalion Wiltshire Regiment
Hall, John	Driver T4/356394	ASC
Hall, Thomas	Private 38377	Gloucestershire Regiment
Handy, Albert	Private 437-114	440th Agricultural Company, Labour Corps
Hensley, George	Private M2/148096	Mechanical Transport Company, ASC
Hensley, Hubert Edward	144379	13th (Works) Battalion Devonshire Regiment
Hewitt, John	Private 48490	1/7th Battalion Royal Warwickshire Regiment
Hill, Alfred Charles	Private 12730	9th (Service) Battalion Gloucestershire Regiment
Holder, Percival R.J.	Private 130653	Machine Gun Corps
Holibar, George Francis	Private M2/053625	Mechanical Transport Company, ASC
Hopkins, William	Unknown	1 Mess, Royal Navy (HMS Vendetta)

Name	Rank and Number	Battalion and Regiment or Corps
Horne, David Francis	Sapper WR/255444	30th Labour Battalion (Railway Construction)
Horne, William	Sergeant 65047	RFA
Hughes, John	172375	8th Company, 13th (Works) Battalion Devonshire Regiment
Ingles, Charles Henry	Gunner 81678	484th Siege Battery, RGA
Ingles, Dennis George	394245	111th Employment Company, Labour Corps
Ingles, Francis Henry	Private TF/241275	'C' Company, 7th Battalion The Queen's Own (Royal West Kent Regiment)
Ingles, Stephen John	Driver 239782	RFA
Ingram, Arthur James	Driver T3/030717	1st Cavalry Division Supply Column, ASC
Invine, Thomas Edwin	Private 17016	2nd Battalion Coldstream Guards
Invine, William John	414758	Lowland Division, Royal Engineers
James, Gilbert Clement	Driver 840525	'D' Battery, RFA
Jarrett, John William Charles	Private 14969	2nd Battalion Worcestershire Regiment
Jarrett, William James	Private 497283	83rd Field Ambulance RAMC
Jenner, Ernest Edmund Holland	Air Mechanic 3rd Class 267799	RFC
Jones, Nelson	Unknown	HMHS Berbice
Jordan, Charles	Private 42364	6th Battalion King's Royal Rifle Corps
Kempson, Leonard	Private 19084	9th (Service) Battalion Gloucestershire Regiment
Keyte, Algernon John	Private 9573	Royal Warwickshire Regiment
Keyte, Arthur Harold	Private 34322	Royal Sussex Regiment
Keyte, George	Gunner 154649	49th Reserve Battery, RFA
Keyte, George Leigh	Private 43954	1st Battalion Royal Berkshire Regiment
Keyte, Heber John	Private 33142 (formerly 3757)	264th Protection Company, Royal Defence Corps
Keyte, James Richard	Private 24502	10th (Service) Battalion Gloucestershire Regiment
Keyte, Wilson	Private 30818	11th Battalion Worcestershire Regiment
Kilby, Benjamin	Private 13734	1st Garrison Battalion Royal Warwickshire Regiment
King, Lewis	149909	51 Auxiliary (Omnibus) Company, ASC
Kinsman, Albert	Private 26172	'D' Company, Garrison Battalion Oxfordshire & Buckinghamshire Light Infantry
Knight, Francis	Private 47034	Labour Corps
Knight, Harry	Farrier 241132	Worcestershire Regiment
Knight, Sydney Edward	Signalman	Royal Navy (HMS Kent)
Knight, William Lloyd	Private 1743	Warwickshire Yeomanry
Ladbrooke, Jesse	Gunner 59029	31st Reserve Battery, RFA
Lambley, Alfred	Private 262581	RFC/RAF
Lissaman, John Alex	Private DM2/151634	626th Company, 19 Motor Ambulance Company ASC
Lloyd, Sidney Evan	476679	241st Company ASC
Macfarlane, James	Second Lieutenant	15th Battalion Royal Warwickshire Regiment

Name	Rank and Number	Battalion and Regiment or Corps
Macfarlane, Robert	Second Lieutenant	14th Battalion Royal Warwickshire Regiment
Malin, John	Private 597101	424th Agricultural Company, Labour Corps
Malin, Walter	Driver T4/239930	4th Divisional Transport Company, ASC
Malin, William Henry	Private 19266	Worcestershire Regiment
Mayne, William	Pioneer 335116	Royal Enginers
Meadows, Walter	Private 9576	1st Battalion Royal Warwickshire Regiment
Morris, Arthur Oliver Philip	Acting Corporal 5409	Army Pay Corps
Morris, Crescens Lindsay	Corporal 3199	Royal Defence Corps
Naden, Bernard Grove	Private 657	'A' Company, 3rd Battalion Royal Warwickshire Regiment
Nash, William	Private 189715	200th Company, Labour Corps
Newbury, James	Private 10149	2/5th Battalion Gloucestershire Regiment
Parker, Arthur	24387	7th Battalion Rifle Brigade
Parker, Charles Henry	Private 599947	Labour Corps
Parker, Hubert	Gunner 192700	No. 15 Company, RGA
Parker, Theodore	Private M2/033499	Mechanical Transport Company, ASC
Parker, Walter William	Private 9565	10th (Service) Battalion Gloucestershire Regiment
Paskin, Geoffrey Wallgrave	Lieutenant	Royal Engineers
Payne, John Frederick	Private 118917	No. 1 Depot Company, Mechanical Transport Division, ASC
Phillips, Frank Alfred	Private 9572	Royal Warwickshire Regiment (Prisoner of War)
Phillips, Robert Francis	239285	Mechanical Transport Company ASC
Porter, Albert Arthur	Lance Corporal 10504	9th Battalion Royal Warwickshire Regiment
Porter, Wilson	Private 281907	2 Air Force Reserve Depot
Rastall, Harry	Private 92702	Labour Corps
Reid, Robert	Private T3/024120	Head Quarters, 19th Divisional Train, ASC
Riley, Robert	Sapper 239218	119th Company, Royal Engineers
Roberts, Frederick	Private 36696	8th Battalion Royal Berkshire Regiment
Roberts, John	Private 3/5615	1st Battalion Duke of Cornwall's Light Infantry
Roberts, William	Gunner 121176	RFA
Roberts, William Vernon	Gunner 246757	RFA
Robinson, Frank	Corporal 266459	9th Battalion Royal Warwickshire Regiment
Rose, Samuel	Private 46975	5th (Reserve) Battalion Royal Warwickshire Regiment
Russell, Algernon John	Private 267356	1/6th Battalion Devonshire Regiment
Russell, Donald George Shefford	Second Lieutenant	7th Battalion Worcestershire Regiment
Russell. Reginald Oscar	Private 4355101	RAMC
Russell, Sydney Gordon	Second Lieutenant	1st Battalion Worcestershire Regiment
Sandals, George Henry	Private 34212	13th Battalion Gloucestershire Regiment
Sanford, Henry Ayshford	Captain	Worcestershire Regiment

Name	Rank and Number	Battalion and Regiment or Corps
Savage, Arthur Edward	Private 452934	651st Agricultural Company, Labour Corps
Shillam, Walter	Private 436326	447th Agricultural Company, Labour Corps
Sims, Arthur Edwin	Air Mechanic 2nd Class 405964	Aircraft Repair Section, 21 Squadron RFC
Smith, George	Private 9563	'A' Company, 2/6th Royal Warwickshire Regiment
Sollis, James Wood	Private 245195	2/2nd (City of London) Battalion Royal Fusiliers
Stainforth, John Ronald	Lieutenant	Irish Guards
Staite, David William	Private 224661	88th Company, Labour Corps
Stanley, Alec Silvester	Private 42530	'B' Company, 7th Platoon, 2nd Battalion Worcestershire Regiment
Stanley, Joseph	Driver 210952	14th Divisional Signals Company, Royal Engineers
Stephens, Francis	241553	2/8th Worcestershire Regiment
Stephens, James	Private 205848	13th (Home Service) Battalion Royal Scots Fusiliers
Stephens, Thomas	2305	23rd (Service) Battalion (2nd Football) Middlesex Regiment
Stokes, Reginald Walter	241492	12th (Service) Battalion (Bermondsey) East Surrey Regiment
Tooley, Francis William	Second Lieutenant	Irish Guards
Tooley, Victor Allan	Sergeant 45329	'C' Company, 52nd (Graduated) Royal Sussex Regiment
Towersey, Arthur George	Second Lieutenant	Unknown
Tracy-Arkell, Leonard William	Lieutenant	12th (Reserve) Battalion Welsh Regiment
Trayler, James	123839	RAMC
Tredwell, Arthur	Private M2/101891	Mechanical Transport Company, ASC
Turner, Edgar	Lance Corporal 240817	1/8th Worcestershire Regiment
Turner, Harold C.	Private 316803	13th Battalion Royal Hussars
Turner, Percival Joseph	Private 260135	1/5th Battalion Gloucestershire Regiment
Tustin, Algernon Ernest	Private 281909	2 Air Force Reserve Depot
Vellender, William	Private 17279	4th Battalion Worcestershire Regiment
Wallis, Albert	Private 95550	RAMC
Watts, William Edward	Monitor 23	Royal Navy (HMS Attentive)
Webb, George Harvey	Private S/33470	2/8th (City of London) Battalion (Post Office Rifles) London Regiment
West, William	Private S4/041832	ASC
Whitaker, Charles Henry	Unknown	HM Airship Station, Anglesey
Whittle, Thomas	Private 271030	1/1st Northumberland Yeomanry (Northumberland Hussars)
Woodward, Walter Henry	Sapper 283619	Royal Engineers
Yorke, Alfred Christopher	Nagsman RTS/2355	Remounts Service, ASC

Sources

Articles and Books

A Short History of the 39th (Deptford) Divisional Artillery 1915-1918. Lieutenant Colonel H.W. Wiebkin, M.C. (Late R.F.A.) (1923)

Deeds and Words in the Suffrage Military Hospital in Endell Street, Med Hist. 2007 January 1; 51(1): 79-98

Gallipoli. Peter Hart (2011)

The British Campaign in France and Flanders. Sir Arthur Conan Doyle (1915)

The Diary of A Yeomanry M.O. (Egypt, Gallipoli, Palestine and Italy). Captain O. Teichman, DSO, MC, Croix de Guerre, Croce di Guerra, Royal Army Medical Corps (T.F.) (1921)

The Escape of a Princess Pat. George Pearson (1918)

The Great War: Gallipoli and Mesopotamia, The Story of The Royal Warwickshire Regiment. C.L. Kingsford (1921)

The Great War Handbook. Geoff Bridger (2009)

The Minutes of the Broadway War Memorial Committee 1919-1920

The Queens Own Royal West Kent Regiment 1914 to 1919. Captain C.T. Atkinson (1924)

Worcestershire Regiment in the Great War 1914-1919. Captain H. FitzM Stacke (1927)

Databases

UK, Soldiers Died in the Great War, 1914-1919

Libraries, Museums, Records Offices and Societies

Amblecote History Society – www.amblecotehistorysociety.org.uk

Badsey Society – www.badsey.net

Broadway Library

Chipping Campden History Society – www.chippingcampdenhistory.org.uk

Evesham Public Library

Ford Park Cemetery Trust

Gloucestershire Archives

Jesus College Archive, Cambridge University

London Metropolitan Archives

Malvern College

Old Caterhamian's Association

Royal Welch Fusiliers Museum

Sedbergh School Archive and Heritage Centre

The Hive, Worcester

The National Archives, Kew

The Shakespeare Birthplace Trust

Newspapers

Berrows Worcester Journal - all pictures from the Berrows Worcester Journal are copyright and courtesy of the Berrows Worcester Journal (Berrows Worcester Journal)
Evesham Journal - all pictures and quotes from the Evesham Journal are copyright and courtesy of the Evesham Journal (Evesham Journal)

Websites

Ancestry.co.uk - www.ancestry.co.uk
Anglo Boer War – www.angloboerwar.com
Canadian Great War Project – www.canadiangreatwarproject.com
Commonwealth War Graves Commission – www.cwgc.org
Find a Grave – www.findagrave.com
FreeBMD - www.freebmd.org.uk
Lightbobs – www.lightbobs.com
Remember the Fallen – www.rememberthefallen.co.uk
Rootschat.com – www.rootschat.com
The Great War Forum – www.1914-1918.invisionzone.com/forums
The Long Long Trail – www.1914-1918.net
The Royal Victoria Hospital & Military Cemetery Netley – www.netley-military-cemetery.co.uk
The Western Front Association – www.westernfrontassociation.com
The Worcestershire Regiment – www.worcestershireregiment.com
WW1Daily.com - www.ww1daily.com

Index